To You With Love: A TREASURY OF GREAT ROMANTIC LITERATURE

To You With Love:

Drawings by Evelyn Copelman

A TREASURY OF GREAT
ROMANTIC LITERATURE

EDITED BY SEON MANLEY AND GOGO LEWIS

MACRAE SMITH COMPANY   *Philadelphia*

This book is for our husbands,
ROBERT R. MANLEY *and*
WILLIAM W. LEWIS,
with all our love

Acknowledgments

We are grateful to the authors, agents, and publishers who have given permission to reprint the following selections:

"Sixteen" by Maureen Daly. Reprinted by permission of Scholastic Magazines, Inc. Copyright 1938 by the Scholastic Corporation, © renewed 1966 by Maureen Daly.

"One Day in April" by Anita Rowe Block, Copyright 1948 by The Hearst Corporation. From LOVE IS A FOUR LETTER WORD by Anita Rowe Block. Reprinted by permission of Doubleday & Company, Inc.

"My Longing to Talk to Someone" from ANNE FRANK: THE DIARY OF A YOUNG GIRL by Anne Frank. Copyright 1952 by Otto H. Frank. Reprinted by permission of Doubleday & Company, Inc. and Vallentine, Mitchell & Co. Ltd.

"Still, Still So" from COLLECTED STORIES, Volume I by Mark Van Doren. © 1962 by Mark Van Doren. Reprinted by permission of Hill and Wang, Inc.

Chapter IV. "Fifteen: Summer," originally titled "Mr. Cornelius, I Love You," copyright, 1952, by Jessamyn West. Reprinted from her volume CRESS DELAHANTY, by permission of Harcourt, Brace & World, Inc.

"The Love Letter" by Jack Finney. Copyright 1959 by Jack Finney. Reprinted by permission of Harold Matson Company, Inc.

"The Gift of the Magi" from THE FOUR MILLION by O. Henry. Reprinted by permission of Doubleday & Company, Inc.

"The First Prom's the Hardest" from WE SHOOK THE FAMILY TREE by Hildegarde Dolson. Copyright 1941, 1942, 1946 by Hildegarde Dolson. Reprinted by permission of Random House, Inc.

"The Singing Lesson." Copyright 1922 by Alfred A. Knopf, Inc. and renewed, 1950 by J. Middleton Murry. Reprinted from THE SHORT STORIES OF KATHERINE MANSFIELD, by permission of the publisher. Permission to include this story has also been granted by The Society of Authors as the literary representative of the Estate of Katherine Mansfield.

"Lady Daisy and Her Crazy Dog" by William Saroyan. Copyright 1958 by William Saroyan. Reprinted by permission of the author.

"Araby" by James Joyce. From DUBLINERS by James Joyce. Originally pub-

Contents

In the rich pages of romantic literature, sometimes the very best stories, letters or poems are those that are old favorites. Just as all the expressions of love are centuries old, so are the feelings. They are probably the most universal of all feelings: the awakening of first love, the hesitation, the shyness, the beauty—yes, even the anxiety. Such emotions are as poignant and perishable as the spring flowers, but the writing about such emotions is enduring. Good writing appeals strongly to each new generation, and some stories, the following particularly, belong to the young in heart.

Now a well-known short story writer and novelist, Maureen Daly wrote "Sixteen" when she was sixteen years old in high school at St. Mary's Springs Academy in Fond du Lac, Wisconsin. It is now recognized as one of the leading stories of our time. Perhaps the fashions, the tweed skirts, for example, and the ankle socks, are no longer in, but the emotions, the clothes we wear inside ourselves, never change.

SIXTEEN

MAUREEN DALY

Now don't get me wrong. I mean, I want you to understand from the beginning that I'm not really so dumb. I know what a girl should do and what she shouldn't. I get around. I read. I listen to the radio. And I have two older sisters. So you see, I know what the score is. I know it's smart to wear tweedish skirts and shaggy sweaters with the sleeves pushed up, and pearls and ankle socks and saddle shoes that look as if they've seen the world. And I know that your hair should be long—almost to your shoulders—and sleek as a wet seal—just a little fluffed at the ends—and you should wear a campus hat or a dink, or else a peasant hankie if you've that sort of face. Properly, a peasant hankie should make you think of edelweiss, mist and sunny mountains, yodeling and Swiss cheese. You know, that kind of peasant. Now, me—I never wear a hankie. It makes my face seem wide and Slavic, and I always look like a picture in one of those magazine articles that run: ". . . and Stalin says the future of Russia lies in its women . . . In its women who have tilled its soil, raised its children . . ." Well, anyway. I'm not exactly too small-town either. I read Winchell's column. You get to know what New York boy is that way about some pineapple princess on the West Coast, and what paradise pretty is currently the prettiest, and why someone eventually will play Scarlett O'Hara. It gives you that cosmopolitan feeling. And I know that anyone who orders a strawberry sundae in a drugstore instead of a lemon Coke would probably be dumb enough to wear colored ankle socks with high-heeled pumps, or use Evening in Paris with a tweed suit. But I'm sort of drifting. This isn't what I wanted to tell you. I just wanted to give you the general idea of how I'm not so dumb. It's important that you understand that.

You see, it was funny how I met him. It was a winter night like any other winter night. And I didn't have my Latin done either. But the way the moon tinseled the twigs and silver-plated the snowdrifts, I just couldn't stay inside. The skating rink isn't far from our house—you can make it in five minutes if the sidewalks aren't slippery —so I went skating. I remember it took me a long time to get ready that night because I had to darn my skating socks first. I don't know why they always wear out so fast—just in the toes, too. Maybe it's because I have metal protectors on the toes of my skates. That probably *is* why. And then I brushed my hair—hard—so hard it clung to my hand and stood up around my head in a hazy halo.

My skates were hanging by the back door all nice and shiny, for I'd just gotten them for Christmas, and they smelled so queer—just like fresh smoked ham. My dog walked with me as far as the corner. She's a red chow, very polite and well-mannered, and she kept pretending it was me she liked, when all the time I knew it was the ham smell. She panted along beside me, and her hot breath made a frosty little balloon balancing on the end of her nose. My skates thumped me good-naturedly on my back as I walked. The night was breathlessly quiet, and the stars winked down like a million flirting eyes. It was all so lovely.

It was all so lovely I ran most of the way, and it was lucky the sidewalks had ashes on them or I'd have slipped surely. The ashes crunched like cracker-jack, and I could feel their cindery shape through the thinness of my shoes. I always wear old shoes when I go skating.

I had to cut across someone's back garden to get to the rink, and last summer's grass stuck through the thin ice, brown and discouraged. Not many people came through this way, and the crusted snow broke through the little hollows between corn stubbles frozen hard in the ground. I was out of breath when I got to the shanty— out of breath with running and with the loveliness of the night. Shanties are always such friendly places—the floor all hacked to wet splinters from skate runners, and the wooden wall frescoed with symbols of dead romance. There was a smell of singed wool as someone got too near the glowing isinglass grin of the iron stove. Girls burst through the door laughing, with snow on their hair, and tripped over shoes scattered on the floor. A pimply-faced boy grabbed the hat from the frizzled head of an eighth-grade blonde and stuffed it into an empty galosh to prove his love, and then hastily bent to examine his skate strap with innocent unconcern.

It didn't take me long to get my own skates on, and I stuck my shoes under the bench—far back where they wouldn't get knocked around and would be easy to find when I wanted to go home. I walked out on my toes, and the shiny runners of my new skates dug deep into the sodden floor.

It was snowing a little outside—quick, eager little Lux-like flakes that melted as soon as they touched your hand. I waited a moment. You know, to start to skate at a crowded rink is like jumping on a moving merry-go-round. The skaters go skimming round in a colored blur, like gaudy painted horses, and the shrill musical jabber re-echoes in the night from a hundred human caliopes. Once in, I went all right. At least after I found out exactly where that rough ice was. It was *round, round—jump the rut; round, round, round—jump the rut; round, round* . . .

And then he came. All of a sudden his arm was around my waist so warm and tight, and he said very casually, "Mind if I skate with you?" Then he took my other hand. That's all there was to it. Just that, and then we were skating. It wasn't that I'd never skated with a boy before. Don't be silly. I told you before I get around. But this was different. He was a smoothie! He was a big shot up at school. He went to all the big dances and he was the best dancer in town—except Harold Wright, who didn't count because he'd been to college in New York for two years. Don't you see? This was different.

At first I can't remember what we talked about; I can't even remember if we talked at all. We just skated and skated, and laughed every time we came to that rough spot—and pretty soon we were laughing all the time at nothing at all. It was all so lovely.

Then we sat on the big snowbank at the edge of the rink and just watched. It was cold at first—even with my skating pants on—sitting on that hard heap of snow, but pretty soon I got warm all over. He threw a handful of snow at me, and it fell in a little white shower on my hair. He leaned over to brush it off. I held my breath. The night stood still.

The moon hung just over the warming shanty like a big quarter slice of muskmelon, and the smoke from the pipe chimney floated up in a sooty fog. One by one the houses around the rink twinkled out their lights, and somebody's hound wailed a mournful apology to a star as he curled up for the night. It was all so lovely.

Then he sat up straight and said, "We'd better start home." Not, "Shall I take you home?" or "Do you live far?" but, "We'd better start home." See, that's how I know he wanted to take me home. Not because he *had* to, but because he *wanted* to. He went to the shanty to get my shoes.

"Black ones," I told him. "Same size as Garbo's." And he laughed again. He was still smiling when he came back and took off my skates and tied the wet skate strings in a soggy knot and put them over his shoulder. Then he held out his hand, and I slid off the snowbank and brushed off the seat of my pants, and we were ready.

It was snowing harder now. Big, quiet flakes that clung to twiggy bushes and snuggled in little drifts against the tree trunks. The night was an etching in black and white. It was all so lovely I was sorry I lived only a few blocks away. He talked softly as we walked, as if every little word were a secret. Did I like Wayne King, and did I plan to go to college next year, and had I a cousin who lived in Appleton and knew his brother? A very respectable Emily Post sort of conversation, and then finally how nice I looked with snow in my hair, and had I ever seen the moon so close?—for the moon was following us as we walked, and ducking playfully behind a chimney every time I turned to look at it. And then we were home.

The porch light was on. My mother always puts the porch light on when I go away at night. And we stood there a moment by the front steps, the snow turned pinkish in the glow of the colored light, and a few feathery flakes settled on his hair. Then he took my skates and put them over my shoulder and said, "Good night now. I'll call you." . . . "I'll call you," he said.

I went inside then, and in a moment he was gone. I watched him from my window as he went down the street. He was whistling softly, and I waited until the sound faded away so I couldn't tell if it was he or my heart whistling out there in the night. And then he was gone—completely gone.

I shivered. Somehow the darkness seemed changed. The stars were little hard chips of light far up in the sky, and the moon stared down with a sullen yellow glare. The air was tense with sudden cold, and a gust of wind swirled his footprints into white oblivion. Everything was quiet.

But he'd said, "I'll call you." That's what he said: "I'll call you." I couldn't sleep all night.

And that was last Thursday. Tonight is Tuesday. Tonight is Tuesday, and my homework's done, and I darned some stockings that didn't really need it, and I worked a cross-word puzzle, and I listened to the radio, and now I'm just sitting. I'm just sitting because I can't think of anything else to do. I can't think of anything—anything but snowflakes and ice skates and yellow moons and Thursday night. The telephone is sitting on the corner table with its old black face turned to the wall, so I can't see its leer. I don't even jump when it rings anymore. My heart still prays, but my mind just laughs. Outside the night is still—so still I think I'll go crazy—and the white snow's all dirtied and smoked into grayness, and the wind is blowing the arc lamp so it throws weird, waving shadows from the trees onto the lawn—like thin, starved arms begging for I don't know what. And so I'm just sitting here, and I'm not feeling anything. I'm not even sad, because all of a sudden I know. All of a sudden I know. I can sit here now forever, and laugh and laugh and laugh while the tears run salty in the corners of my mouth. For all of a sudden I know. I know what the stars knew all the time: he'll never, never call—never.

"Man's love," wrote Lord Byron, "is a man's life, a thing apart; 'tis woman's whole existence." Perhaps that is the reason why it is so much more difficult for a boy or man to say I love you. In this haunting and very beautiful story some of that hesitation is captured as delightfully as an April day captures sunlight.

ONE DAY IN APRIL

ANITA ROWE BLOCK

It was that kind of day. The sun was warm through a hazy cloud that spread over the town. The birds chirped lazily, and the sprinklers on the lawns twirled in slow, muted unison, their sprays of water multicolored. Screen doors banged less frequently, and usually frisking dogs lay inert on back porches, their eyes drowsy with presummer lassitude. The smell of grass and budding trees was fresh and sweet, as befitted late April, and here and there blankets were airing and slip covers drooped from upstairs windows. Tomorrow might dawn clear and crisp, and for weeks actual summer might linger somewhere far away before it came to settle. But today there was that kind of lazy, warm peacefulness that stilled energetic hands and dulled aches and brought ease and relaxation.

Ricky lounged indolently in a chair on the back lawn. His socks tumbled effortlessly against his ankles, and his stained gabardine pants hiked halfway up his thin legs. He wore size-twelve sneakers, split at the seams and indeterminate in color. His arms hung loosely at his sides, and his eyes stared unseeingly straight ahead. He was a perfect picture of graceless repose.

His mother called from the kitchen window. "What are you doing, Ricky?"

"Nothin'."

He heard her discussing the marketing with Anna, heard Anna's harsh guttural tones and his mother's soft gentle ones. Then he heard his mother walk out to the back porch. "If you have nothing to do, perhaps you'd like to ride your bike down to the grocer's and pick up some things for me."

His eyes turned to her, but he hardly moved his head a fraction of an inch. "Sorry, Mom. I gotta date."

"But you're just *sitting*."

"I'm gonna go in a sec."

His mother sighed, expressing the inevitable bewilderment of parents.

Ricky grinned. "Some hunk o' day, huh?"

His mother looked surprised. "To look at you I wouldn't think you'd even *notice* the day. You're so—so—Ricky, how do you manage to look *boneless*?"

He stood up in one fluid movement. He yawned and slouched over to the railing of the back porch. His mother stood two steps above him, but her eyes were on a level with his. He leaned over and kissed the tip of her nose, but it was not actually a kiss. It was more like a lick from a friendly puppy. "S'long, Duchess."

"Darling, please stand up straight. Your posture is positively frightening. You've grown too fast, and I honestly think you're getting a curvature."

He straightened his shoulders briefly, slouched comfortably again. "Want me to stop by the grocer's this aft?"

Her look was a mixture of adoration and tenderness, irritation and annoyance. "Of course not. It would be too late, and you'd probably forget anyway. Where are you going?"

"Pick up Marge." He raised two fingers in a half salute, smiled engagingly, and slouched off.

He got his bike and rode down the driveway, his long legs doubled up over the pedals, one hand barely touching the handle bar, the other in his pocket carelessly. He looked too tall for the bike, too big to be riding it. He was sixteen and on weekends he was allowed to drive his father's car, just as long as he kept to the suburbs and didn't go downtown into traffic. Most of the boys had that same arrangement. They rode their bikes with disgraceful, reckless ease that

threatened the lives of any passing pedestrians. On Saturdays and Sundays they drove their fathers' cars with serious absorption and also threatened pedestrians' lives. No matter how you looked at it, the poor pedestrian didn't stand a chance. Ricky turned a corner with "no hands," a childish habit he still retained. There were many childish habits he had not outgrown, despite his man's size and the fuzz on his upper lip and the cigarette case he had just received for his birthday.

He left his bike against Marge's stoop and went up to the porch. He rang the bell—two longs and a short—and then opened the door and went inside.

Mrs. Crane was writing letters at the desk in the living room. She looked up vaguely and said, "Oh, good morning, Ricky. Margery is out back feeding the dog."

"Thanks." He went through the kitchen. There were strawberries in a bowl, and he took one and ate it. It was tart and needed sugar. He made a face and then looked out of the kitchen window. Margery was on her knees, coaxing an ugly dachshund to eat. She put one finger in the bowl of milk and soggy cereal and wriggled it. "Come on, Snitz, try it." The dog sniffed at her hand and turned away.

Ricky tiptoed to the door. He crouched and then, with a sudden bloodcurdling yell, he pushed open the door, his face grimaced menacingly, his fingers curled like claws. The dog whimpered in fright and cringed, terrified. Margery looked up placidly. " 'Lo, Spider."

"Hi." He lounged against the door. "Whatsa matter?"

"Snitz won't eat anything since Mathilda went to visit her sister." Mathilda was their maid.

"Leave him alone."

"But he'll get sick if he doesn't eat. Mother's wild. She said if he gets sick again she's going to *give* him to Mathilda's sister and let *her* worry about him."

"He won't eat if ya hang around," Ricky said sagely. "Leave it there and pretend to go away."

They left the bowl and walked away, carefully casual. They hid behind a bush and after a few minutes the dachshund lapped at the cereal and milk hungrily.

Margery said, "The faker."

"Dogs don't like people to look at them eat," he said with assurance. "Wha' do ya wanna do?"

"Mother's got a meeting here this morning. We can't hang around."

"Get your bike and we'll see."

"All right." She went to tell her mother, and then they bicycled down the quiet streets. When they got to the countryclub grounds they turned up a rocky dirt road and went single file. The stones clattered against the spokes of the wheels, and the handle bars shook unsteadily. Once he called, " 'S a hole ahead," and she swung way to the right, following his lead. When they came to a clearing they left the bicycles and sprawled on the grass. Snitz had followed them, and now caught up, tongue hanging.

It was still early, and the sun had not risen enough to penetrate the tall trees. It was cool and damp, and they sat where they could hear the happy murmur of a nearby brook. Margery wore faded blue denim pedal-pushers, black moccasins, white socks. Her dark hair, shoulder-length, was combed in bangs. Her cheeks were red from the ride and her nose was a little sunburned and beginning to peel. A light film of perspiration lined her upper lip. She said, "Billy and Anita are going to the movies this aft. Want to go?"

"What's playing?"

"Cary Grant and Katharine Hepburn in *Holiday*. It's a revival."

He shrugged. "Maybe. It'll be mushy." He lay flat and squinted up at the branches of the trees. There were many spaces where the leaves weren't out yet and though the sun peeked through, it didn't hit his body. He would have gone to the movies if Billy and Anita weren't going along. Anita was a drip. She giggled and did funny things with her mouth that she thought made her look like Joan Crawford, and she and Billy were always holding hands and whispering. He glanced at Margery. She was different from the rest—different, the way he was. She used lipstick and when they came home from a party sometimes she kissed him good night—but it was different. She could ride for miles without getting tired, and she talked about the kind of things he liked. Besides, he had known her ever since he could remember. Maybe that was it. Maybe that was why he never had to say silly things or pretend with her.

She wriggled the braces on her teeth and took her finger and slid them off. "I have to go to the dentist tomorrow."

He clucked sympathetically. "I gotta go next week. I gotta cavity."

"If he'd only take these things off. They pinch."

"That's 'cause you're always sliding 'em up and down. Put 'em back." Sometimes he had to be firm with her. She was like that about some things—childish. She slipped the braces back in and "clicked" them. Then she lay down next to him. She was very close and he could smell the starched odor of her blouse. It smelled just like his shirts when they came back from the laundry.

He felt wonderful, and he whistled tunelessly. At times he wondered at the nice feeling he got when she was very close to him—or when he didn't expect to see her and suddenly she was near. Like the day she was home from school and he was going through the hall, from geometry to Latin, and she just showed up. "My mother took me to the doctor, and he said there was nothing wrong—that I should go to school." He hadn't been able to explain the sense of—of *goodness* that made him slap the books from the arm of the boy ahead of him and laugh uproariously at the boy's surprise. When he was at a loss to explain some emotions he always told himself it was "one of those things." He was still at the age where he would accept blindly the soft, intimate intricacies that were confusing to him and yet fight tenaciously the unalterable, irrevocable ones like having his dog run over, or the kid in his class who had heart trouble and had to be put in a hospital. Things like that he hated fiercely, and he tried in a million ways to rectify them; wild implausible plans to fill his thoughts. But the others—like Margery; and the day he overheard his father say to his mother, "This may sound sentimental, or even biased, but Ricky is honestly everything I've ever dreamed my son would be —everything I'd want him to be. Sure he's sloppy and at times lazy, but that's superficial. Basically—he's all there." The feelings that suffused him, the ones that made him want to shout or sing at the top of his lungs, the ones he couldn't pigeonhole or label, he lumped into the phrase, "one of those things." They would become clear later— maybe when he was older. He moved his arm closer to Margery's, touching Margery's. She didn't notice, didn't mind, and it felt good.

"Ugh—school Monday." She wasn't too good a student, and he helped her with her homework all the time.

"Easter vacation's always short—seems."

"And exams. My father said if I don't pass everything this year I can't get into college."

Funny the way he hated to think of college. One more year at school—and then college. He was going, of course, but he really didn't like to think of it all.

"Where are you going, Spider?"

"Harvard—if I get in. It's tough."

"Aren't you excited? I mean, it's not so far off."

"Nope."

"Why not?"

"I don't know—just one of those things." College meant going away—for years. Oh, you came home for vacations and probably summers but . . .

"Maybe if I didn't go to Harvard we could go to the same place— coed—maybe Cornell." It was a good idea, and he rolled over and stared at her. He'd help her with her homework, and then they could ride home for vacations on the train together. "Say—what about it? I could talk my parents into it—maybe."

"If I get in," she said doubtfully. "I'll probably fail chemistry this year."

"No, you won't. I'll coach you."

She laughed suddenly, deliciously. "Can you take Regents for me too?"

He doubled up, he laughed loud and hard, he beat the ground with his hand. That was the killing story about Gail and Mary Jane, the twins. Last year Mary Jane had taken Latin Regents for Gail—signing her name and everything—and not a single teacher had found out.

Margery pulled at long piece of grass carefully and chewed on its root.

"Why don't you like Billy?"

"He's okay—except when he's around Anita he's a drip."

"She's pretty."

"Pretty!" He made grotesque faces. "She's Dracula."

"Everybody thinks she's pretty."

"Not me."

"You're funny."

"No, I'm not," he said. "I think you're pretty."

She thought about it, her eyes candid and reflective.

Suddenly he leaned over and kissed her. It was awkward, for he needed his elbow to support himself and his arm tangled with hers. But gradually the awkwardness left because it was a long kiss—different from the other times he had kissed her. Her braces felt hard and lumpy beneath her lips, but he didn't mind.

When she got up he coughed nervously. She was very quiet, plucking at her wool socks with her fingers.

"Margery?"

"Yes."

"Look—let's go to college together. I mean we could be together —huh?"

"All right—if I can."

The feeling grew, the wild exultant *good* feeling, and he said very loudly, "'S getting hot. Whadya say we skip the movies. Let's stop at the delicatessen and get sandwiches. I can charge them and we can go to the beach. My father's coming home early today, and I know I can use the car."

"I'll take Snitz. He loves the water."

They got up and walked back to the clearing. It was very hot in the sun, and the crickets made ceaseless noises. And then, just as she was about to grasp the handle bars and pedal off, he said, "Marge!"

"Yes?"

A hot stiffness caught at his chest, and his tongue felt like a piece of cotton in his mouth. The crickets dinned wildly in his ears. His voice sounded as if he were choking. "I love you."

A great stillness touched him. Nothing moved—not a tree, not a branch. He was afraid to look at her, afraid she would laugh, afraid she would cry.

She said, "Thank you, Spider." And the earth moved normally.

He slapped at a tall weed and got on his bike and they pedaled back. Something rare and wonderful had happened to him. It was over, and he was kind of glad it was past. He couldn't understand why he had had to say what he had said—and why it had become an idea, out of a formless mass, but anyway it was over and he felt fine, and it was one of those things.

Love is so powerful an emotion that it can transcend many of the more painful realities of life. This truth is nowhere more obvious than in the beautiful diaries of Anne Frank, the adolescent girl who was to die later in a German concentration camp during the Second World War. In her early adolescence her family sought refuge in an attic, where they lived without any communication with the outside world except for some neighbors who had joined them in their refuge. The boy Peter was such a neighbor.

Anne Frank thought of her diary as a friend. She called it "Kitty" and poured into it her deepest feelings. She wrote, "I want to go on living even after my death." Indeed, her diary has done just that, a living memorial to youth and courage.

MY LONGING TO TALK
TO SOMEONE

ANNE FRANK

Dear Kitty, Thursday, 6 January, 1944

My longing to talk to someone became so intense that somehow or other I took it into my head to choose Peter.

Sometimes if I've been upstairs into Peter's room during the day, it always struck me as very snug, but because Peter is so retiring and would never turn anyone out who became a nuisance, I never dared stay long, because I was afraid he might think me a bore. I tried to think of an excuse to stay in his room and get him talking, without its being too noticeable, and my chance came yesterday. Peter has a mania for crossword puzzles at the moment and hardly does anything else. I helped him with them, and we soon sat opposite each other at his little table, he on the chair and me on the divan.

It gave me a queer feeling each time I looked into his deep blue eyes, and he sat there with that mysterious laugh playing round his lips. I was able to read his inward thoughts. I could see on his face that look of helplessness and uncertainty as to how to behave, and, at the same time, a trace of his sense of manhood. I noticed his shy manner and it made me feel very gentle; I couldn't refrain from meeting those dark eyes again and again, and with my whole heart I almost beseeched him: oh, tell me, what is going on inside you, oh, can't you look beyond this ridiculous chatter?

But the evening passed and nothing happened, except that I told him about blushing—naturally not what I have written but just so that he would become more sure of himself as he grew older.

When I lay in bed and thought over the whole situation, I found it far from encouraging, and the idea that I should beg for Peter's patronage was simply repellent. One can do a lot to satisfy one's longings, which certainly sticks out in my case, for I have made up my mind to go and sit with Peter more often and to get him talking somehow or other.

Whatever you do, don't think I'm in love with Peter—not a bit of it! If the Van Daans had had a daughter instead of a son, I should have tried to make friends with her too.

I woke at about five to seven this morning and knew at once, quite positively, what I had dreamed. I sat on a chair and opposite me sat Peter . . . Wessel. We were looking together at a book of drawings by Mary Bos. The dream was so vivid that I can still partly remember the drawings. But that was not all—the dream went on. Suddenly Peter's eyes met mine and I looked into those fine, velvet-brown eyes for a long time. Then Peter said very softly, "If I had only known, I would have come to you long before!" I turned around brusquely because the emotion was too much for me. And after that I felt a soft, and oh, such a cool kind cheek against mine and it felt so good, so good. . . .

I awoke at this point, while I could still feel his cheek against mine and felt his brown eyes looking deep into my heart, so deep, that there he read how much I had loved him and how much I still love him. Tears sprang into my eyes once more, and I was very sad

My Longing to Talk to Someone ✑ 25

that I had lost him again, but at the same time glad because it made me feel quite certain that Peter was still the chosen one.

It is strange that I should often see such vivid images in my dreams here. First I saw Grandma [1] so clearly one night that I could even distinguish her thick, soft, wrinkled velvety skin. Then Granny appeared as a guardian angel; then followed Lies, who seemed to be a symbol to me of the sufferings of all my girl friends and all Jews. When I pray for her, I pray for all Jews and all those in need. And now Peter, my darling Peter—never before have I had such a clear picture of him in my mind. I don't need a photo of him, I can see him before my eyes, and oh, so well!

Yours, Anne

Friday, 7 January, 1944

Dear Kitty,

What a silly ass I am! I am quite forgetting that I have never told you the history of myself and all my boy friends.

When I was quite small—I was even still at a kindergarten—I became attached to Karel Samson. He had lost his father, and he and his mother lived with an aunt. One of Karel's cousins, Robby, was a slender, good-looking dark boy, who aroused more admiration than the little, humorous fellow, Karel. But looks did not count with me and I was very fond of Karel for years.

We used to be together a lot for quite a long time, but for the rest, my love was unreturned.

Then Peter crossed my path, and in my childish way I really fell in love. He liked me very much, too, and we were inseparable for one whole summer. I can still remember us walking hand in hand through the streets together, he in a white cotton suit and me in a short summer dress. At the end of the summer holidays he went into the first form of the high school and I into the sixth form of the lower school. He used to meet me from school and, vice versa, I would meet him. Peter was a very good-looking boy, tall, handsome, and slim, with an earnest, calm, intelligent face. He had dark hair, and wonderful brown eyes, ruddy cheeks, and a pointed nose. I was mad about his laugh, above all, when he looked so mischievous and naughty!

I went to the country for the holidays; when I returned, Peter had

[1]Grandma is grandmother on Father's side, Granny on Mother's side.

in the meantime moved, and a much older boy lived in the same house. He apparently drew Peter's attention to the fact that I was a childish little imp, and Peter gave me up. I adored him so that I didn't want to face the truth. I tried to hold on to him until it dawned on me that if I went on running after him I should soon get the name of being boy-mad. The years passed. Peter went around with girls of his own age and didn't even think of saying "Hello" to me any more; but I couldn't forget him.

I went to the Jewish Secondary School. Lots of boys in our class were keen on me—I thought it was fun, felt honored, but was otherwise quite untouched. Then later on, Harry was mad about me, but, as I've already told you, I never fell in love again.

There is a saying "Time heals all wounds," and so it was with me. I imagined that I had forgotten Peter and that I didn't like him a bit any more. The memory of him, however, lived so strongly in my subconscious mind that I admitted to myself sometimes I was jealous of the other girls, and that was why I didn't like him any more. This morning I knew that nothing has changed; on the contrary, as I grew older and more mature my love grew with me. I can quite understand now that Peter thought me childish, and yet it still hurt that he had so completely forgotten me. His face was shown so clearly to me, and now I know that no one else could remain with me as he does.

I am completely upset by the dream. When Daddy kissed me this morning, I could have cried out: "Oh, if only you were Peter!" I think of him all the time and I keep repeating to myself the whole day, "Oh, Petel, darling, darling darling Petel . . . !"

Who can help me now? I must live on and pray to God that He will let Peter cross my path when I come out of here, and that when he reads the love in my eyes he will say, "Oh, Anne, if I had only known, I would have come to you long before!"

I saw my face in the mirror and it looks quite different. My eyes look so clear and deep, my cheeks are pink—which they haven't been for weeks—my mouth is much softer; I look as if I am happy, and yet there is something so sad in my expression and my smile slips away from my lips as soon as it has come. I'm not happy, because I might know that Peter's thoughts are not with me, and yet I still feel his wonderful eyes upon me and his cool soft cheek against mine.

Oh, Petel, Petel, how will I ever free myself of your image? Wouldn't any other in your place be a miserable substitute? I love you,

My Longing to Talk to Someone ✑ 27

and with such a great love that it can't grow in my heart any more but has to leap out into the open and suddenly manifest itself in such a devastating way!

A week ago, even yesterday, if anyone had asked me, "Which of your friends do you consider would be the most suitable to marry?" I would have answered, "I don't know"; but now I would cry, "Petel, because I love him with all my heart and soul. I give myself completely!" But one thing, he may touch my face, but no more.

Once, when we spoke about sex, Daddy told me that I couldn't possibly understand the longing yet; I always knew that I did understand it and now I understand it fully. Nothing is so beloved to me now as he, my Petel.

Yours, Anne

Monday, 24 January, 1944

Dear Kitty,

Something has happened to me; or rather, I can hardly describe it as an event, except that I think it is pretty crazy. Whenever anyone used to speak of sexual problems at home or at school, it was something either mysterious or revolting. Words which had any bearing on the subject were whispered, and often if someone didn't understand he was laughed at. It struck me as very odd and I thought, "Why are people so secretive and tiresome when they talk about these things?" But as I didn't think that I could change things, I kept my mouth shut as much as possible, or sometimes asked girl friends for information. When I had learned quite a lot and had also spoken about it with my parents, Mummy said one day, "Anne, let me give you some good advice; never speak about this subject to boys and don't reply if they begin about it." I remember exactly what my answer was: I said, "No, of course not! The very idea!" And there it remained.

When we first came here, Daddy often told me about things that I would really have preferred to hear from Mummy, and I found out the rest from books and things I picked up from conversations. Peter Van Daan was never as tiresome over this as the boys at school—once or twice at first perhaps—but he never tried to get me talking.

Mrs. Van Daan told us that she had never talked about these things to Peter, and for all she knew neither had her husband. Apparently she didn't even know how much he knew.

Yesterday, when Margot, Peter, and I were peeling potatoes,

somehow the conversation turned to Boche. "We still don't know what sex Boche is, do we?" I asked.

"Yes, certainly," Peter answered. "He's a tom."

I began to laugh. "A tomcat that's expecting, that's marvelous!"

Peter and Margot laughed too over this silly mistake. You see, two months ago, Peter had stated that Boche would soon be having a family, her tummy was growing visibly. However, the fatness appeared to come from the many stolen bones, because the children didn't seem to grow fast, let alone make their appearance!

Peter just had to defend himself. "No," he said, "You can go with me yourself to look at him. Once when I was playing around with him, I noticed quite clearly that he's a tom."

I couldn't control my curiosity, and went with him to the warehouse. Boche, however, was not receiving visitors, and was nowhere to be seen. We waited for a while, began to get cold, and went upstairs again. Later in the afternoon I heard Peter go downstairs for the second time. I mustered up all my courage to walk through the silent house alone, and reached the warehouse. Boche stood on the packing table playing with Peter, who had just put him on the scales to weigh him.

"Hello, do you want to see him?" He didn't make any lengthy preparations, but picked up the animal, turned him over on his back, deftly held his head and paws together, and the lesson began. "These are the male organs, these are just a few stray hairs, and that is his bottom." The cat did another half turn and was standing on his white socks once more.

If any other boy had shown me "the male organs," I would never have looked at him again. But Peter went on talking quite normally on what is otherwise such a painful subject, without meaning anything unpleasant, and finally put me sufficiently at my ease for me to be normal too. We played with Boche, amused ourselves, chattered together, and then sauntered through the large warehouse towards the door.

"Usually, when I want to know something, I find it in some book or other, don't you?" I asked.

"Why on earth? I just ask upstairs. My father knows more than me and has had more experience in such things."

We were already on the stairs, so I kept my mouth shut after that.

"Things may alter," as Brer Rabbit said. Yes. Really I shouldn't have discussed these things in such a normal way with a girl. I

My Longing to Talk to Someone ⇜ 29

know too definitely that Mummy didn't mean it that way when she warned me not to discuss the subject with boys. I wasn't quite my usual self for the rest of the day though, in spite of everything. When I thought over our talk, it still seemed rather odd. But at least I'm wiser about one thing, that there really are young people—and of the opposite sex too—who can discuss these things naturally without making fun of them.

I wonder if Peter really does ask his parents much. Would he honestly behave with them as he did with me yesterday? Ah, what would I know about it!

Yours, Anne

Sunday, 13 February, 1944

Dear Kitty,

Since Saturday a lot has changed for me. It came about like this. I longed—and am still longing—but . . . now something has happened, which has made it a little, just a little, less.

To my great joy—I will be quite honest about it—already this morning I noticed that Peter kept looking at me all the time. Not in the ordinary way, I don't know how, I just can't explain.

I used to think that Peter was in love with Margot, but yesterday I suddenly had the feeling that it is not so. I made a special effort not to look at him too much, because whenever I did, he kept on looking too and then—yes, then—it gave me a lovely feeling inside, but which I mustn't feel too often.

I desperately want to be alone. Daddy has noticed that I'm not quite my usual self, but I really can't tell him everything. "Leave me in peace, leave me alone," that's what I'd like to keep crying out all the time. Who knows, the day may come when I'm left alone more than I would wish!

Yours, Anne

Tuesday, 28 March, 1944

Dearest Kitty,

I could write a lot more about politics, but I have heaps of other things to tell you today. First, Mummy has more or less forbidden me to go upstairs so often, because, according to her, Mrs. Van Daan is jealous. Secondly, Peter has invited Margot to join us upstairs; I don't know whether it's just out of politeness or whether he really means it. Thirdly, I went and asked Daddy if he thought I need pay any regard to Mrs. Van Daan's jealousy, and he didn't think so. What next?

Mummy is cross, perhaps jealous too. Daddy doesn't grudge us these times together, and thinks it's nice that we get on so well. Margot is fond of Peter too, but feels that two's company and three's a crowd.

Mummy thinks that Peter is in love with me; quite frankly, I only wish he were, then we'd be quits and really be able to get to know each other. She also says that he keeps on looking at me. Now, I suppose that's true, but still I can't help it if he looks at my dimples and we wink at each other occasionally, can I?

I'm in a very difficult position. Mummy is against me and I'm against her, Daddy closes his eyes and tries not to see the silent battle between us. Mummy is sad, because she does really love me, while I'm not in the least bit sad, because I don't think she understands. And Peter—I don't want to give Peter up, he's such a darling. I admire him so; it can grow into something beautiful between us; why do the "old 'uns" have to poke their noses in all the time? Luckily I'm quite used to hiding my feelings and I manage extremely well not to let them see how mad I am about him. Will he ever say anything? Will I ever feel his cheek against mine, as I felt Petel's cheek in my dream? Oh, Peter and Petel, you are one and the same! They don't understand us; won't they ever grasp that we are happy, just sitting together and not saying a word. They don't understand what has driven us together like this. Oh, when will all these difficulties be overcome? And yet it is good to overcome them, because then the end will be all the more wonderful. When he lies with his head on his arm with his eyes closed, then he is still a child; when he plays with Boche, he is loving; when he carries potatoes or anything heavy, then he is strong; when he goes and watches the shooting, or looks for burglars in the darkness, then he is brave; and when he is so awkward and clumsy, then he is just a pet.

I like it much better if he explains something to me than when I have to teach him; I would really adore him to be my superior in almost everything.

What do we care about the two mothers? Oh, but if only he would speak!

Yours, Anne

Monday, 17 April, 1944

Dear Kitty,

Do you think that Daddy and Mummy would approve of my sitting and kissing a boy on a divan—a boy of seventeen and a half and a girl of just under fifteen? I don't really think they would, but I must rely on myself over this. It is so quiet and peaceful to lie in his arms and to dream, it is so thrilling to feel his cheek against mine, it is so lovely to know that there is someone waiting for me. But there is indeed a big "but," because will Peter be content to leave it at this? I haven't forgotten his promise already, but . . . he *is* a boy!

I know myself that I'm starting very soon, not even fifteen, and so independent already! It's certainly hard for other people to understand, I know almost for certain that Margot would never kiss a boy unless there had been some talk of an engagement or marriage, but neither Peter nor I have anything like that in mind. I'm sure too that Mummy never touched a man before Daddy. What would my girl friends say about it if they knew that I lay in Peter's arms, my heart against his chest, my head on his shoulder and with his head against mine!

Oh, Anne, how scandalous! But honestly, I don't think it is; we are shut up here, shut away from the world, in fear and anxiety, especially just lately. Why, then, should we who love each other remain apart? Why should we wait until we've reached a suitable age? Why should we bother?

I have taken it upon myself to look after myself; he would never want to cause me sorrow or pain. Why shouldn't I follow the way my heart leads me, if it makes us both happy? All the same, Kitty, I believe you can sense that I'm in doubt, I think it must be my honesty which rebels against doing anything on the sly! Do you think it's my duty to tell Daddy what I'm doing? Do you think we should share our secret with a third person? A lot of the beauty would be lost, but would my conscience feel happier? I will discuss it with "him."

Oh, yes, there's still so much I want to talk to him about, for I don't see the use of only just cuddling each other. To exchange our thoughts, that shows confidence and faith in each other, we would both be sure to profit by it!

Yours, Anne

Friday, 28 April, 1944

Dear Kitty,

I have never forgotten my dream about Peter Wessel (see beginning of January). If I think of it, I can still feel his cheek against mine now, and recall that lovely feeling that made everything good.

Sometimes I have had the same feeling here with Peter, but never to such an extent, until yesterday, when we were, as usual, sitting on the divan, our arms around each other's waists. Then suddenly the ordinary Anne slipped away and a second Anne took her place, a second Anne who is not reckless and jocular, but one who just wants to love and be gentle.

I sat pressed closely against him and felt a wave of emotion come over me, tears sprang into my eyes, the left one trickled onto his dungarees, the right one ran down my nose and also fell onto his dungarees. Did he notice? He made no move or sign to show that he did. I wonder if he feels the same as *I* do? He hardly said a word. Does he know that he has two Annes before him? These questions must remain unanswered.

At half past eight I stood up and went to the window, where we always say good-by. I was still trembling, I was still Anne number two. He came towards me, I flung my arms around his neck and gave him a kiss on his left cheek, and was about to kiss the other cheek, when my lips met his and we pressed them together. In a whirl we were clasped in each other's arms, again and again, never to leave off. Oh, Peter does so need tenderness. For the first time in his life he has discovered a girl, has seen for the first time that even the most irritating girls have another side to them, that they have hearts and can be different when you are alone with them. For the first time in his life he has given of himself and, having never had a boy or girl friend in his life before, shown his real self. Now we have found each other. For that matter, I didn't know him either, like him having never had a trusted friend, and this is what it has come to. . . .

Once more there is a question which gives me no peace: "Is it right? Is it right that I should have yielded so soon, that I am so ardent, just as ardent and eager as Peter himself? May I, a girl, let myself go to this extent?" There is but *one* answer: "I have longed so much and for so long—I am so lonely—and now I have found consolation."

In the mornings we just behave in an ordinary way, in the afternoons more or less so (except just occasionally); but in the evenings the suppressed longings of the whole day, the happiness and the blissful memories of all the previous occasions come to the surface and we only think of each other. Every evening, after the last kiss, I would like to dash away, not to look into his eyes any more—away, away, alone in the darkness.

And what do I have to face, when I reach the bottom of the staircase? Bright lights, questions, and laughter; I have to swallow it all and not show a thing. My heart still feels too much; I can't get over a shock such as I received yesterday all at once. The Anne who is gentle shows herself too little anyway and, therefore, will not allow herself to be suddenly driven into the background. Peter has touched my emotions more deeply than anyone has ever done before—except in my dreams. Peter has taken possession of me and turned me inside out; surely it goes without saying that anyone would require a rest and a little while to recover from such an upheaval?

Oh Peter, what have you done to me? What do you want of me? Where will this lead us? Oh, now I understand Elli; now, now that I am going through this myself, now I understand her doubt; if I were older and he should ask me to marry him, what should I answer? Anne, be honest! You would not be able to marry him, but yet, it would be hard to let him go. Peter hasn't enough character yet, not enough will power, too little courage and strength. He is still a child in his heart of hearts, he is no older than I am; he is only searching for tranquillity and happiness.

Am I only fourteen? Am I really still a silly little schoolgirl? Am I really so inexperienced about everything? I have more experience than most; I have been through things that hardly anyone of my age has undergone. I am afraid of myself, I am afraid that in my longing I am giving myself too quickly. How, later on, can it ever go right with other boys? Oh, it is so difficult, always battling with one's heart and reason; in its own time, each will speak, but do I know for certain that I have chosen the right time?

Yours, Anne

Tuesday, 2 May, 1944

Dear Kitty,

On Saturday evening I asked Peter whether he thought that I ought to tell Daddy a bit about us; when we'd discussed it a little, he came to the conclusion that I should. I was glad, for it shows that he's an honest boy. As soon as I got downstairs I went off with Daddy to get some water; and while we were on the stairs I said, "Daddy, I expect you've gathered that when we're together Peter and I don't sit miles apart. Do you think it's wrong?" Daddy didn't reply immediately, then said, "No, I don't think it's wrong, but you must be careful, Anne; you're in such a confined space here." When we went upstairs, he said something else on the same lines. On Sunday morning he called me to him and said, "Anne, I have thought more about what you said." I felt scared already. "It's not really very right—here in this house; I thought that you were just pals. Is Peter in love?"

"Oh, of course not," I replied.

"You know that I understand both of you, but you must be the one to hold back. Don't go upstairs so often, don't encourage him more than you can help. It is the man who is always the active one in these things; the woman can hold him back. It is quite different under normal circumstances, when you are free, you see other boys and girls, you can get away sometimes, play games and do all kinds of other things; but here, if you're together a lot, and you want to get away, you can't; you see each other every hour of the day—in fact, all the time. Be careful, Anne, and don't take it too seriously!"

"I don't, Daddy, but Peter is a decent boy, really a nice boy!"

"Yes, but he is not a strong character; he can be easily influenced, for good, but also for bad; I hope for his sake that his good side will remain uppermost, because, by nature, that is how he is."

We talked on for a bit and agreed that Daddy should talk to him too.

On Sunday morning in the attic he asked, "And have you talked to your father, Anne?"

"Yes," I replied, "I'll tell you about it. Daddy doesn't think it's bad, but he says that here, where we're so close together all the time, clashes may easily arise."

"But we agreed, didn't we, never to quarrel; and I'm determined to stick to it!"

"So will I, Peter, but Daddy didn't think that it was like this, he just thought we were pals; do you think that we still can be?"

"I can—what about you?"

"Me too, I told Daddy that I trusted you. I do trust you, Peter, just as much as I trust Daddy, and I believe you to be worthy of it. You are, aren't you, Peter?"

"I hope so." (He was very shy and rather red in the face.)

"I believe in you, Peter," I went on, "I believe that you have good qualities, and that you'll get on in the world."

After that, we talked about other things. Later I said, "If we come out of here, I know quite well that you won't bother about me any more!"

He flared right up. "That's not true, Anne, oh no, I won't let you think that of me!"

Then I was called away.

Daddy has talked to him; he told me about it today. "Your father thought that the friendship might develop into love sooner or later," he said. But I replied that we would keep a check on ourselves.

Daddy doesn't want me to go upstairs so much in the evenings now, but I don't want that. Not only because I like being with Peter; I have told him that I trust him. I do trust him and I want to show him that I do, which can't happen if I stay downstairs through lack of trust.

No, I'm going!

In the meantime the Dussel drama has righted itself again. At supper on Saturday evening he apologized in beautiful Dutch. Van Daan was nice about it straight away; it must have taken Dussel a whole day to learn that little lesson off by heart.

Sunday, his birthday, passed peacefully. We gave him a bottle of good 1919 wine, from the Van Daans (who could give their presents now after all), a bottle of piccalilli and a packet of razor blades, a jar of lemon jam from Kraler, a book, *Little Martin*, from Miep, and a plant from Elli. He treated each one of us to an egg.

Yours, Anne

Friday, 5 May, 1944

Dear Kitty,

Daddy is not pleased with me; he thought that after our talk on Sunday I automatically wouldn't go upstairs every evening. He doesn't want any "necking," a word I can't bear. It was bad enough talking about it, why must he make it so unpleasant now? I shall talk to him today. Margot has given me some good advice, so listen; this is roughly what I want to say:

"I believe, Daddy, that you expect a declaration from me, so I will give it you. You are disappointed in me, as you had expected more reserve from me, and I suppose you want me to be just as a fourteen-year-old should be. But that's where you're mistaken!

"Since we've been here, from July 1942 until a few weeks ago, I can assure you that I haven't had any easy time. If you only knew how I cried in the evenings, how unhappy I was, how lonely I felt, then you would understand that I want to go upstairs!

"I have now reached the stage that I can live entirely on my own, without Mummy's support or anyone else's for that matter. But it hasn't just happened in a night; it's been a bitter, hard struggle and I've shed many a tear, before I became as independent as I am now. You can laugh at me and not believe me, but that can't harm me. I know that I'm a separate individual and I don't feel in the least bit responsible to any of you. I am only telling you this because I thought that otherwise you might think that I was underhand, but I don't have to give an account of my deeds to anyone but myself.

"When I was in difficulties you all closed your eyes and stopped up your ears and didn't help me; on the contrary, I received nothing but warnings not to be so boisterous. I was only boisterous so as not to be miserable all the time. I was reckless so as not to hear that persistent voice within me continually. I played a comedy for a year and a half, day in, day out, I never grumbled, never lost my cue, nothing like that—and now, now the battle is over. I have won! I am independent both in mind and body. I don't need a mother any more, for all this conflict has made me strong.

"And now, now that I'm on top of it, now that I know that I've fought the battle, now I want to be able to go on in my own way too, the way that I think is right. You can't and mustn't regard me as fourteen, for all these troubles have made me older; I shall not be sorry for what I have done, but shall act as I think I can. You can't coax me into not going upstairs; *either* you forbid it, *or* you trust me through thick and thin, but then leave me in peace as well!"

Yours, Anne

Saturday, 6 May, 1944

Dear Kitty,

I put a letter, in which I wrote what I explained to you yesterday, in Daddy's pocket before supper yesterday. After reading it, he was, according to Margot, very upset for the rest of the evening. (I was upstairs doing the dishes.) Poor Pim, I might have known what the effect of such an epistle would be. He is so sensitive! I immediately told Peter not to ask or say anything more. Pim hasn't said any more about it to me. Is that yet in store, I wonder?

Here everything is going on more or less normally again. What they tell us about the prices and the people outside is almost unbelievable, half a pound of tea costs 350 florins,[1] a pound of coffee 80 florins, butter 35 florins per pound, an egg 1.45 florin. People pay 14 florins for an ounce of Bulgarian tobacco! Everyone deals in the black market, every errand boy has something to offer. Our baker's boy got hold of some sewing silk, 0.9 florin for a thin little skein, the milkman manages to get clandestine ration cards, the undertaker delivers the cheese. Burglaries, murders, and theft go on daily. The police and night watchmen join in just as strenuously as the professionals, everyone wants something in their empty stomachs and because wage increases are forbidden the people simply have to swindle. The police are continually on the go, tracing girls of fifteen, sixteen, seventeen, and older, who are reported missing every day.

Yours, Anne

Sunday morning, 7 May, 1944

Dear Kitty,

Daddy and I had a long talk yesterday afternoon, I cried terribly and he joined in. Do you know what he said to me, Kitty? "I have received many letters in my life, but this is certainly the most unpleasant! You, Anne, who have received such love from your parents, you, who have parents who are always ready to help you, who have always defended you whatever it might be, can you talk of feeling no responsibility towards us? You feel wronged and deserted; no, Anne, you have done us a great injustice!

"Perhaps you didn't mean it like that, but it is what you wrote; no, Anne, we haven't deserved such a reproach as this!"

Oh, I have failed miserably; this is certainly the worst thing I've ever done in my life. I was only trying to show off with my crying and my tears, just trying to appear big, so that he would respect me. Certainly, I have had a lot of unhappiness, but to accuse the good Pim, who has done and still does do everything for me—no, that was too low for words.

It's right that for once I've been taken down from my inaccessible pedestal, that my pride has been shaken a bit, for I was becoming much too taken up with myself again. What Miss Anne does is by no means always right! Anyone who can cause such unhappiness to

[1]A florin is equal to approximately twenty-eight cents.

someone else, someone he professes to love, and on purpose, too, is low, very low!

And the way Daddy has forgiven me makes me feel more than ever ashamed of myself, he is going to throw the letter in the fire and is so sweet to me now, just as if he had done something wrong. No, Anne, you still have a tremendous lot to learn, begin by doing that first, instead of looking down on others and accusing them!

I have had a lot of sorrow, but who hasn't at my age? I have played the clown a lot too, but I was hardly conscious of it; I felt lonely, but hardly ever in despair! I ought to be deeply ashamed of myself, and indeed I am.

What is done cannot be undone, but one can prevent its happening again. I want to start from the beginning again and it can't be difficult, now that I have Peter. With him to support me, I can and will!

I'm not alone any more; he loves me. I love him, I have my books, my storybook and my diary, I'm not so frightfully ugly, not utterly stupid, have a cheerful temperament and want to have a good character!

Yes, Anne, you've felt deeply that your letter was too hard and that it was untrue. To think that you were even proud of it! I will take Daddy as my example, and I *will* improve.

Yours, Anne

Saturday, 15 July, 1944

Dear Kitty,

We have had a book from the library with the challenging title of: *What Do You Think of the Modern Young Girl?* I want to talk about this subject today.

The author of this book criticizes "the youth of today" from top to toe, without, however, condemning the whole of the young brigade as "incapable of anything good." On the contrary, she is rather of the opinion that if young people wished, they have it in their hands to make a bigger, more beautiful and better world, but that they occupy themselves with superficial things, without giving a thought to real beauty.

In some passages the writer gave me very much the feeling she was directing her criticisms at me, and that's why I want to lay myself completely bare to you for once and defend myself against this attack.

I have one outstanding trait in my character, which must strike

anyone who knows me for any length of time, and that is my knowledge of myself. I can watch myself and my actions, just like an out-
sider. The Anne of every day I can face entirely without prejudice,
without making excuses for her and watch what's good and what's
bad about her. This "self-consciousness" haunts me, and every time I
open my mouth I know as soon as I've spoken whether "that ought
to have been different" or "that was right as it was." There are so
many things about myself that I condemn; I couldn't begin to name
them all. I understand more and more how true Daddy's words
were when he said: "All children must look after their own upbring-
ing." Parents can only give good advice or put them on the right
paths, but the final forming of a person's character lies in their own
hands.

In addition to this, I have lots of courage, I always feel so strong
and as if I can bear a great deal, I feel so free and so young! I was
glad when I first realized it, because I don't think I shall easily bow
down before the blows that inevitably come to everyone.

But I've talked about these things so often before. Now I want to
come to the chapter of "Daddy and Mummy don't understand me."
Daddy and Mummy have always thoroughly spoiled me, were
sweet to me, defended me, and have done all that parents could do.
And yet I've felt so terribly lonely for a long time, so left out, neglected, and misunderstood. Daddy tried all he could to check my rebel-
lious spirit, but it was no use, I have cured myself, by seeing for myself what was wrong in my behavior and keeping it before my eyes.

How is it that Daddy was never any support to me in my struggle,
why did he completely miss the mark when he wanted to offer me
a helping hand? Daddy tried the wrong methods; he always talked
to me as a child who was going through difficult phases. It sounds
crazy, because Daddy's the only one who has always taken me into
his confidence, and no one but Daddy has given me the feeling that
I'm sensible. But there's one thing he's omitted: you see, he hasn't
realized that for me the fight to get on top was more important than
all else. I didn't want to hear about "symptoms of your age," or
"other girls," or "it wears off by itself"; I didn't want to be treated
as a girl-like-all-others, but as Anne-on-her-own-merits. Pim didn't understand that. For that matter, I can't confide in anyone, unless they
tell me a lot about themselves, and as I know very little about Pim, I
don't feel that I can tread upon more intimate ground with him. Pim
always takes up the older, fatherly attitude, tells me that he too has

had similar passing tendencies. But still he's not able to feel with me like a friend, however hard he tries. These things have made me never mention my views on life nor my well-considered theories to anyone but my diary and, occasionally, to Margot. I concealed from Daddy everything that perturbed me; I never shared my ideals with him. I was aware of the fact that I was pushing him away from me.

I couldn't do anything else. I have acted entirely according to my feelings, but I have acted in the way that was best for my peace of mind. Because I should completely lose my repose and self-confidence, which I have built up so shakily, if, at this stage, I were to accept criticisms of my half-completed task. And I can't do that even from Pim, although it sounds very hard, for not only have I not shared my secret thoughts with Pim but I have often pushed him even further from me, by my irritability.

This is a point that I think a lot about: why is it that Pim annoys me? So much so that I can hardly bear him teaching me, that his affectionate ways strike me as being put on, that I want to be left in peace and would really prefer it if he dropped me a bit, until I felt more certain in my attitude towards him? Because I still have a gnawing feeling of guilt over that horrible letter that I dared to write him when I was so wound up. Oh, how hard it is to be really strong and brave in every way!

Yet this was not my greatest disappointment; no, I ponder far more over Peter than Daddy. I know very well that I conquered him instead of he conquering me. I created an image of him in my mind, pictured him as a quiet, sensitive, lovable boy, who needed affection and friendship. I needed a living person to whom I could pour out my heart; I wanted a friend who'd help to put me on the right road. I achieved what I wanted, and, slowly but surely, I drew him towards me. Finally, when I had made him feel friendly, it automatically developed into an intimacy which, on second thought, I don't think I ought to have allowed.

We talked about the most private things, and yet up till now we have never touched on those things that filled, and still fill, my heart and soul. I still don't know quite what to make of Peter, is he superficial, or does he still feel shy, even of me? But dropping that, I committed one error in my desire to make a real friendship: I switched over and tried to get at him by developing it into a more intimate relation, whereas I should have explored all other possibilities. He longs

My Longing to Talk to Someone ᴈ§ 41

to be loved and I can see that he's beginning to be more and more in love with me. He gets satisfaction out of our meetings, whereas they just have the effect of making me want to try it out with him again. And yet I don't seem able to touch on the subjects that I'm so longing to bring out into the daylight. I drew Peter towards me, far more than he realizes. Now he clings to me, and for the time being, I don't see any way of shaking him off and putting him on his own feet. When I realized that he could not be a friend for my understanding, I thought I would at least try to lift him up out of his narrow-mindedness and make him do something with his youth.

"For in its innermost depths youth is lonelier than old age." I read this saying in some book, and I've always remembered it and found it to be true. Is it true then that grownups have a more difficult time here than we do? No. I know it isn't. Older people have formed their opinions about everything and don't waver before they act. It's twice as hard for us young ones to hold our ground and maintain our opinions, in a time when all ideals are being shattered and destroyed, when people are showing their worst side and do not know whether to believe in truth and right and God.

Anyone who claims that the older ones have a more difficult time here certainly doesn't realize to what extent our problems weigh down on us, problems for which we are probably much too young, but which thrust themselves upon us continually, until, after a long time, we think we've found a solution, but the solution doesn't seem able to resist the facts which reduce it to nothing again. That's the difficulty in these times: ideals, dreams, and cherished hopes rise within us, only to meet the horrible truth and be shattered.

It's really a wonder that I haven't dropped all my ideals, because they seem so absurd and impossible to carry out. Yet I keep them, because in spite of everything I still believe that people are really good at heart. I simply can't build up my hopes on a foundation consisting of confusion, misery, and death. I see the world gradually being turned into a wilderness, I hear the ever approaching thunder, which will destroy us too, I can feel the sufferings of millions and yet, if I look up into the heavens, I think that it will all come right, that this cruelty too will end, and that peace and tranquillity will return again.

In the meantime, I must uphold my ideals, for perhaps the time will come when I shall be able to carry them out.

Yours, Anne

Can you fall in love with someone whose name you do not know, whose house you cannot find, whose parents will not accept you, who is indeed just a face you have seen? Many great writers have said yes. They have turned such a feeling into both poetry and prose. The poet Dante was inspired by the young girl Beatrice, whom he was never to meet officially. Our own contemporary Mark Van Doren, a Pulitzer Prize winner, has also captured the shadow and substance of such an encounter.

STILL, STILL SO

MARK VAN DOREN

The afternoons were darker now when he came up out of the subway at 12th Street to walk the four long blocks home. He noticed it for the first time yesterday, telling himself as he did so that fog must be the reason for those lights under the marquee of the movie house. But there was no fog. There was merely November—itself, he thought as he swung his briefcase around the corner and started west, itself the fog of the year, when thick air filled the streets and dusk rose sooner and softer from the areaways of the houses, as if the stoop and obscure basement passage had undertaken to engender it for a purpose of their own. The year was old, even if the twilights were still temperate. Most days he wore no topcoat up to college, and he had not yet looked into closets for his hat. This evening was mild enough so that he could go slowly, as he liked; slowly, thinking of calculus and Shakespeare; or, and this was just as good, thinking not at all.

As he crossed Waverly Place and entered the second

block he heard his heart informing him how loudly he lied. He had not been thinking of fog and the time of the year. He had been thinking only of her whom he had reason to believe he would see at the end of this block, just two houses before the intersection. And once more he felt in his pocket for the envelope he had taken with him this morning.

She was never there in the morning, but for a month now she had stood where he knew she would be standing—he slowed almost to a halt—at the top of eight stone steps, by the right column of a dimly lighted doorway, looking quietly over his head as he approached, and never dropping her eyes to show his own eyes that they had yet been noticed, let alone read and understood. They were capable of being read. One who ran might read them, and certainly one who stood. As she did, so quietly and beautifully that the act of standing became in her an act indeed, with more of graceful motion in it than most girls, even in their dreams of running, would ever achieve.

There she was. He must stop now. He must go by, and he must barely hesitate as he laid the envelope on the third step without looking up to her or uttering a word. The third step, at the level of his hand, and well into the angle between stone and iron, so that she could leave it there if she chose, and so that if she did leave it there it would not be trampled by strangers to its contents.

Its contents. That was the thing. Would they be understood? They were the highest compliment, he believed, a prince had ever paid a princess. He passed the stoop, his heart pounding out the message that at last he told the truth, and—and dropped rather than laid the envelope where it should go. But it remained in place, he saw, and he hastened to the intersection. Two more blocks to go before he was at home where nothing of this was guessed, and nothing, of course, was to be disclosed.

The prince and the princess had been disguised: he by his own intention, she by her ignorance that she was anything but the shepherd's daughter she had always seemed to be. And the compliment had to do with how she moved.

> *What you do*
> *Still betters what is done. When you speak, sweet,*
> *I'd have you do it ever; when you sing,*
> *I'd have you buy and sell so, so give alms,*
> *Pray so; and for the ord'ring your affairs,*
> *To sing them too. When you do dance, I wish you*

A wave o' the sea, that you might ever do
Nothing but that; move still, still so,
And own no other function. Each your doing,
So singular in each particular,
Crowns what you are doing in the present deeds,
That all your acts are queens.

With how she moved. This girl stood still. Not statuesquely, for she was neither marble nor wax. Nor was she tall. She wore a woolen jacket, with always a green scarf falling softly down the front of it, as far as the waist which the jacket, being always open, always revealed. She simply stood still.

But that was what he wanted to tell her, with Shakespeare's wonderful help—he would have her still, still so, since it was by her so doing that he had been made to love her. For he loved her, the young man said as he turned the corner to his father's house; he loved her, and he always would, even if she never gave him the briefest word or glance. He had not supposed love would lie in wait for him like this, exerting its power so quietly, and promising no return. But that was how it was, and it was how he would take it if he had to.

He was glad two of his father's friends were coming for dinner. He would not have to talk very much, then, even with his mother, who was fond of these doctors and would be happily occupied as hostess. He scarcely talked at all. He went to his room and opened *The Winter's Tale*, trying to imagine, as he read the words again, what it would be like never to have seen them until now. That was her case, probably. Then would she understand? He would not find out until tomorrow. Just how he would find out he put off explaining. Sufficient to the moment was the clarity thereof. Pleased with being able to put it thus, he got out his calculus and lost himself in magnitudes—or smallnesses, an Englishman had said—until long after midnight, when with a free heart he went to bed.

The next evening was colder, and a wind from the river blew alien dust along the streets. The weather was changing at last; he should have worn his topcoat. He walked briskly as far as Waverly Place, then checked himself and forgot the weather.

Would she be there at all? And if so, would her eyes lower themselves to his, even for an instant, saying she had understood? Her eyes —it was not that they were cold or superior. Their very warmness was why he loved them, as he loved all of her, he said, however little she might be for him. She had never rejected his glance. She had never even ignored it, if ignoring can be an act. She simply hadn't known he was there. Nor had she seemed to be expecting someone else. At first he feared so, but weeks of watching had given him the more comfortable conviction. She was there for her own purposes, which no living person shared. Would she still be there?

She was, and the wind was ruffling her scarf with a rudeness which the young man set down at once as his own fault. She was waiting for him in the cold. The excitement of believing this was immediately replaced by the thought: I am responsible for her being cold. If the wind is rude to her, last evening I was ruder. I left something on the step for her, I tossed something there, for all the world as if I supposed she was a hungry animal that would slink down, after I was safely gone, and lick it up. I have insulted this queen; and now I seem to be coming by so that I may reap the spectacle of her humiliation. Even if I am to be punished, I forced her to wait until now—until now—to punish me.

But her eyes were on his as he came. It was they that had been waiting, and there was no anger in them. This was a fact more tremendous than wrath or recrimination would have been. It was a fact that filled him with confused, with terrifying joy. He did not know what to do with joy like this. He only knew he was not a stranger to her. Yet her eyes were saying he must not stop or speak. And in his confusion he blessed them for such kindness.

They glanced back to the curtained window over the areaway, returned to his, then dropped to the end of the step where he had left his envelope. A piece of white paper, folded once or twice, was wedged in a crack between the stone and the rusty iron upright. He was to take that—quickly, she made him understand, as if he took nothing—and keep on. And not look back. He was certain she was telling him not to look back.

As he reached for the paper he was aware that her feet turned and took her through to the inner door of the vestibule, which soon he heard opening and closing. The paper in his hand—he would not open it till he was home. Much as he wanted to, he would not. Yet in a way he did not have the wish. It might say too little. It might say too much. He realized that he had no notion, even the faintest, what it would say. Anything, the squares of the sidewalk repeated as he counted them to his door, anything might be too much. Anything might be too much.

He was so pale that his mother exclaimed as she kissed him, and asked him what was wrong. Nothing, he told her from the top of the stairs, but he would take a nap before dinner.

He locked himself in, lighted his lamp, unfolded the paper—a sheet torn from a tablet, with faint rulings between the lines of carefully written words—and read:

> *Thank you.*
> But my father is out of work and sick, and he does not want anybody to come here. He knows about you, he watched you from the window.
> What you wrote was beautiful if I understand it, but you must not write again.
> Tomorrow we are moving. Do not inquire here, it will do no good.
> My father has found out who you are. He says rich people are not to be trusted. He does not trust poor people either.
> I am very sorry. Thank you, sir.
> *Goodbye.*

When his mother knocked he was still staring at what he held in his hands. And when he let her in he found it hard to convince her that he had been refreshed by an hour's sleep. "Goodness!" she said. "No color at all. I must have your father look at you. If he will. What is it, dear? Have you been overworking?"

He let it go at that, and was relieved when his father let it go with a few remarks about sleeping enough, especially now that winter, man's old enemy, had returned to the attack.

But what an emptiness all night. For he could not go where she still was and insist upon seeing her and saying—saying what? That was it. He did not know how to go, and he did not know what he ought to say. It was worse to stay where he was, in the silence of his room. Yet he stayed.

And what an acrid sense of sorrow when he passed her window in the morning and saw by the drawn shade either that they had gone or that they wanted to appear so.

He hesitated at the bottom of the stoop, then went on. Since he had never ascended those eight steps, he would not do so now. Why had he never gone up and said one solitary word? And why had she been there? He knew why he hadn't spoken. She really wished he wouldn't. Her avoidance of his eyes was not an invitation. And if now he took no relish in the noble rôle he had played, he thought he did not know why she was there. It had been her one free hour of the day, when perhaps her father slept, or when she knew that they would quarrel if she didn't leave him for a while. It was better, she must have decided, to leave him at a stated hour, since invalids prefer routine.

If he ever saw her again he would ask her if this weren't a good guess, and whether she was sorry now that she had picked *his* hour, his hour for coming from the subway. Also, he would find out more about her father; would ask to see him, would insist, and if this succeeded, would tell him how wrong he had been to call his people rich.

If he ever saw her again. It was mad of him to run on imagining what the two of them would talk about in such a case. The case would never be. He didn't even know her name; and there were millions of places in New York where she could be without his finding her, by foot or by conveyance. Taxis, buses, trolleys, subways, elevateds, hansom cabs, and the convertibles of his friends—for he had none, he was not rich—he imagined himself in them all; and was most successful in imagining her just gone from some apartment house at which, stepping from a cross-town bus and walking three blocks up or down, he eagerly inquired, giving her name—which he had learned at last—and waiting for the word that would save or break him.

It broke him, and he stumbled at the curb he was about to mount, which jolted him into attention, so that he turned back and ran to her house, and took the stone steps two at a time.

Above one of the bells there was a blank rectangle where the name must have been only yesterday. He pushed the superintendent's button, and when a woman with untidy black hair opened the door under the stoop, he went down to her at once.

"Can you give me—excuse me for bothering you, but *will* you give me the name of the man and his daughter who moved out this morning?"

She stared at him as she snapped, "I don't have to."

"Please. It's important."

"I don't have to." And she shut the door in his face.

It was no use. She had her directions, and he had his reward. By staying in his room last night he had lost the one thing he wanted. The one person that mattered to him was a Missing Person. The official phrase was musty; not meant for him or her. He used it, then cast it from his tongue, wryly, as he resumed his walk to the movie house and went on to the subway entrance.

He read the plate on the first car of the express that roared in. Van Cortlandt Park. She would not be there, he decided. That was open country, more or less, with grass between some of the houses, and long views east and west. No, they would have escaped into closer streets, into a thicker anonymity than "rich people" would ever solve.

Mike Stillman hailed him when he appeared out of the exit uptown, at the corner where trolleys clanked going north and south, and walked with him to the Hall. There should have been much to say to his closest friend, and this morning in particular there was. But he could not say it, of course. The subject was not only secret, it was sore. So he said nothing, or almost nothing; and later, sitting in the calculus class, he found himself utterly unable to focus on the symbols on the board. At noon, too, things were difficult and different. He knew he could not eat, just as he knew he could not talk, with Mike or anybody. He knew this so well that he slipped out of his last class of the morning a minute early, as if he had an engagement with the dean, and half tumbled, half floated down four flights of stairs.

He was a weightless body now—weightless with the purpose he discovered in himself. He had got off the subway too soon this morning. If he had gone on, and waited till a hunch came, and got off then—he knew not at what station, but surely he would have known when he arrived there—he would now be in her neighborhood, with some slim chance of finding her and saying—of saying, he fumbled, whatever it was it would then be proper to say. Until this happened he would recognize no other duty of god or devil. He had to make this happen. And he dropped his dime into the turnstile without hearing its click, and without feeling any pressure from the crossbar as he waded through into the tunnel world where he would live till he found her.

But there was no hunch. He rode to the end of the line without it, sat staring in the car, and returned downtown. Past the college he rattled, without a thought for the claims it had upon him; past his home station at 12th Street; past name after name, until he was under the East River, and then under Brooklyn.

Then back, and still without his inspiration. At Times Square he ran up to the surface and took a trolley east, watching the avenues as he crossed them and wondering which of them might take him north, by bus or elevated, to where she had arrived a few hours before him, and was only now settling her father in his chair by some window which would be, perhaps, without a curtain; and if so, would keep out no such glance as he would send through, burning with triumph and adoration. Yet not so burning, he checked himself and said, that it would frighten her. Or disgust her. That was the more likely danger. And he looked at himself in the mirror over the motorman's head. He must compose himself a little, he must manage to look less pale. He must get off and eat, for it was the middle of the afternoon. He must be the person he really was, not this frantic fellow whose hair needed combing and the collar of whose topcoat was meaninglessly awry.

But he knew he could not eat, and though he tugged at his collar he did not get it straight. There was no time for this; Third Avenue was coming, and he had his inspiration. He would take the El uptown. There was a lot to see from it, and something told him he would know where to get off so that he could descend into her street.

He raced up the long stairs and waited for a train to come rocking in, slowing smoothly, then jerking to its stop. While he waited he studied the people on the opposite platform. Would it ever be possible that one of those—at this station or some other—was she standing there even now, standing there in her green scarf while a train from the north rumbled along to take her away from him before he could race down and across and up and say whatever it was he would say? They were all so different from her over there—so different, and so dull—that the very intensity of his disappointment created her image for him in the now darkening afternoon. He knew she was not there, and yet he saw her.

And he knew she didn't see him. If she did, he said, she would not ignore him. No, not now. She might drop her eyes, or frown, or shake her head, or step back into the deeper shadows of the platform. But she would not ignore him.

Then her train would be coming in. And just before it did, obscuring her sweet figure, she would point to a poster—that poster, just behind her—would point to one of its lower corners, seeming to say that in this corner, on the white paper where there was no picture, he would find some words if he crossed over after she had gone and bent low enough to read them.

He almost stepped off the platform in his eagerness to go straight there and confirm his faith. An old man at his side was startled, and peered at him as if he thought him mad. He was, he said to himself, he was; and he rubbed his face hard with his right hand, hoping that this would restore the color to it, and shook his shoulders bitterly.

When his train came in from the south he took it with relief, though as he sat on its cane seat, watching the lights that grew rapidly in number between him and the East River, he dwelt again upon those words.

"'Three-eight-two East one-oh-eight," he thought they said. "But please don't come. Thank you. Goodbye."

Numbers, and the name of a street! If she had written those, did she *mean* he shouldn't come? How could she? For then she wouldn't have written the address.

There was no address, there was no address. There had been no such person. There had been only the poster with its empty corner where words might be. He shut his eyes fiercely and opened them again. This rested them, but he still saw a series of elevated platforms —or subway platforms—down which posters followed in file. In front of them stood she, bending and scribbling with the stump of a pencil she had taken from her purse; and afterwards he came, reading and hurrying on. He never caught up with her, however much he hurried. But New York was a tablet on which they corresponded. For finally he was bending and writing, too, and she was coming after him, to read and then run on.

382 East 108th Street. Could there be anything in that? Could it be his hunch? For the numerals had come to him without effort, almost as if he had heard them spoken. He doubted, yet he almost believed, and got precipitately out at 110th Street, and went as precipitately down the cold iron stairs.

There was no house at the address. Only a lot with scraps of dirty paper blowing over it, and heaps of rubble where a garage had been —he saw the torn tin of a blue and red gasoline sign.

He dragged himself back to Third Avenue and paused before a lunch room whose front window was clouded with steam. Coffee, anyway. He needed that to go on. For he would go on. And while the coffee cooled in its thick cup he telephoned his mother to say that he would spend the night with Mike. If she sounded worried, as she certainly did, he could do nothing about it. He could not go home. He could not go anywhere but where his hunch might lead him. If he got his hunch. If he could keep on going.

More and more people stared at him in trains and trolleys as the evening grew old. He must be a sight, he said. But what of that? Then as midnight passed he got to falling into dozes, leaning and lurching with the cars whose corners he haunted, but waking up suddenly with a sense of terrible guilt because he had dreamed he was there at last, yet did not get off to say certain words that formed, then faded, in his mind.

Once a cool current of under-river air roused him to see, or think he saw, her green scarf hanging quietly before him. She was there—the only other person in the car—waiting till he should wake. And when he did so she bent over, reading his face and answering with smiles the words she found written on it. With smiles that were both close and far away, as if she wanted him to say more and yet was telling him to be silent, silent, silent, until——

He reached out a hand and felt nothing; looked up, and saw nothing but his white reflection in the window opposite. The guard was yawning twenty feet away, indifferent to his one passenger. The night was old and gray. What next, when it would be morning?

For still he could not go home, and never again would he go where young men who knew nothing of all this sat in rows and listened, listened. What were they listening to? Nothing, if it was not this. And he slept until the early morning crowd trampled his tired feet.

He had coffee at Columbus Circle, and had nothing else. The park looked silvery in the sun, inviting him to enter it. He did so and wandered there most of the morning; parks, too, were for lovers, who sat under statues and talked—talked as now he said *they* would talk if they ever came together again.

If they ever did. But his faith, grown automatic overnight, shrugged off the doubt as if it barely existed. If he could keep going he would find her. So much faith meant something, he said. So much faith. The words sounded lonely in his ears. So many miles to travel. So many miles.

The more miles, he began chanting to himself, the more I shall convince her. The more trouble, the deeper love is proved.

When you speak, sweet

Oh, if he could only hear her say one word. Even "no." Even "go," or "blow," or "woe." The syllables pursued one another in senseless rhyme, which he rejected, saying he must be practical now. He must not stay in the park all day. He could do so, for it was large, but he had established that she was not here, and so he must go on. Yes, he must ride again, and wait for the hunch. Not lunch. Rhyme again. A thing to be rigidly suppressed. But he knew he was not hungry. He would not eat till he found her. Then they two would sit and eat, and bless each other's bread.

He couldn't keep his words from making a kind of poetry on his tongue. Not good poetry, but at least it came in waves, and sometimes rhymed. It came with the flushes that visited his face and wrists, so that he wondered if his father would say he had a temperature. He thought he had none really. Yet the flushes kept on coming, and when they were hottest he had the least control over his feet, which stumbled at curbs and occasionally were unwilling to lift him or advance him at all.

At five it was dark on 72nd Street, and suddenly he knew he was going home in spite of everything. It was practical, wasn't it, to make perfectly sure he had no fever? His father could tell him that at once. Then if he had none he would start off again—perhaps downtown from there, to the financial district (rich people), and then to the Staten Island Ferry. He hadn't been on a single ferry. The omission shocked him, and he blamed himself furiously for a fool as he put his last dime in the subway turnstile.

Another practical consideration. He was out of money. It took a little money (rich people) to live a little life. And to look for a wife. He shook off the rhyme but not the word. It was a new word at which he stared, trying it again and again to see how it sounded.

Perhaps he moved his lips, perhaps he said the word aloud. For between 23d Street and home he was glanced at five times by curious passengers. He didn't care now. What they would make of the mixture on his face—the misery, the fatigue, and yet the happiness that played about this word—they were welcome to make, as they were welcome to go on beyond the station where he planned to get off.

At Waverly Place he wondered if he would have the courage to look up and see how empty that step was, how empty of her whom he had driven away.

When he saw her coming down to meet him, he was certain that it was another of those mirages, those visitations on platforms and in the corridors of cars. She couldn't be here.

But she was speaking. She was standing one step higher than where he swayed on the concrete—for the wind in the street found him as insubstantial as paper torn from a poster. She was standing there and gazing at him in consternation. Yet in pity, too. And with a kind of happiness that warmed him as he listened to her words. For she was really speaking.

"You didn't come by last night. I thought—tonight again. So I was going."

He trembled with the strength he used to stand there calmly, or what he thought was calmly.

She spoke again, close to his face and eyes.

"I came back last night, just to—because—and I came again tonight because you weren't here, and I was worried. I wouldn't have come another time."

"I've been looking for you," he said at last.

"I know."

She stepped down to the sidewalk and started off west with him, supporting him with a hand from which she drew a mitten that matched her scarf.

He did not see, held tightly in the other mitten, a small piece of paper, folded. But she had come with that, and it was for him, though not just yet.

"Your hand," he said, wondering at the way she had taken charge of him without announcing that she would. "It's so cold."

"Yours is cold, too."

"I had to see you again."

"I know."

"Did you want to see me?"

She was silent. They were at the intersection, and she was looking left and right for cars.

"Did you?"

Still no answer.

"But you came." She nodded. "And now I'm going to take you home."

"Oh, no!" She drew her hand away, though only for a moment. "It's too far, it's way uptown. Tomorrow—or when you are well ——"

She broke off, tightening her free mitten on the fugitive thing it held.

"I mean where *I* live."

She stopped and shook her head.

"Yes," he said. But now his words sounded weak in his own ears. "You must. You know," and he tried to laugh, "I don't guess I can get there by myself."

She had let him go on a step or two, but now she was at his side again. "I'll take you to the door."

"And in." The blood inside his head was happy; if he was swaying now, he didn't care.

"No, not in. They would never understand."

"They would. They will. I'll make them."

At the shiny black door he fumbled for his keys but could not even find his pocket. She pushed the bell.

"Now I'll run," she whispered.

But she had thrust the piece of paper into his hand, and his hand held it. Then he lifted it to look.

When the door opened, he stared in at his mother with a green scarf dangling from the other hand.

"Thank goodness!" she cried. "Dear boy! Where have you really been? Mike says—what's *that?*"

"It's what I have left of *her*. She ran away."

"Her? Who, dear?" She was helping him in. "Why you're——"

"But I have two things. She promised I would see her—still, still so. Tomorrow. And I know where."

He looked down at the scrap of white he held more tightly than he held the scarf. He looked down at it as at something too precious to let go.

They laid him on the downstairs sofa to get his first rest, the rest he needed most. He would say more tomorrow, his mother thought. Tonight he was saying nothing, and hearing and seeing nothing.

But the paper was safe in his pocket.

*And then there is that love which can never be fulfilled
—the love of a young person for an older one, a love
which expects no fulfillment. Indeed, it would be frightening if it were to be fulfilled. Jessamyn West, one of
our greatest writers, has created a superb portrait of adolescence in her character Cress Delahanty. Here, in a
haunting story, she portrays not only an aspect of love
but also a quality of life itself that is immediate and
precious.*

MR. CORNELIUS, I LOVE YOU

JESSAMYN WEST

$Mr.$ and Mrs. Delahanty, Cress, and Cress's friends, Jo
Grogan and Bernadine Deevers, sat down to the Delahanty dinner table on Wednesday evening. The table
was round, with a white cloth that dipped at its four
corners to the floor, so that in the dusk of the dining
room the cloth seemed actually to be supporting the table. Mrs. Delahanty, who hadn't even expected Cress
home for dinner, let alone Jo and Bernadine, felt apologetic about the food which, besides being rather unin-
viting, was skimpy in amount: a small salmon loaf, Harvard beets, mashed potatoes, and for dessert a cabinet
pudding which did nothing to redeem the meal that had
gone before. But the girls didn't seem to know or care
what they put in their mouths and she decided that
strawberries and fresh asparagus would have been wasted
on them.

A mockingbird was singing in the orange grove outside
the opened windows and the girls listened, a spoonful of
cabinet pudding lifted to their opened lips—then, as the

song ceased, put the spoons down without having tasted a bite. Mr. and Mrs. Delahanty had given up trying to carry on a conversation with them and treated them as so many portraits ranged round their dining room—"Girls at Dusk," or "Reveries of Youth." They talked their own talk and let the girls dream their dreams, wrap their feet around the rungs of their chairs, and listen (mouths open, eyes closed) to the bird song.

"I saw Doc Mendenhall in town today," Mr. Delahanty said.

Mrs. Delahanty said "Yes?" waiting for whatever it was that made this fact worth reporting, but Bernadine interrupted his train of thought, if he had one, by extending her long arms toward the darkening windows and singing very softly, "Oh night of love, oh beauteous night." Bernadine was barefooted (it was the spring's great fad at high school) though she was eighteen, and wore an elaborate blue voile dress which drifted about her like a sky-stained cloud. Bernadine was to be married the day after school was out and sometimes, Mrs. Delahanty felt, overplayed her role of bride-to-be.

It was already, unbelievably, the last week of school, which in Southern California is the second week in June, a time climatically as well as scholastically neither one thing nor another, neither spring nor summer, neither truly school nor truly vacation. Class routines had been relaxed but not abandoned. Gradewise, the feeling among the students was that the year was already water over the dam; still they couldn't be positive; some of the teachers were still going through the motions of setting down grades in their record books. Climatically the days started spring-like, damp and gray with threat even of one more unseasonal rain; at 1 P.M. exactly the day did an about-face, took on September inclinations. At that hour the overcast burned away and the tawny grasses, sun-bleached foothills, and smoldering flowers of full summer emerged. It was very confusing, after getting up into a dripping cold which made sweaters and open fires necessary, to finish the day barefooted, hot-cheeked, and as naked as possible.

Cress and Jo both wore shorts and halters. Cress had shasta daisies tucked in the V of her halter and Jo Grogan, with those three flame-colored hibiscus in her short dark hair, might have been August itself on any calendar of girls. As the day darkened the white tablecloth grew silvery, the mockingbird retreated deeper into the orchard, and Mrs. Delahanty felt that the whole scene might be unreal, a mirage cast up into the present out of either the past or the future—that girls *had* sat in many a darkening room in years gone by and would so sit in the future; but that "now," the present minute, was unreal, only the past whisking by on its way to the future, or the future casting a long prophetic shadow to rearwards.

"Jo," she said briskly, "if you'll put some more custard on your pudding you might be able to eat it."

"I beg your pardon," said Jo. "Were you speaking to me?"

"Never mind," Mrs. Delahanty told her. "I was only urging you to eat."

"Oh food!" said Cress. "Food. Who cares about food?"

"I do," said Bernadine. "Howie adores puddings. Will you copy down this recipe for me, Mrs. Delahanty? I plan to serve Howie a different pudding every single night for thirty nights. I already have twenty-two recipes."

"Tapioca, jello, and bread," said Jo, sing-songing. "If puddings be the food of love, cook on."

The mockingbird had ceased to sing. The leaves of the bougainvillaea vine which clambered over the dining-room wall rustled faintly. Mrs. Delahanty began taking the spoons from the serving dishes.

Mr. Delahanty remarked, in the voice of a man who has had the words in mind for some time, "Doc Mendenhall says that Frank Cornelius had a bad hemorrhage this morning."

Mrs. Delahanty laid the spoons down clattering. "Oh John!" she said. "I understood he was getting better."

There was a note in her voice of condemnation, as if Mr. Cornelius had not tried hard enough, as if he were a turncoat, a traitor to his generation—and hers. When old people sickened and died, men and women in their seventies and eighties, that was to be expected. But thirty-eight! That was a direct threat to her and John.

"I don't think he's taken very good care of himself," Mr. Delahanty explained. "You can't throw off TB just by wishing. You've got to co-operate, rest, stay put. I've seen Cornelius about town off and on all spring. Baseball, things like that. Staggering around half-alive. I saw him yesterday, sitting along the road out by his place. Today, a hemorrhage. He was asking for . . ."

Cress sprang to her feet, interrupting her father. "You mustn't say that. You have no right to say that." She pulled the daisies from the neck of her halter and passed them from hand to hand distractedly. "You don't have any idea what it's like to be dying. Do you?" she insisted.

Mr. Delahanty agreed instantly. "No, I don't, Crescent. The worst I ever had was a touch of shingles."

"Don't be funny," Cress said, her chin quivering. "Don't be funny about death. How can you understand how terrible it is for Mr. Cornelius to think he may die, no matter how much he takes care of himself? And that if he doesn't go out and see the sunshine and people and trees today he may never see them again. Never, never. And you were never a great athlete like Mr. Cornelius, so it's a thousand times worse for him than it would be for you to stay in bed. And you blame him. You blame him for not giving in. You blame him—" She paused, trying to steady her voice. "I hate—I hate *people* who say cruel things like that." She looked at her father, and Mr. Delahanty looked back. Then she dropped her daisies onto her plate amidst the uneaten salmon and beets and ran from the room.

Mrs. Delahanty, after the sound of the slammed door had stopped echoing, leaned over and began to gather up the daisies. The two girls excused themselves and left the room.

"What did I say?" Mr. Delahanty asked. "To cause all that?"

Mrs. Delahanty continued without speaking to shake bits of food from the flowers. "Gertrude, did what I said sound cruel and hateful to you?"

"No, John, not to me," she answered. "But then I'm not in love with Mr. Cornelius."

In her bedroom, Cress sat on the floor, her head on the window sill. When she felt an arm about her shoulders, Jo's by the weight and pressure, she said, "Go away, please go away and leave me alone." The arm remained where it was. Jo knew, and so did Bernadine. Not much, because there wasn't much to know, except that she had seen Mr. Cornelius three times to look at him and had spoken to him twice and that she loved him and would willingly die for him.

There was "not much to know" in what was called the outside world; but inside herself, in her dreams and imaginings there was nothing *but* Mr. Cornelius. She had decided out of her experience of loving Mr. Cornelius that the knowledge people had of one another, parents of children, anyway, was almost nothing. She could sit at the dinner table with her father and mother, answering their questions about school but being in reality thousands of miles away in some hot dry land, nursing Mr. Cornelius back to health; and her father and mother never noticed her absence in the least.

In her dreams she and Mr. Cornelius sometimes went away together, Mr. Cornelius saying, "Cress, without knowing it I have
been searching for you all of my life. My sickness is no more than the
sum of my disappointment, and without you I can never get well."

Sometimes in her dreams Mrs. Cornelius came to her, and the gist
of what she said was, "My life with Mr. Cornelius has been a failure.
He has not many months to live. I do not want to stand between
him and his happiness in the little time that is left. Go, with my
blessing."

But for the most part Mrs. Cornelius and the Cornelius boys did
not exist in her dreams; even the world, as she knew it in what
was called "real life," was greatly altered; or, perhaps, simplified.
Changed, anyway, so that it consisted of nothing but sunshine, a
background of sand or water, and a grassy or sandy bank against
which Mr. Cornelius reclined, getting well. And as he got well she
waited on him, and talked to him. As a matter of fact, every thought
in her mind had become part of an unending monologue directed toward the omnipresent mental image of Mr. Cornelius. Everything
she saw immediately became words in a report to Mr. Cornelius;
and if, by chance, some experience was so absorbing as to momentar-
ily obscure his image, she made up for it by living the whole scene
through once again just for him. Sometimes she imagined that Mr.
Cornelius kissed her. She had to be careful about these imaginings
however. She had never been kissed—family didn't count, of course—
and since she supposed that when you were kissed by the man you
loved, the sensations were near to swooning, swooning was what
she nearly did whenever she had imaginings of this kind.

Most often she simply helped Mr. Cornelius as he reclined in the
midst of the sunny simplified landscape, his thin beautiful face becoming tanned and fuller as his health improved; but not more beautiful.
That was impossible. She doted on his hawk-nose and dark crest; she
dismissed every other face she saw as pudgy and ill-shaped by comparison. In her dream she picked flowers for Mr. Cornelius, went to
the library for him, read to him, smoothed his brow, sometimes
kissed him and always, always gazed at him with enraptured eyes.
But all the time she was imagining this life with Mr. Cornelius she
suffered, because Mr. Cornelius was dying and there was nothing
she could do about it; she suffered because she had feelings which she
did not know how to express, suffered because she had put the core
of her life outside its circumference.

She sat up, and Jo took her arm away. It was still light enough to see Bernadine on the floor leaning against the bed, and Jo by her side. The pitcher of white stock on her desk reflected what light there was, like a moon. The room was quiet and warm and full of misery.

"There is nothing you can do, Cress," Jo said. "You love him and he is dying. You can't do anything about either one. All you can do is to endure it."

"I can do something," Cress said.

"What?" Jo asked.

"I can go to Mr. Cornelius and tell him I love him."

"Oh no," Bernadine said, very shocked. "You can't do that."

"Why not?" Cress asked.

"You don't know whether he loves you or not."

"What does that have to do with it? I'm not going to him to ask him if he loves me. I'm going to tell him that I love him."

"Is that what you really want to do, Cress?" Jo asked.

"No—if you mean by want to, do I feel good about going. I feel awful about going. It makes me feel sick to my stomach to even think about it. It gives me the shakes."

Jo once again put an arm around Cress's shoulders. "It's a fact," she reported to Bernadine. "She's shaking like a leaf."

"Look, Cress," Bernadine said. "I'm almost married myself. It's just a matter of days. For all practical purposes I *am* married. You must think of Mr. Cornelius, Cress, and what he'd feel. I know if Howie was sick and maybe dying he wouldn't want some other woman coming to his sick bed and saying, 'I love you.' The first thing he'd do, I know, is say to me, 'Bernadine, throw this madwoman out.' And that's exactly what Mr. Cornelius is liable to say to you."

"I know it," Cress said bleakly.

"Well, then?" Bernadine asked, pride of reasoning in her voice. "Are you still going?"

Cress huddled silent, unanswering.

"It's probably not a very kind thing to do," Jo suggested in her deep, thoughtful voice. "Go to see him now when he's so sick."

"Oh I *know* that. If I just asked myself what was kind I would never do it. But what has kindness got to do with love? I'm not doing it to be kind to Mr. Cornelius. I'm doing it because I have to."

"Have to?" Jo reminded her, steadily. "You don't have to. Sit right here. Sit still. By morning everything will be different."

"By morning Mr. Cornelius may be dead."

"Well then," Bernadine said, "all your problems will be over. Mr. Cornelius will be dead and you'll be sad. But you won't have bothered him or made a fool of yourself."

"I don't care about making a fool of myself."

"You do care. You're still shaking. And think about Mrs. Cornelius. How's she going to feel about someone barging in on her sick husband, making passionate declarations of love?"

"It wouldn't be passionate. I would just say, very quietly, the minute I got there, 'I love you, Mr. Cornelius.' Then leave."

"Cress," Bernadine said, "what actually do you see yourself doing? You get there, the whole family is around the bed, and doctors and priests too, maybe. What are your plans? To say 'I beg your pardon but I've a little message for Mr. Cornelius'? Then push your way through them all to the bedside, drop on your knee, kiss his wasted hand and say, 'Mr. Cornelius, I love you.' Is that it?"

"Oh, don't heckle her, Bernadine," Jo said.

"What I see myself doing," said Cress, "is telling Mr. Cornelius something I have to tell him."

"How," asked Bernadine, "do you see yourself getting there?" Bernadine had Howie's car while he was in the army and she had driven the girls home from school. "Do you see yourself walking eight miles?"

"If I have to," Cress said.

"O.K.," Bernadine told her. "I'll drive you. And let's go right away and get it over with."

Mr. Cornelius was still living in the small one-room tent-house at the edge of the walnut grove in which his home stood. Here he was away from the noises of his family and was able to get the fresh air he needed. It was nine o'clock when Bernadine stopped the car in front of the Cornelius ranch. A dim light was burning inside the tent-house, but there was nothing to indicate the presence of the crowd of people she had prophesied. "Here we are," she said, turning off the engine.

Cress wished for any catastrophe, however great, which would prevent her from having to leave the car. She felt real hatred for Bernadine and Jo. Why, if they were convinced that she shouldn't come, hadn't they remained steadfast? What kind of friends were they, to give way to their better judgment so weakly? And what were her parents thinking about? Why had they permitted her to go riding off into the night? To tell a strange man she loved him? True, she hadn't told them where she was going nor that she loved a strange man. But what were parents for if not to understand without being told? She blamed them for her fright and unhappiness.

Still anything that *happened* would be better than continuing to live in a make-believe world in which she only dreamed that she told Mr. Cornelius she loved him. And she knew that if Bernadine were to start the car now she would jump out and run toward the tent-house and the declaration which would start her to living inside her dream. She opened the car door and stepped out into the night air which, after the warmth of the car, was damp and cold against her bare legs and arms.

"Cheerio," said Bernadine quite calmly as she was walking away from the car under the dark canopy of the big trees toward the dimly lighted room. Why was it so hard to do what she had set her heart on doing?

She stood at the screened door looking into the room as into a picture. Why did it seem like a picture? The small number of furnishings? Their neat arrangement, dresser balanced by table, chair by bed? The light falling from a bulb, shaded by blue paper, so that part of the room was in deep shadow? But most of all, was it picturelike because she had imagined the room and Mr. Cornelius for so long that a frame had grown up about them in her mind? Now, would it be possible to break that frame? She opened the screen door, stepped into the room and became a part of the picture by that easy act.

Mr. Cornelius lay on a high narrow bed. He lay very straight, his head supported by three or four pillows and his hands folded across an ice pack which he held to his chest. His eyes were closed and his face, in spite of his illness, was warm with color. At the sight of him all of Cress's doubts left her. Oh Mr. Cornelius, she thought, I do truly love you and I have come at last to tell you.

Without opening his eyes Mr. Cornelius said, "Joyce, I think I'm going to be sick."

Joyce. Cress was surprised at the name. It seemed too gentle for the bus driver. "It's not Joyce, Mr. Cornelius," Cress said. "It's me."

Then Mr. Cornelius opened his eyes and Cress was enchanted all over again by the enormous blaze of being alive and searching and understanding which she saw there.

"It's Cress," he said, in a very low careful voice, "the trackmeet girl." Then he closed his eyes. "I'm going to be sick," he said. "Hand me the basin."

The basin, Cress saw, was an enamel wash bowl on the night stand by the bed. She got it, put it on the bed beside Mr. Cornelius.

"Help me," Mr. Cornelius said, and Cress helped him the way her mother had helped her when she was sick after her tonsils were out, by putting an arm around his shoulders and supporting him.

"Don't be scared," Mr. Cornelius whispered. "It's not a hemorrhage. I'm just going to lose my supper."

He did, and afterwards he lay back against his pillows for a minute or two, then he reached up his hand and rang the bell which was suspended from the headboard of his bed.

"A glass of water," he told Cress, and Cress was holding it for him to rinse his mouth when Mrs. Cornelius arrived. Mrs. Cornelius paid no more attention to her than if she'd been some kind of device to help Mr. Cornelius—like the ice pack or the bell. She took the glass from Cress's hand, slipped her arm around her husband's shoulders and said, "Frank, Frank. Oh thank God, Frank, no more blood. Just your supper and that doesn't matter. I made you eat too much. This was to be expected. If you can swallow a bite or two later I'll fix you another. How do you feel now, honey?"

Cress had backed away from the bed. Mrs. Cornelius was wearing a housecoat or dressing gown of deep red, lightened by wreaths of tiny yellow and white flowers. What she looked like now was not a General in the Russian army but Robert Louis Stevenson's wife, "trusty, dusky, vivid and true with eyes of gold and bramble dew." Her bosom, which had spoiled the lines of her chauffeur's coat, was exactly right for pillowing an invalid's head, and her chestnut hair, curled corkscrew crisp, said "Never give up," as plain as any words; said "Fight on"; said "Defy the universe." And all the time she was cradling Mr. Cornelius in her arms and helping him rinse his mouth she was pressing her cheek to his hair and speaking comforting words through which there ran a mixture of laughing and joking.

"Take this to the bathroom and empty it," she said to Cress when Mr. Cornelius had finished rinsing his mouth. She handed the basin to Cress and nodded toward a door at the back of the room. Cress, ordinarily too squeamish to pull off her own Band-Aids, marched away with it without a word.

When she returned, Mr. Cornelius was once more against his pillows and Mrs. Cornelius was wiping his face with a damp cloth.

"Where'd you come from?" she asked Cress as she took the basin from her.

"From out there," Cress said, nodding toward the road. "The girls are waiting for me. In the car," she explained.

Mrs. Cornelius paused in her washing. "What did you come *for?*"

Cress welcomed the question. It was a wonderful help, like the upward spring of the diving board against her feet when she was reluctant to take off into deep water. Though she no longer had so great a need to say what she had come to say, some change had taken place in her since she had come into the room; what had been locked inside her and had been painful, because unsaid, had somehow, without a word being spoken, gotten itself partially expressed. She was not sure how. Nevertheless she had come to speak certain words. They were the answer to Mrs. Cornelius' question. They were *why* she had come.

So, louder than was necessary, and in a voice cracking with strain she said, "I came to tell Mr. Cornelius I loved him." Then she turned, resolutely, and said the words directly to Mr. Cornelius. "Mr. Cornelius, I love you."

At that Mrs. Cornelius laughed, not jeering, not angry, not unbelieving, but in the soft delighted way of a person who has received an unexpected gift, a pleasure never dreamed of but one come in the nick of time and most acceptable.

"Oh, Frankie," she said, running her hand through Mr. Cornelius' thick black hair, "look at what we've got here."

"What *we've* got," was what she'd said—as if, Cress thought, I'd said I loved them both. And then, watching Mr. Cornelius reach for his wife's hand, she saw that there was nothing she could give to Mr. Cornelius without giving it also to Mrs. Cornelius. Because they were not two separated people. They were really one, the way the Bible said. It was an astounding discovery. It was almost too much for her. It held her motionless and speculating. She felt as if her mind, by an infusion of light and warmth, was being forced to expand to accommodate this new idea. And it was an idea which, contrary to all her expectations, she liked. It was exactly what she wanted. Not Mr. Cornelius alone on a stretch of desert sand and she kissing his wasted hand—in spite of her six months' dreaming. What she wanted was Mr. and Mrs. Cornelius. She was so happy for Mrs. Cornelius' presence she almost took and kissed *her* plump brown unwasted hand.

Mrs. Cornelius, however, was continuing her laughing murmur to her husband. "Frankie," she said, "oh Frankie, you old jackanapes. You old irresistible. What's all this talk about being on your last legs? Done for? Caved in? With school girls coming with professions of love? Pretty school girls. Boy, we're not cashing in our checks just yet. Not us. What's your name, dear?" she asked Cress.

Mr. Cornelius answered in his low half-whispering voice. "She's John Delahanty's daughter, Crescent. They call her Cress at school."

"Well," said Mrs. Cornelius. "I've heard the boys mention you. Where'd you see Frank?"

"At a track meet."

"I stared at her some," Mr. Cornelius said. "Reminded me of you at her age. So alive."

"Was I ever like that?" Mrs. Cornelius asked her husband.

"That's what *I* thought about Mr. Cornelius," Cress said.

"Alive?" asked Mrs. Cornelius.

"Oh yes. More than anyone there. More than the boys. I thought his eyes fed on the sights," she said, daring the poetry of her thoughts.

"Fed?" Mrs. Cornelius studied the word then accepted it. "I see what you mean. Now, Frank," she said, "will you lie still and take care of yourself? Unknown school girls loving you and wanting you to get well. You do, don't you?" she asked Cress.

"Oh yes," Cress said. "I was willing to die for him."

Her voice evidently convinced Mrs. Cornelius. "Oh, Frank," she said, "school girls willing to die for you and you not half trying."

"Mrs. Cornelius," Cress said, wanting, since even partial confession made her feel so much better, to tell everything, "I ought to tell you something else." She stumbled for words. "I ought to tell you what else I planned."

"I bet you planned to run away with Frank and nurse him back to health."

Cress was amazed. "Yes," she said, her face burning with guilt and foolishness, "yes, I did. How did you know?"

"Oh Frank, don't it bring it all back to you? No wonder you were reminded of me. *I* was going to run away with the minister," she said, turning to Cress. "Save him from his wife and family. And he *was* the most beautiful man in the world, Frank. You can't hold a candle to your father—never could."

Cress wanted to say something, but she couldn't settle on what. She had too many emotions to express. Exhilaration at being released from the isolation of her dreaming; relief to find that other girls had loved secretly too, but most of all joy to have acted, to have made for herself a single undivided world in which to live.

"Oh Mrs. Cornelius," she said, "oh Mrs. Cornelius . . ."

"Cress," asked Mrs. Cornelius, "can you play cards? Or checkers?"

"Yes," Cress said, "I can. I like to."

"And read out loud? Of course you can do that, can't you? Why don't you come read to Frank? And play cards with him? It gets so darn lonesome for him. I work. The boys work, and besides they haven't got enough patience to sit still. And the good people come in and tell Frank how their uncles or mothers passed away with consumption and for him to be resigned. He needs somebody interested in living, not dying. Would you come?"

"Oh yes. If you want me—if he wants me. I could come every day all summer."

"O.K.," Mrs. Cornelius said, "we'll plan on it. Now you'd better run on. Frank's had a bad day. He's worn out."

Cress looked at Mr. Cornelius. His eyes were closed but he opened them at Mrs. Cornelius' words and made a good-by flicker with the lids.

"Good night," Cress said.

Mrs. Cornelius went to the door with her. "We'll count on you," she said once again and put a hand on Cress's shoulder and gave her a kind of humorous loving shake before she turned away.

Cress flew to the car, propelled, it seemed, by the beat of her heart as a bird is propelled by the beat of its wings. The walnut leaves were alive and fluttering in the warm air, and all about her mockingbirds were singing like nightingales. As she emerged from the grove she saw the June stars big and heavy-looking like June roses. This is the happiest hour of my life, she thought, and she yearned to do something lovely for the girls, something beautiful and memorable; but all she could think of was to ask them to go to town for milk shakes.

"I could stand some food," Bernadine said, "after all that waiting."

"He was sick," Cress explained, "and Mrs. Cornelius and I had to take care of him."

"Mrs. Cornelius? Did she come out?"

"Of course," Cress answered. "Wouldn't you, if Howie was sick?"

Bernadine had no answer to this. She started the car and after they had gone a mile or so Jo asked, "Did you tell him?"

"Of course."

"Does he love you?" Bernadine asked.

Cress felt sorry for Bernadine. "You're a fine one to be getting married," she said. "Of course he doesn't. He loves Joyce."

"Joyce? Who's Joyce?"

"Mrs. Cornelius. I remind him some of her. I adore Mrs. Cornelius. She is like Mrs. Robert Louis Stevenson and *they* are one person. Mr. and Mrs. Cornelius, I mean. They are truly married. I don't suppose you understand," she said, arrogant with new knowledge, "but what is for the one is for the other. I am going to help her take care of him this summer. Isn't that wonderful? Maybe I can really help him get well. Isn't this the most gloriously beautiful night? Oh, I think it's the most significant night of my life." The two girls were silent, but Cress was too full of her own emotions to notice.

When they went into the soda fountain, she looked at their reflection in the mirror and liked what she saw. The three of them had always been proud of one another. Bernadine had glamour, Jo character, and Cress personality; that was the division they made of themselves. "Look at Bernadine, listen to Cress, and let Jo act," someone had said. Oh, but I've broken through that, Cress thought; I can act, too. She searched for some understanding of the part Mrs. Cornelius had played in that breakthrough. If she had said "You wicked girl" or made her feel that loving was a terrible thing, would she have been pushed back, fearful, into the narrowness of dreaming, and into dreaming's untruths? She didn't know. She couldn't hold her mind to such abstractions.

"What we want," she said to Lester Riggins, the boy at the fountain, "is simply the most stupendous, colossal, overpowering concoction you ever served."

"This a special night?" Lester asked.

"Super-special."

"How come?"

"Bernadine's going to be married."

"Known that for six months."

"Jo's been accepted for Stanford. With special praise."

"Old stuff."

"Then there's me."

"What about you?"

"I'm alive."

"That's different," Lester said. "Why didn't you tell me in the first place? How do you like it?"

"Being alive? Fine," said Cress. "Better than shooting stars."

"O.K., O.K.," Lester said. "This obviously merits the Riggins' special. Expense any issue?"

"No issue," Cress said.

He brought them something shaped, roughly, like the Eiffel Tower, but more dramatically colored.

"Here it is, girls. Here's to being alive!"

They sank their spoons in it and ate it down, their appetites equal to the whole of it, color, size, sweetness and multiplicity of ingredients.

*Can we be haunted by a love from the past, a person we
have never known, one who lived in another century,
another generation, another time? Once again, writers
have thought so, and surely nearly all of us have felt at
one time or another that we would be happier and more
fulfilled in another age. We pick up a book and feel that
there is a mind in tune with ours; those are emotions
that we have shared; those are feelings that we have
known.*

*Here a young man falls in love with a girl who once
wrote a love letter long before he was born.*

THE LOVE LETTER

JACK FINNEY

I've heard of secret drawers in old desks, of course; who
hasn't? But the day I bought my desk I wasn't thinking
of secret drawers, and I know very well I didn't have any
least premonition or feel of mystery about it. I spotted it
in the window of a secondhand store near my apartment,
went in to look it over, and the proprietor told me where
he got it. It came from one of the last of the big old mid-
Victorian houses in Brooklyn; they were tearing it down
over on Brock Place, a few blocks away, and he'd bought
the desk along with some other furniture, dishes, glass-
ware, light fixtures, and so on. But it didn't stir my
imagination particularly; I never wondered or cared who
might have used it long ago. I bought it and lugged it
home because it was cheap and because it was small; a
legless little wall desk that I fastened to my living-room
wall with heavy screws directly into the studding.

I'm twenty-four years old, tall and thin, and I live in

Brooklyn to save money and work in Manhattan to make it. When you're twenty-four and a bachelor, you usually figure you'll be married before much longer, and since they tell me that takes money, I'm reasonably ambitious and bring work home from the office every once in a while. And maybe every couple weeks or so I write a letter to my folks in Florida. So I'd been needing a desk; there's no table in my phone-booth kitchenette, and I'd been trying to work at a wobbly little end table I couldn't get my knees under.

So I bought the desk one Saturday afternoon and spent an hour or more fastening it to the wall. It was after six when I finished. I had a date that night, and so I had time to stand and admire it for only a minute or so. It was made of heavy wood, with a slant top like a kid's school desk, and with the same sort of space underneath to put things into. But the back of it rose a good two feet above the desk top and was full of pigeonholes like an old-style roll-top desk. Underneath the pigeonholes was a row of three brass-knobbed little drawers. It was all pretty ornate; the drawer ends carved, some fancy scrollwork extending up over the back and out from the sides to help brace it against the wall. I dragged a chair up, sat down at the desk to try it for height, then got showered, shaved and dressed and went over to Manhattan to pick up my date.

I'm trying to be honest about what happened, and I'm convinced that includes the way I felt when I got home around two or two-thirty that morning; I'm certain that what happened wouldn't have happened at all if I'd felt any other way. I'd had a good enough time that evening; we'd gone to an early movie that wasn't too bad, then had dinner, a drink or so and some dancing afterward. And the girl, Roberta Haig, is pretty nice—bright, pleasant, good-looking. But walking home from the subway, the Brooklyn streets quiet and deserted, it occurred to me that while I'd probably see her again, I didn't really care whether I did or not. And I wondered, as I often had lately, whether there was something wrong with me; whether I'd ever meet a girl I desperately wanted to be with—the only way a man can get married, it seems to me.

So when I stepped into my apartment I knew I wasn't going to feel like sleep for a while. I was restless, half-irritated for no good reason, and I took off my coat and yanked down my tie, wondering whether I wanted a drink or some coffee. Then—I'd half forgotten about it—I saw the desk I'd bought that afternoon and walked over and sat down at it, thoroughly examining it for the first time.

I lifted the top and stared down into the empty space underneath it. Lowering the top, I reached into one of the pigeonholes, and my hand and shirt cuff came out streaked with old dust; the holes were a good foot deep. I pulled open one of the little brassknobbed drawers, and there was a shred of paper in one of its corners, nothing else. I pulled the drawer all the way out and studied its construction, turning it in my hands; it was a solidly made, beautifully mortised little thing. Then I pushed my hand into the drawer opening; it went in to about the middle of my hand before my fingertips touched the back; there was nothing in there.

For a few moments I just sat at the desk, thinking vaguely that I could write a letter to my folks. And then it suddenly occurred to me that the little drawer in my hand was only half a foot long, while the pigeonholes just above the drawer extended a good foot back.

Shoving my hand into the opening again, exploring with my finger tips, I found a tiny, grooved indentation and pulled out the secret drawer which lay in back of the first. For an instant I was excited at the glimpse of papers inside it. Then I felt a stab of disappointment as

I saw what they were. There was a little sheaf of folded writing paper, plain white but yellowed with age at the edges, and the sheets were all blank. There were three or four blank envelopes to match, and underneath them a small, round, glass bottle of ink; and because it had been upside down, the cork remaining moist and tight in the bottle mouth, a good third of the ink had remained unevaporated still. Beside the bottle lay a plain black wooden pen holder, the pen point reddish-black with old ink. Three was nothing else in the drawer.

And then, putting the things back into the drawer, I felt the slight extra thickness of one blank envelope, saw that it was sealed, and ripped it open to find the letter inside. The folded paper opened stiffly, the crease permanent with age, and even before I saw the date I knew this letter was old. The handwriting was obviously feminine, and beautifully clear—it's called Spencerian, isn't it?—the letters perfectly formed and very ornate, the capitals especially being a whirl of dainty curlicues. The ink was rust-black, the date at the top of the page was May 14, 1882, and reading it, I saw that it was a love letter. It began:

> Dearest! Papa, Mamma, Willy and Cook are long retired and to sleep. Now, the night far advanced, the house silent, I alone remain awake, at last free to speak to you as I choose. Yes, I am willing to say it! Heart of mine, I crave your bold glance, I long for the tender warmth of your look; I welcome your ardency, and prize it; for what else should these be taken but sweet tribute to me?

I smiled a little; it was hard to believe that people had once expressed themselves in elaborate phrasings of this kind, but they had. The letter continued, and I wondered why it had never been sent:

> Dear one: Do not ever change your ways. Never address me other than with what consideration my utterances should deserve. If I be foolish and whimsical, deride me sweetly if you will. But if I speak with seriousness, respond always with what care you deem my thoughts worthy. For, oh my beloved, I am sick to death of the indulgent smile and tolerant glance with which a woman's fancies are met. As I am repelled by the false gentleness and nicety of manner which too often ill conceal the wantonness they attempt to mask. I speak of the man I am to marry; if you could but save me from that!
>
> But you cannot. You are everything I prize; warmly and honestly ardent, respectful in heart as well as in manner, true and

loving. You are as I wish you to be—for you exist only in my mind. But figment though you are, and though I shall never see your like, you are more dear to me than he to whom I am betrothed.

I think of you constantly. I dream of you. I speak with you, in my mind and heart; would you existed outside them! Sweetheart, good night; dream of me, too.

With all my love, I am
your Helen

At the bottom of the page, as I'm sure she'd been taught in school, was written, "Miss Helen Elizabeth Worley, Brooklyn, New York," and as I stared down at it now I was no longer smiling at this cry from the heart in the middle of a long-ago night.

The night is a strange time when you're alone in it, the rest of your world asleep. If I'd found that letter in the daytime, I'd have smiled and shown it to a few friends, then forgotten it. But alone here now, a window partly open, a cool late-at-night freshness stirring the quiet air—it was impossible to think of the girl who had written this letter as a very old lady, or maybe long since dead. As I read her words, she seemed real and alive to me, sitting—or so I pictured her—pen in hand at this desk, in a long, white, old-fashioned dress, her young hair piled on top of her head, in the dead of a night like this, here in Brooklyn almost in sight of where I now sat. And my heart went out to her as I stared down at her secret, hopeless appeal against the world and time she lived in.

I am trying to explain why I answered that letter. There in the silence of a timeless spring night it seemed natural enough to uncork that old bottle, pick up the pen beside it, and then, spreading a sheet of yellowing old notepaper on the desk top, to begin to write. I felt that I was communicating with a still-living young woman when I wrote:

Helen: I have just read the letter in the secret drawer of your desk, and I wish I knew how I could possibly help you. I can't tell what you might think of me if there were a way I could reach you. But you are someone I am certain I would like to know. I hope you are beautiful, but you needn't be; you're a girl I could like, and maybe ardently, and if I did I promise you I'd be true and loving. Do the best you can, Helen Elizabeth Worley, in the time and place you are; I can't reach you or help you. But I'll think of you. And maybe I'll dream of you, too.

Yours,
Jake Belknap

I was grinning a little sheepishly as I signed my name, knowing I'd read through what I'd written, then crumple the old sheet and throw it away. But I was glad I'd written it—and I didn't throw it away. Still caught in the feeling of the warm, silent night, it suddenly seemed to me that throwing my letter away would turn the writing of it into a meaningless and foolish thing; though maybe what I did seems more foolish still. I folded the paper, put it into one of the envelopes and sealed it. Then I dipped the pen into the old ink, and wrote "Miss Helen Worley" on the face of the envelope.

I suppose this can't be explained. You'd have to have been where I was and felt as I did to understand it; but I wanted to mail that letter. I simply quit examining my feelings and quit trying to be rational; I was suddenly determined to complete what I'd begun, just as far as I was able to go.

My parents sold their old home in New Jersey when my father retired two years ago, and now they live in Florida and enjoy it. And when my mother cleared out the old house I grew up in, she packed up and mailed me a huge package of useless things I was glad to have. There were class photographs dating from grammar school through college, old books I'd read as a kid, Boy Scout pins; a mass of junk of that sort, including a stamp collection I'd had in grade school. Now I found these things on my hall-closet shelf, in the box they'd come in, and I found my old stamp album.

It's funny how things can stick in your mind over the years; standing at the open closet door, I turned the pages of that beat-up old album directly to the stamps I remembered buying from another kid with seventy-five cents I'd earned cutting grass. There they lay, lightly fastened to the page with a little grummed-paper hinge; a pair of two, mint condition two-cent United States stamps, issued in 1869. And standing there in the hallway looking down at them, I once again got something of the thrill I'd had as a kid when I acquired them. It's a handsome stamp, square in shape, with an ornate border and a tiny engraving in the center; a rider on a galloping post horse. And for all I knew they might have been worth a fair amount of money by now, especially an unseparated pair of two stamps. But back at the desk I pulled one of them loose, tearing carefully through the perforation, licked the back and fastened it to the faintly yellowing old envelope.

I'd thought no further than that; by now, I suppose, I was in almost a kind of trance. I shoved the old ink bottle and pen into a hip pocket, picked up my letter and walked out of my apartment.

Brock Place, three blocks away, was deserted when I reached it; the parked cars motionless at the curbs, the high, late moonlight softening the lines of the big concrete-block supermarket at the corner. Then, as I walked on, my letter in my hand, there stood the old house, just past a little shoe-repair shop. It stood far back from the broken cast-iron fence in the center of its wide weed-grown lot, black-etched in the moonlight, and I stopped on the walk and stood staring up at it.

The high-windowed old roof was gone, the interior nearly gutted, the yard strewn with splintered boards and great chunks of torn plaster. The windows and doors were all removed, the openings hollow in the clear wash of light. But the high old walls, last of all to go, still stood, tall and dignified in their old-fashioned strength and outmoded charm.

Then I walked through the opening where a gate had once hung, up the cracked and weed-grown brick pavement toward the wide old porch. And there on one of the ornate fluted posts, I saw the house number deeply and elaborately carved into the old wood. At the wide flat porch rail leading down to the walk, I brought out my ink and pen, and copied the number carefully onto my envelope; 972 I printed under the name of the girl who had once lived here, BROCK PLACE, BROOKLYN, NEW YORK. Then I turned toward the street again, my envelope in my hand.

There was a mailbox at the next corner, and I stopped beside it. But to drop this letter into that box, knowing in advance that it could go only to the dead-letter office, would again, I couldn't help feeling, turn the writing of it into an empty, meaningless act; and after a moment I walked on past the box, crossed the street and turned right, suddenly knowing exactly where I was going.

I walked four blocks through the night, passing a hack stand with a single cab, its driver asleep with his arms and head cradled on the wheel; passing a night watchman sitting on a standpipe protruding from the building wall, smoking a pipe; he nodded as I passed, and I nodded in response. I turned left at the next corner, walked half a block more, then turned up onto the worn stone steps of the Wister postal substation.

It must easily be one of the oldest postal substations in the borough; built, I suppose, not much later than during the decade following the Civil War. And I can't imagine that the inside has changed much at all. The floor is marble; the ceiling high; the woodwork dark and carved. The outer lobby is open at all times, as are post-office lobbies everywhere, and as I pushed through the old swinging doors I saw that it was deserted. Somewhere behind the opaque blind windows a light burned dimly far in the rear of the post office, and I had an impression of subdued activity back there. But the lobby itself was dim and silent, and as I walked across the worn stone of its floor, I knew I was seeing all around me precisely what Brooklynites had seen for no telling how many generations long dead.

The Post Office has always seemed an institution of vague mystery to me; an ancient and worn but still functioning mechanism that is not operated, but only tended by each succeeding generation of men to come along. It is a place where occasionally plainly addressed letters with clearly written return addresses go astray and are lost, to end up no one knows where and for reasons impossible to discover, as the postal employee from whom you inquire will tell you. And its vague air of mystery, for me, is made up of stories—well, you've read them, too, from time to time; the odd little stories in your newspaper. A letter bearing a postmark of 1906 written half a century ago, is delivered today—simply because inexplicably it arrived at some post office along with the other mail, with no explanation from anyone now alive. Or sometimes it's a postcard of greeting—from the Chicago World's Fair of 1893, maybe. And once, tragically, as I remember reading, it was an acceptance of a proposal of marriage offered in 1901—and received today, a lifetime too late, by the man who made it and who married someone else and is now a grandfather.

I pushed the worn brass plate open, dropped my letter into the silent blackness of the slot and it disappeared forever with no sound. Then I turned and left to walk home; with a feeling of fulfillment; of having done, at least, everything I possibly could in response to the silent cry for help I'd found in the secrecy of the old desk.

Next morning I felt the way almost anyone might. Standing at the bathroom mirror shaving, remembering what I'd done the night before, I grinned, feeling foolish but at the same time secretly pleased with myself. I was glad I'd written and solemnly mailed that letter, and now I realized why I'd put no return address on the envelope. I didn't want it to come forlornly back to me with NO SUCH PERSON, or whatever the phrase is, stamped on the envelope. There'd once been such a girl, and last night she still existed for me. And I didn't want to see my letter to her—rubber-stamped, scribbled on and unopened—to prove that there no longer was.

I was terrifically busy all the next week. I work for a wholesale-grocery concern; we got a big new account, a chain of supermarkets, and that meant extra work for everyone. More often than not I had lunch at my desk in the office and worked several evenings besides. I had dates the two evenings I was free. On Friday afternoon I was at the main public library in Manhattan, at Fifth Avenue and Forty-second, copying statistics from half a dozen trade publications for a memorandum I'd been assigned to write over the weekend on the new account.

Late in the afternoon the man sitting beside me at the big reading-room table closed his book, stowed away his glasses, picked up his hat from the table and left. I sat back in my chair, glancing at my watch. Then I looked over at the book he'd left on the table. It was a big one-volume pictorial history of New York put out by Columbia University, and I dragged it over, and began leafing through it.

I skimmed over the first sections on colonial and precolonial New York pretty quickly, but when the old sketches and drawings began giving way to actual photographs, I turned the pages more slowly. I leafed past the first photos, taken around the mid-century, and then past those of the Civil War period. But when I reached the first photograph of the 1870's—it was a view of Fifth Avenue in 1871—I began reading the captions under each one.

I knew it would be too much to hope to find a photograph of Brock Place, in Helen Worely's time especially, and of course I didn't. But I knew there'd surely be photographs taken in Brooklyn during the 1880's, and a few pages farther on I found what I'd hoped I might. In clear, sharp detail and beautifully reproduced lay a big half-page photograph of a street less than a quarter mile from Brock Place; and staring down at it, there in the library, I knew that Helen Worley must often have walked along this very sidewalk. "Varney Street, 1881," the caption said; "A typical Brooklyn residential street of the period."

Varney Street today—I walk two blocks of it every night coming home from work—is a wasteland. I pass four cinder-packed used-car lots; a shabby concrete garage, the dead earth in front of it littered with rusting car parts and old tires; and a half dozen or so nearly paintless boardinghouses, one with a soiled card in its window, reading MASSAGE. It's a nondescript, joyless street, and it's impossible to believe that there has ever been a tree on its entire length.

But there has been. There in sharp black-and-white, in the book on the table before me, lay Varney Street, 1881, and from the wide grass-covered parkways between the cut-stone curb and sidewalks, the thick old long-gone trees rose high on both sides to meet, intertwine and roof the wide street with green. The photograph had been taken, apparently, from the street—it had been possible to do that then, in a day of occasional slow-trotting horses and buggies—and the camera was aimed at an angle to one side, toward the sidewalk and the big houses beyond it, looking down the walk for several hundred feet.

The old walk, there in the foreground under the great trees, appeared to be at least six feet wide; spacious enough easily for a family to walk down it four or five abreast—as families did, in those times, walk together down the sidewalks under the trees. And beyond the walk, widely separated and set far back across the fine old lawns, rose the great houses, the ten-, twelve- and fourteen-room family houses, two or more stories high, and with attics above them for children to play in and discover the relics of childhoods before them. Their windows were tall, and they were framed on the outside with ornamented wood. And in the solid construction of every one of those lost houses in that ancient photograph there had been left over the time, skill, money and inclination to decorate their eaves with scrollwork; to finish a job with craftsmanship and pride. And time, too, to build huge wide porches on which families sat on summer evenings with palm-leaf fans.

Far down that lovely tree-sheltered street—out of focus and indistinct—walked the retreating figure of a long-skirted puff-sleeved woman, her summer parasol open at her back. Of the thousands of long-dead girls it might have been, I knew this could not be Helen Worley. Yet it wasn't completely impossible, I told myself; this was a street, precisely as I saw it now, down which she must often have walked; and I let myself think that yes, this was she. Maybe I live in what is for me the wrong time, and I was filled now with the most desperate yearning to be there, on the peaceful street—to walk off, past the edges of the scene on the printed page before me, into the old and beautiful Brooklyn of long ago. And to draw near and overtake that bobbing parasol in the distance; and then turn and look into the face of the girl who held it.

I worked that evening at home, sitting at my desk, with a can of beer on the floor beside me; but once more now Helen Elizabeth

Worley was in my mind. I worked steadily all evening, and it was around twelve-thirty when I finished; eleven handwritten pages, which I'd get typed at the office on Monday. Then I opened the little center desk drawer into which I'd put a supply of rubber bands and paper clips, took out a clip and fastened the pages together, and sat back in my chair, taking a swallow of beer. The little center desk drawer stood half open as I'd left it, and then, as my eye fell on it, I realized suddenly that of course it, too, must have another secret drawer behind it.

I hadn't thought of that. It simply hadn't occurred to me the week before, in my interest and excitement over the letter I'd found behind the first drawer of the row; and I'd been too busy all week to think of it since. But now I set down my beer, pulled the center drawer all the way out, reached behind it and found the little groove in the smooth wood I touched. Then I brought out the second secret little drawer.

I'll tell you what I think, what I'm certain of, though I don't claim to be speaking scientifically; I don't think science has a thing to do with it. The night *is* a strange time; things *are* different at night, as every human being knows somewhere deep inside him. And I think this: Brooklyn has changed over seven decades; it is no longer the same place at all. But here and there, still, are little islands—isolated remnants of the way things once were. And the Wister postal substation is one of them; it has changed really not at all. And I think that at night—late at night, the world asleep, when the sounds of things as they are now are nearly silent, and the sight of things as they are now is vague in the darkness—the boundary between here and then wavers. At certain moments and places it fades. I think that there in the dimness of the old Wister post office, in the dead of night, lifting my letter to Helen Worley toward the old brass door of the letter drop—I think that I stood on one side of that slot in the year 1959, and that I dropped my letter, properly stamped, written and addressed in the ink and on the very paper of Helen Worley's youth, into the Brooklyn of 1882 on the other side of that worn old slot.

I believe that—I'm not even interested in proving it—but I believe it. Because now, from that second secret little drawer, I brought out the paper I found in it, opened it, and in rust-black ink on yellowing old paper I read:

Please, oh, please—who are you? Where can I reach you? Your letter arrived today in the second morning post, and I have wandered the house and garden ever since in an agony of excitement. I cannot conceive how you saw my letter in its secret place, but since you did, perhaps you will see this one too. Oh, tell me your letter is no hoax or cruel joke! Willy, if it is you; if you have discovered my letter and think to deceive your sister with a prank, I pray you to tell me! But if it is not—if I now address someone who has truly responded to my most secret hopes—do not longer keep me ignorant of who and where you are. For I, too—and I confess it willingly—long to see you! And I, too, feel and am most certain of it, that if I could know you, I would love you. It is impossible for me to think otherwise.

I must hear from you again; I shall not rest until I do.

I remain, most sincerely,

Helen Elizabeth Worley

After a long time, I opened the first little drawer of the old desk and took out the pen and ink I'd found there, and a sheet of the note paper.

For minutes then, the pen in my hand, I sat there in the night staring down at the empty paper on the desk top; finally, then, I dipped the pen into the old ink and wrote:

Helen, my dear: I don't know how to say this so it will seem even comprehensible to you. But I do exist, here in Brooklyn, less than three blocks from where you now read this—in the year 1959. We are separated not by space, but by the years which lie between us. Now I own the desk which you once had, and at which you wrote the note I found in it. Helen, all I can tell you is that I answered that note, mailed it late at night at the old Wister station, and that somehow it reached you, as I hope this will too. This is no hoax! Can you imagine anyone playing a joke that cruel? I live in a Brooklyn, within sight of your house, that you cannot imagine. It is a city whose streets are now crowded with wheeled vehicles propelled by engines. And it is a city extending far beyond the limits you know, with a population of millions, so crowded there is hardly room any longer for trees. From my window as I write I can see—across Brooklyn Bridge, which is hardly changed from the way you, too, can see it now— Manhattan Island, and rising from it are the lighted silhouettes of stone-and-steel buildings more than one thousand feet high.

You must believe me. I live, I exist, seventy-seven years after you read this; and with the feeling that I have fallen in love with you.

I sat for some moments staring at the wall, trying to figure out how to explain something I was certain was true. Then I wrote:

> *Helen:* there are three secret drawers in our desk. Into the first you put only the letter I found. You cannot now add something to that drawer and hope that it will reach me. For I have already opened that drawer and found only the letter you put here. Nothing else can now come down through the years to me in that drawer, for you cannot now alter what you have already done.
>
> Into the second drawer, in 1882, you put the note which lies before me, which I found when I opened that drawer a few minutes ago. You put nothing else into it, and now that, too, cannot be changed.
>
> But I haven't opened the third drawer, Helen. Not yet! It is the last way you can still reach me, and the last time. I will mail this as I did before, then wait. In a week I will open that last drawer.
>
> Jake Belknap

It was a long week. I worked, I kept busy daytimes, but at night I thought of hardly anything but the third secret drawer in my desk. I was terribly tempted to open it earlier, telling myself that whatever might lie in it had been put there decades before and must be there now, but I wasn't sure, and I waited.

Then, late at night, a week to the hour after I'd mailed my second letter at the old Wister post office, I pulled out the third drawer, reached in and brought out the last little secret drawer which lay behind it. My hand was actually shaking, and for a moment I couldn't bear to look directly—something lay in the drawer—and I turned my head away. Then I looked.

I'd expected a long letter; very long, of many pages, her last communication with me, and full of everything she wanted to say. But there was no letter at all. It was a photograph, about three inches square, a faded sepia in color, mounted on heavy stiff cardboard, and with the photographer's name in tiny gold script down in the corner: *Brunner & Holland, Parisian Photography, Brooklyn, N.Y.*

The photograph showed the head and shoulders of a girl in a high-necked dark dress with a cameo brooch at the collar. Her dark hair was swept tightly back, covering the ears, in a style which no longer suits our ideas of beauty. But the stark severity of that dress and hair style couldn't spoil the beauty of the face that smiled out at me from that old photograph. It wasn't beautiful in any classic sense, I suppose. The brows were unplucked and somewhat heavier than we are used to. But it is the soft warm smile of her lips, and her eyes—large and serene as she looks out at me over the years—that make Helen Elizabeth Worley a beautiful woman. Across the bottom of her photograph she had written, "I will never forget." And as I sat there at the old desk, staring at what she had written, I understood that, of course, that was all there was to say—what else?—on this, the last time, as she knew, that she'd ever be able to reach me.

It wasn't the last time, though. There was one final way for Helen Worley to communicate with me over the years, and it took me a long time, as it must have taken her, to realize it. Only a week ago, on my fourth day of searching, I finally found it. It was late in the evening, and the sun was almost gone, when I found the old headstone among all the others stretching off in rows under the quiet trees. And then I read the inscription etched in the weathered old stone: HELEN ELIZABETH WORLEY—1861–1934. Under this were the words I NEVER FORGOT.

And neither will I.

Loving is giving. It is a desire to exchange the gifts of words, the gifts of feelings, the gifts of belonging and the gifts of communicating. Our very first attempt to express our love is often a very mundane gift, exchange of friendship rings or pins, or whatever else becomes the coin of love as times change, but the desire to give something concrete has never been more beautifully expressed than in O. Henry's magical story "The Gift of the Magi."

THE GIFT OF THE MAGI

O. HENRY

One dollar and eighty-seven cents. That was all. And sixty cents of it was in pennies. Pennies saved one and two at a time by bulldozing the grocer and the vegetable man and the butcher until one's cheeks burned with the silent imputation of parsimony that such close dealing implied. Three times Della counted it. One dollar and eighty-seven cents. And the next day would be Christmas.

There was clearly nothing to do but flop down on the shabby little couch and howl. So Della did it. Which instigates the moral reflection that life is made up of sobs, sniffles, and smiles, with sniffles predominating.

While the mistress of the home is gradually subsiding from the first stage to the second, take a look at the home. A furnished flat at $8 per week. It did not exactly beggar description, but it certainly had that word on the lookout for the mendicancy squad.

In the vestibule below was a letter-box into which no letter would go, and an electric button from which no mortal finger could coax a ring. Also appertaining thereunto was a card bearing the name "Mr. James Dillingham Young."

The "Dillingham" had been flung to the breeze during a former period of prosperity when its possessor was being paid $30 per week. Now, when the income was shrunk to $20, the letters of "Dillingham" looked blurred, as though they were thinking seriously of contracting to a modest and unassuming D. But whenever Mr. James Dillingham Young came home and reached his flat above he was called "Jim" and greatly hugged by Mrs. James Dillingham Young, already introduced to you as Della. Which is all very good.

Della finished her cry and attended to her cheeks with the powder rag. She stood by the window and looked out dully at a gray cat walking a gray fence in a gray backyard. Tomorrow would be Christmas Day and she had only $1.87 with which to buy Jim a present. She had been saving every penny she could for months, with this result. Twenty dollars a week doesn't go far. Expenses had been greater than she had calculated. They always are. Only $1.87 to buy a present for Jim. Her Jim. Many a happy hour she had spent planning for something nice for him. Something fine and rare and sterling—something just a little bit near to being worthy of the honor of being owned by Jim.

There was a pier-glass between the windows of the room. Perhaps you have seen a pier-glass in an $8 flat. A very thin and very agile person may, by observing his reflection in a rapid sequence of longitudinal strips, obtain a fairly accurate conception of his looks. Della, being slender, had mastered the art.

Suddenly she whirled from the window and stood before the glass. Her eyes were shining brilliantly, but her face had lost its color within twenty seconds. Rapidly she pulled down her hair and let it fall to its full length.

Now, there were two possessions of the James Dillingham Youngs in which they both took a mighty pride. One was Jim's gold watch that had been his father's and his grandfather's. The other was Della's hair. Had the Queen of Sheba lived in the flat across the airshaft, Della would have let her hair hang out the window some day to dry just to depreciate Her Majesty's jewels and gifts. Had King Solomon been the janitor, with all his treasures piled up in the basement, Jim would have pulled out his watch every time he passed, just to see him pluck at his beard from envy.

So now Della's beautiful hair fell about her rippling and shining like a cascade of brown waters. It reached below her knee and made itself almost a garment for her. And then she did it up again nervously and quickly. Once she faltered for a minute and stood still while a tear or two splashed on the worn red carpet.

On went her old brown jacket; on went her old brown hat. With a whirl of skirts and with the brilliant sparkle still in her eyes, she fluttered out the door and down the stairs to the street.

Where she stopped the sign read: "Mme. Sofronie. Hair Goods of All Kinds." One flight up Della ran, and collected herself, panting. Madame, large, too white, chilly, hardly looked the "Sofronie."

"Will you buy my hair?" asked Della.

"I buy hair," said Madame. "Take yer hat off and let's have a sight at the looks of it."

Down rippled the brown cascade.

"Twenty dollars," said Madame, lifting the mass with a practiced hand.

"Give it to me quick," said Della.

Oh, and the next two hours tripped by on rosy wings. Forget the hashed metaphor. She was ransacking the stores for Jim's present.

She found it at last. It surely had been made for Jim and no one else. There was no other like it in any of the stores, and she had turned all of them inside out. It was a platinum fob chain simple and chaste in design, properly proclaiming its value by substance alone and not by meretricious ornamentation—as all good things should do. It was even worthy of The Watch. As soon as she saw it she knew that it must be Jim's. It was like him. Quietness and value—the description applied to both. Twenty-one dollars they took from her for it, and she hurried home with the 87 cents. With that chain on his watch Jim might be properly anxious about the time in any company. Grand as the watch was, he sometimes looked at it on the sly on account of the old leather strap that he used in place of a chain.

When Della reached home her intoxication gave way a little to prudence and reason. She got out her curling irons and lighted the gas and went to work repairing the ravages made by generosity added to love. Which is always a tremendous task, dear friends—a mammoth task.

Within forty minutes her head was covered with tiny, close-lying curls that made her look wonderfully like a truant schoolboy. She looked at her reflection in the mirror long, carefully, and critically.

"If Jim doesn't kill me," she said to herself, "before he takes a second look at me, he'll say I look like a Coney Island chorus girl. But what could I do—oh! what could I do with a dollar and eighty-seven cents?"

At 7 o'clock the coffee was made and the frying-pan was on the back of the stove hot and ready to cook the chops.

Jim was never late. Della doubled the fob chain in her hand and sat on the corner of the table near the door that he always entered. Then she heard his step on the stair away down on the first flight, and she turned white for just a moment. She had a habit of saying little silent prayers about the simplest everyday things, and now she whispered: "Please God, make him think I am still pretty."

The door opened and Jim stepped in and closed it. He looked thin and very serious. Poor fellow, he was only twenty-two—and to be burdened with a family! He needed a new overcoat and he was without gloves.

Jim stepped inside the door, as immovable as a setter at the scent of quail. His eyes were fixed upon Della, and there was an expression in them that she could not read, and it terrified her. It was not anger, nor surprise, nor disapproval, nor horror, nor any of the sentiments that she had been prepared for. He simply stared at her fixedly with that peculiar expression on his face.

Della wriggled off the table and went for him.

"Jim, darling," she cried, "don't look at me that way. I had my hair cut off and sold it because I couldn't have lived through Christmas without giving you a present. It'll grow out again—you won't mind, will you? I just had to do it. My hair grows awfully fast. Say 'Merry Christmas!' Jim, and let's be happy. You don't know what a nice—what a beautiful, nice gift I've got for you."

"You've cut off your hair?" asked Jim, laboriously, as if he had not arrived at that patent fact yet even after the hardest mental labor.

"Cut it off and sold it," said Della. "Don't you like me just as well, anyhow? I'm me without my hair, ain't I?"

Jim looked about the room curiously.

"You say your hair is gone?" he said, with an air almost of idiocy.

"You needn't look for it," said Della. "It's sold, I tell you—sold and gone, too. It's Christmas Eve, boy. Be good to me, for it went for you. Maybe the hairs on my head were numbered," she went on with a sudden serious sweetness, "but nobody could ever count my love for you. Shall I put the chops on, Jim?"

Out of his trance Jim seemed quickly to wake. He enfolded his Della. For ten seconds let us regard with discreet scrutiny some inconsequential object in the other direction. Eight dollars a week or a million a year—what is the difference? A mathematician or a wit would give you the wrong answer. The magi brought valuable gifts, but that was not among them. This dark assertion will be illuminated later on.

Jim drew a package from his overcoat pocket and threw it upon the table.

"Don't make any mistake, Dell," he said, "about me. I don't think there's anything in the way of a haircut or a shave or a shampoo that could make me like my girl any less. But if you'll unwrap that package you may see why you had me going a while at first."

White fingers and nimble tore at the string and paper. And then an ecstatic scream of joy; and then, alas! a quick feminine change to hysterical tears and wails, necessitating the immediate employment of all the comforting powers of the lord of the flat.

For there lay The Combs—the set of combs, side and back, that Della had worshipped for long in a Broadway window. Beautiful combs, pure tortoise shell, with jewelled rims—just the shade to wear in the beautiful vanished hair. They were expensive combs, she knew, and her heart had simply craved and yearned over them without the least hope of possession. And now, they were hers, but the tresses that should have adorned the coveted adornments were gone.

But she hugged them to her bosom, and at length she was able to look up with dim eyes and a smile and say: "My hair grows so fast, Jim!"

And then Della leaped up like a little singed cat and cried, "Oh, oh!"

Jim had not yet seen his beautiful present. She held it out to him eagerly upon her open palm. The dull precious metal seemed to flash with a reflection of her bright and ardent spirit.

"Isn't it a dandy, Jim? I hunted all over town to find it. You'll have to look at the time a hundred times a day now. Give me your watch. I want to see how it looks on it."

Instead of obeying, Jim tumbled down on the couch and put his hands under the back of his head and smiled.

"Dell," said he, "let's put our Christmas presents away and keep 'em a while. They're too nice to use just at present. I sold the watch to get the money to buy your combs. And now suppose you put the chops on."

The magi, as you know, were wise men—wonderfully wise

men—who brought gifts to the Babe in the manger. They invented the art of giving Christmas presents. Being wise, their gifts were no doubt wise ones, possibly bearing the privilege of exchange in case of duplication. And here I have lamely related to you the uneventful chronicle of two foolish children in a flat who most unwisely sacrificed for each other the greatest treasures of their house. But in a last word to the wise of these days let it be said that of all who give gifts these two were the wisest. Of all who give and receive gifts, such as they are wisest. Everywhere they are wisest. They are the magi.

Here is another kind of love letter, more delicious than any perhaps, because it was so difficult for the writer to undertake. The writer is, thanks to Charles Dickens who created him, Sam Weller, one of the most delightful characters in the Pickwick Papers. Here, Sam with tremendous persistence, and perhaps more perspiration than inspiration, writes one of the most famous valentines of all time.

SAM WELLER'S VALENTINE

CHARLES DICKENS

Mr. Weller having obtained leave of absence from Mr. Pickwick, who in his then state of excitement and worry was by no means displeased at being left alone, set forth, long before the appointed hour, and having plenty of time at his disposal, sauntered down as far as the Mansion House, where he paused and contemplated, with a face of great calmness and philosophy, the numerous cads and drivers of short stages who assemble near that famous place of resort, to the greater terror and confusion of the old-lady population of these realms. Having loitered here for half an hour or so, Mr. Weller turned and began wending his way towards Leadenhall Market, through a variety of bye streets and courts. As he was sauntering away his spare time, and stopped to look at almost every object that met his gaze, it is by no means surprising that Mr. Weller should have paused before a small stationer's and print-seller's window; but without further explanation it does appear surprising that his eyes should have no sooner rested on certain pictures which were exposed for sale therein, than he gave a sudden start, smote his right leg with great vehemence, and exclaimed with energy, "If it hadn't been for this, I should ha' forgot all about it, till it was too late!"

The particular picture on which Sam Weller's eyes were fixed, as he said this, was a highly colored representation of a couple of human hearts skewered together with an arrow cooking before a cheerful fire, while a male and female cannibal in modern attire: the gentleman being clad in a blue coat and white trousers, and the lady in a deep red pelisse with a parasol of the same: were approaching the meal with hungry eyes, up a serpentine gravel path leading thereunto. A decidedly indelicate young gentleman, in a pair of wings and nothing else, was depicted as superintending the cooking; a representation of the spire of the church in Langham Place, London, appeared in the distance; and the whole formed a "valentine," of which, as a written inscription in the window testified, there was a large assortment within, which the shopkeeper pledged himself to dispose of, to his countrymen generally, at the reduced rate of one and sixpence each.

"I should ha' forgot it; I should certainly ha' forgot it!" said Sam; so saying, he at once stepped into the stationer's shop, and requested to be served with a sheet of the best gilt-edged letter paper, and a hard-nibbed pen which could be warranted not to splutter. These articles having been promptly supplied, he walked on direct towards Leadenhall Market at a good round pace, very different from his recent lingering one. Looking round him, he there beheld a signboard on which the painter's art had delineated something remotely resembling a cerulean elephant with an aquiline nose in lieu of trunk. Rightly conjecturing that this was the Blue Boar himself, he stepped into the house, and inquired concerning his parent.

"He won't be here this three quarters of an hour or more," said the young lady who superintended the domestic arrangements of the Blue Boar.

"Wery good, my dear," replied Sam. "Let me have nine penn'orth o' brandy and water luke, and the inkstand, will you, miss?"

The brandy and water luke and the inkstand having been carried into the little parlor, and the young lady having carefully flattened down the coals to prevent their blazing, and carried away the poker to preclude the possibility of the fire being stirred, without the full privity and concurrence of the Blue Boar being first had and obtained, Sam Weller sat himself down in a box near the stove, and pulled out the sheet of gilt-edged letter paper and the hard-nibbed pen. Then

looking carefully at the pen to see that there were no hairs in it, and dusting down the table, so that there might be no crumbs of bread under the paper, Sam tucked up the cuffs of his coat, squared his elbows, and composed himself to write.

To ladies and gentlemen who are not in the habit of devoting themselves practically to the science of penmanship, writing a letter is no very easy task; it being always considered necessary in such cases for the writer to recline his head on his left arm, so as to place his eyes as nearly as possible on a level with the paper, while glancing sideways at the letters he is constructing, to form with his tongue imaginary characters to correspond. These motions, although unquestionably of the greatest assistance to original composition, retard in some degree the progress of the writer; and Sam had unconsciously been a full hour and a half writing words in small text, smearing out wrong letters with his little finger, and putting in new ones which required going over very often to render them visible through the old blots, when he was roused by the opening of the door and the entrance of his parent.

Sam Weller's Valentine 93

"Vell, Sammy," said the father.

"Vell, my Prooshan Blue," responded the son, laying down his pen. "What's the last bulletin about mother-in-law?"

"Mrs. Veller passed a wery good night, but is uncommon perwerse and unpleasant this mornin'. Signed upon oath, T. Veller, Esquire, Senior. That's the last vun as was issued, Sammy," replied Mr. Weller, untying his shawl.

"No better yet?" inquired Sam.

"All the symptoms aggerawated," replied Mr. Weller, shaking his head. "But wot's that you're a doing of? Pursuit of knowledge under difficulties, Sammy?"

"I've done now," said Sam with slight embarrassment; "I've been a writin'."

"So I see," replied Mr. Weller. "Not to any young 'ooman, I hope, Sammy?"

"Why, it's no use a sayin' it ain't," replied Sam. "It's a walentine."

"A what!" exclaimed Mr. Weller, apparently horror-stricken by the word.

"A walentine," replied Sam.

"Samivel, Samivel," said Mr. Weller, in reproachful accents, "I didn't think you'd ha' done it. Arter the warnin' you've had o' your father's wicious propensities; arter all I've said to you upon this here wery subject; arter activally seein' and bein' in the company o' your own mother-in-law, vich I should ha' thought wos a moral lesson as no man could never ha' forgotten to his dyin' day! I didn't think you'd ha' done it, Sammy. I didn't think you'd ha' done it!" These reflections were too much for the good old man. He raised Sam's tumbler to his lips and drank off its contents.

"Wot's the matter now?" said Sam.

"Nev'r mind, Sammy," replied Mr. Weller, "it'll be a wery agonizin' trial to me at my time of life, but I'm pretty tough, that's vun consolation, as the wery old turkey remarked wen the farmer said he wos afeered he should be obliged to kill him for the London market."

"Wot'll be a trial?" inquired Sam.

"To see you married, Sammy—to see you a dilluded wictim, and thinkin' in your innocence that it's all wery capital," replied Mr. Weller. "It's a dreadful trial to a father's feelin's, that 'ere, Sammy."

"Nonsense," said Sam. "I ain't a goin' to get married, don't you fret yourself about that; I know you're a judge of these things. Order in your pipe, and I'll read you the letter. There!"

We cannot distinctly say whether it was the prospect of the pipe, or the consolatory reflection that a fatal disposition to get married ran in the family and couldn't be helped, which calmed Mr. Weller's feelings, and caused his grief to subside. We should be rather disposed to say that the result was attained by combining the two sources of consolation, for he repeated the second in a low tone, very frequently; ringing the bell meanwhile, to order in the first. He then divested himself of his upper coat; and lighting the pipe and placing himself in front of the fire, with his back towards it, so that he could feel its full heat, and recline against the mantelpiece at the same time, turned towards Sam, and, with a countenance greatly mollified by the softening influence of tobacco, requested him to "fire away."

Sam dipped his pen into the ink to be ready for any corrections, and began with a very theatrical air:

" 'Lovely——' "

"Stop," said Mr. Weller, ringing the bell. "A double glass o' the inwariable, my dear."

"Very well, sir," replied the girl; who with great quickness appeared, vanished, returned, and disappeared.

"They seem to know your ways here," observed Sam.

"Yes," replied his father, "I've been here before, in my time. Go on, Sammy."

" 'Lovely creetur,' " repeated Sam.

" 'Tain't in poetry, is it?" interposed his father.

"No, no," replied Sam.

"Wery glad to hear it," said Mr. Weller. "Poetry's unnat'ral; no man ever talked poetry 'cept a beadle on boxin' day, or Warren's blackin', or Rowland's oil, or some o' them low fellows; never you let yourself down to talk poetry, my boy. Begin again, Sammy."

Mr. Weller resumed his pipe with critical solemnity, and Sam once more commenced, and read as follows:

" 'Lovely creetur i feel myself a dammed'——"

"That ain't proper," said Mr. Weller, taking his pipe from his mouth.

"No; it ain't 'dammed,' " observed Sam, holding the letter up to the light, "it's 'shamed,' there's a blot there—'I feel myself ashamed.' "

"Wery good," said Mr. Weller. "Go on."

" 'Feel myself ashamed, and completely cir—' I forget what this here word is," said Sam, scratching his head with the pen, in vain attempts to remember.

"Why don't you look at it, then?" inquired Mr. Weller.

"So I *am* a lookin' at it," replied Sam, "but there's another blot. Here's a 'c,' and a 'i,' and a 'd.' "

"Circumwented, p'raps," suggested Mr. Weller.

"No, it ain't that," said Sam, " 'circumscribed'; that's it."

"That ain't as good a word as circumwented, Sammy," said Mr. Weller, gravely.

"Think not?" said Sam.

"Nothin' like it," replied his father.

"But don't you think it means more?" inquired Sam.

"Vell p'raps it is a more tenderer word," said Mr. Weller, after a few moments' reflection. "Go on, Sammy."

" 'Feel myself ashamed and completely circumscribed in a dressin' of you, for you *are* a nice gal and nothin' but it.' "

"That's a wery pretty sentiment," said the elder Mr. Weller, removing his pipe to make way for the remark.

"Yes, I think it is rayther good," observed Sam, highly flattered.

"Wot I like in that 'ere style of writin'," said the elder Mr. Weller, "is that there ain't no callin' names in it—no Wenuses, nor nothin' o' that kind. Wot's the good o' callin' a young 'ooman a Wenus or a angel, Sammy?"

"Ah! what, indeed?" replied Sam.

"You might jist as well call her a griffin, or a unicorn, or a king's arms at once, which is wery well known to be a col-lection o' fabulous animals," added Mr. Weller.

"Just as well," replied Sam.

"Drive on, Sammy," said Mr. Weller.

Sam complied with the request, and proceeded as follows, his father continuing to smoke, with a mixed expression of wisdom and complacency, which was particularly edifying.

" 'Afore I see you, I thought all women was alike.' "

"So they are," observed the elder Mr. Weller, parenthetically.

" 'But now,' " continued Sam, " 'now I find what a reg'lar soft-headed, inkred'lous turnip I must ha' been; for there ain't nobody like you, though *I* like you better than nothin' at all.' I thought it best to make that rayther strong," said Sam, looking up.

Mr. Weller nodded approvingly, and Sam resumed.

" 'So I take the privilidge of the day, Mary, my dear—as the gen'l'm'n in difficulties did, ven he valked out of a Sunday—to tell you that the first and only time I see you, your likeness was took on my hart in much quicker time and brighter colors than ever a likeness was took by the profeel macheen (wich p'raps you have heerd on Mary my dear) altho it *does* finish a portrait and put the frame and glass on complete, with a hook at the end to hang it up by, and all in two minutes and a quarter.' "

"I am afeerd that werges on the poetical, Sammy," said Mr. Weller, dubiously.

"No, it don't," replied Sam, reading on very quickly, to avoid contesting the point:

" 'Except of me Mary my dear as your walentine and think over what I've said. My dear Mary I will now conclude.' That's all," said Sam.

"That's rather a sudden pull up, ain't it, Sammy?" inquired Mr. Weller.

"Not a bit on it," said Sam; "she'll vish there wos more, and that's the great art o' letter writin'."

"Well," said Mr. Weller, "there's somethin' in that; and I wish your mother-in-law 'ud only conduct her conwersation on the same genteel principle. Ain't you a goin' to sign it?"

"That's the difficulty," said Sam; "I don't know what *to* sign it."

"Sign it Veller," said the oldest surviving proprietor of that name.

"Won't do," said Sam. "Never sign a walentine with your own name."

"Sign it 'Pickvick,' then," said Mr. Weller; "it's a wery good name, and a easy one to spell."

"The wery thing," said Sam. "I *could* end with a werse; what do you think?"

"I don't like it, Sam," rejoined Mr. Weller. "I never know'd a respectable coachman as wrote poetry, 'cept one as made an affectin' copy o' werses the night afore he vos hung for a highway robbery; and *he* wos only a Cambervell man, so even that's no rule."

But Sam was not to be dissuaded from the poetical idea that had occurred to him, so he signed the letter,

> "*Your love-sick
> Pickwick.*"

How Do I Love Thee:

A GATHERING OF
LOVE POETRY

Love and poetry, of course, go together. Shakespeare said that the lover, the poet, and the madman were all alike. Perhaps in the beginnings of love—in its first torrential feelings—we are all a little mad. Love is exaggerated. The loved one is bigger than life; the feelings are sometimes more than we can bear. Out of these very deep feelings, out of the exaggeration of the emotions, comes poetry; and some of the greatest poetry in the world is love poetry.

HOW DO I LOVE THEE?

ELIZABETH BARRETT BROWNING

How do I love thee? Let me count the ways.
I love thee to the depth and breadth and height
My soul can reach, when feeling out of sight
For the ends of Being and ideal Grace.
I love thee to the level of everyday's
Most quiet need, by sun and candle-light.
I love thee freely, as men strive for Right;
I love thee purely, as they turn from Praise.
I love thee with the passion put to use
In my old griefs, and with my childhood's faith.
I love thee with a love I seemed to lose
With my lost saints—I love thee with the breath,
Smiles, tears, of all my life!—and, if God choose,
I shall but love thee better after death.

SONG

THOMAS LOVELL BEDDOES

How *many times do I love thee, dear?*
Tell me how many thoughts there be
In the atmosphere
Of a new-fall'n year,
Whose white and sable hours appear
The latest flake of Eternity—
So many times do I love thee, dear.

How many times do I love again?
Tell me how many beads there are
In a silver chain
Of evening rain,
Unraveled from the tumbling main,
And threading the eye of a yellow star—
So many times do I love again.

SO WE'LL GO NO MORE A-ROVING

GEORGE GORDON, LORD BYRON

So, *we'll go no more a-roving*
  So late into the night,
Though the heart be still as loving,
  And the moon be still as bright.

For the sword outwears its sheath,
  And the souls wears out the breast,
And the heart must pause to breathe,
  And Love itself have rest.

Though the night was made for loving,
  And the day returns too soon,
Yet we'll go no more a-roving
  By the light of the moon.

TO MY DEAR AND LOVING HUSBAND

ANNE BRADSTREET

If ever two were one, then surely we.
If ever man were lov'd by wife, then thee;
If ever wife was happy in a man,
Compare with me ye women if you can.
I prize thy love more than whole Mines of gold,
Or all the riches that the East doth hold.
My love is such that Rivers cannot quench,
Nor ought but love from thee, give recompence.
Thy love is such I can no way repay,
The heavens reward thee manifold I pray.
Then while we live, in love let's so persever,
That when we live no more, we may live ever.

ONE WORD IS TOO OFTEN PROFANED

PERCY BYSSHE SHELLEY

One *word is too often profaned*
For me to profane it;
One feeling too falsely disdain'd
For thee to disdain it;
One hope is too like despair
For prudence to smother;
And pity from thee more dear
Than that from another.

I can give not what men call love:
But wilt thou accept not
The worship the heart lifts above
And the heavens reject not,
The desire of the moth for the star,
Of the night for the morrow,
The devotion to something afar
From the sphere of our sorrow?

WHO EVER LOVED, THAT LOVED NOT AT FIRST SIGHT?

CHRISTOPHER MARLOWE

It lies not in our power to love or hate,
For will in us is overruled by fate.
When two are stripped, long ere the course begin,
We wish that one should lose, the other win;
And one especially do we affect
Of two gold ingots, like in each respect:
The reason no man knows; let it suffice
What we behold is censured by our eyes.
Where both deliberate, the love is slight:
Who ever loved, that loved not at first sight?

BELIEVE ME, IF ALL THOSE ENDEARING YOUNG CHARMS

THOMAS MOORE

Believe me, if all those endearing young charms,
  Which I gaze on so fondly today,
Were to change by tomorrow, and fleet in my arms,
  Like fairy-gifts fading away,
Thou wouldst still be adored, as this moment thou art,
  Let thy loveliness fade as it will,
And around the dear ruin each wish of my heart
  Would entwine itself verdantly still.

It is not while beauty and youth are thine own,
  And thy cheeks unprofaned by a tear,
That the fervour and faith of a soul can be known,
  To which time will but make thee more dear;
No, the heart that has truly loved never forgets,
  But as truly loves on to the close,
As the sunflower turns on her god, when he sets,
  The same look which she turned when he rose.

IT WAS A LOVER AND HIS LASS

WILLIAM SHAKESPEARE

It was a lover and his lass,
*   With a hey, and a ho, and hey nonino,*
That o'er the green corn-field did pass
*   In the spring time, the only pretty ring time,*
When birds do sing, hey ding a ding, ding:
Sweet lovers love the spring.

Between the acres of the rye,
*   With a hey, and a ho, and a hey nonino,*
These pretty country folk would lie,
*   In the spring time, the only pretty ring time,*
When birds do sing, hey ding a ding, ding:
Sweet lovers love the spring.

This carol they began that hour,
*   With a hey, and a ho, and a hey nonino,*
How that a life was but a flower
*   In the spring time, the only pretty ring time,*
When shepherds pipe on oaten straws,
*   And merry larks are ploughmen's clocks,*
When turtles tread, and rooks, and daws,
*   And maidens bleach their summer smocks,*
The cuckoo then, on every tree,
Mocks married men; for thus sings he,
*   Cuckoo;*
Cuckoo, cuckoo: O word of fear,
Unpleasing to a married ear.

LA BELLE DAME SANS MERCI

JOHN KEATS

O *what* can ail thee, knight-at-arms,
  Alone and palely loitering?
The sedge has withered from the lake,
  And no birds sing.

O *what can ail thee, knight-at-arms,*
  So haggard and so woe-begone?
The squirrel's granary is full,
  And the harvest's done.

I see a lily on thy brow
  With anguish moist and fever dew,
And on thy cheek a fading rose
  Fast withereth too.

I met a lady in the meads,
  Full beautiful—a faery's child;
Her hair was long, her foot was light,
  And her eyes were wild.

I made a garland for her head,
  And bracelets too, and fragrant zone;
She looked at me as she did love,
  And made sweet moan.

I set her on my pacing steed,
  And nothing else saw all day long,

For sidelong would she bend, and sing
    A faery's song.

She found me roots of relish sweet,
    And honey wild, and manna dew,
And sure in language strange she said—
    "I love thee true!"

She took me to her elfin grot,
    And there she wept and sighed full sore,
And there I shut her wild wild eyes
    With kisses four.

And there she lullèd me asleep,
    And there I dreamed—ah! woe betide!
The latest dream I ever dreamed
    On the cold hill's side.

I saw pale kings and princes too,
    Pale warriors, death-pale were they all;
They cried—"La Belle Dame sans Merci
    Hath thee in thrall!"

I saw their starved lips in the gloam,
    With horrid warning gapèd wide,
And I awoke and found me here,
    On the cold hill's side.

And this is why I sojourn here,
    Alone and palely loitering,
Though the sedge is withered from the lake
    And no birds sing.

IF YOU WERE COMING IN THE FALL

EMILY DICKINSON

If you *were coming in the fall,*
I'd brush the summer by
With half a smile and half a spurn,
As housewives do a fly.

If I could see you in a year,
I'd wind the months in balls,
And put them each in separate drawers,
Until their time befalls.

If only centuries delayed,
I'd count them on my hand,
Subtracting till my fingers dropped
Into Van Diemen's land.

If certain, when this life was out,
That yours and mine should be,
I'd toss it yonder like a rind,
And taste eternity.

But now, all ignorant of the length
Of time's uncertain wing,
It goads me, like the goblin bee,
That will not state its sting.

SECRET LOVE

JOHN CLARE

I hid *my love when young till I*
Couldn't bear the buzzing of a fly;
I hid my life to my despite
Till I could not bear to look at light:
I dare not gaze upon her face
But left her memory in each place;
Where'er I saw a wild flower lie
I kissed and bade my love good-bye.

I met her in the greenest dells,
Where dewdrops pearl the wood bluebells;
The lost breeze kissed her bright blue eye,
The bee kissed and went singing by,
A sunbeam found a passage there,
A gold chain round her neck so fair;
As secret as the wild bee's song
She lay there all the summer long.

I hid my love in field and town
Till e'en the breeze would knock me down;
The bees seemed singing ballads o'er,
The fly's bass turned a lion's roar;
And even silence found a tongue,
To haunt me all the summer long;
The riddle nature could not prove
Was nothing else but secret love.

NEVER SEEK TO TELL THY LOVE

WILLIAM BLAKE

Never *seek to tell thy love*
Love that never told can be;
For the gentle wind does move
Silently, invisibly.

I told my love, I told my love,
I told her all my heart,
Trembling, cold, in ghastly fears—
Ah, she doth depart.

Soon as she was gone from me
A traveller came by
Silently, invisibly—
O, was no deny.

OPEN THE DOOR TO ME, OH!

ROBERT BURNS

Oh, open the door, some pity to shew,
  Oh, open the door to me, oh!
Tho' thou hast been false, I'll ever prove true,
  Oh, open the door to me, oh!

Cauld is the blast upon my pale cheek,
  But caulder thy love for me, oh!
The frost that freezes the life at my heart,
  Is nought to my pains fra thee, oh!

The wan moon is setting behind the white wave,
  And time is setting with me, oh!
False friends, false love, farewell! for mair
  I'll ne'er trouble thee, nor thee, oh!

She has open'd the door, she has open'd it wide;
  She sees his pale corse on the plain, oh!
My true love! she cried, and sank down by his side,
  Never to rise again, oh!

GIVE ALL TO LOVE

RALPH WALDO EMERSON

Give *all to love;*
Obey thy heart;
Friends, kindred, days,
Estate, good-fame,
Plans, credit and the Muse,—
Nothing refuse.

'Tis a brave master;
Let it have scope:
Follow it utterly,
Hope beyond hope:
High and more high
It dives into noon,
With wing unspent,
Untold intent;
But it is a god,
Knows its own path
And the outlets of the sky.

It was never for the mean;
It requireth courage stout.
Souls above doubt,
Valor unbending,
It will reward,—
They shall return
More than they were,
And ever ascending.

Leave all for love;
Yet, hear me, yet,
One word more thy heart behoved,
One pulse more of firm endeavor,—
Keep thee to-day,
To-morrow, forever,
Free as an Arab
Of thy beloved.

Cling with life to the maid;
But when the surprise,
First vague shadow of surmise
Flits across her bosom young,
Of a joy apart from thee,
Free be she, fancy-free;
Nor thou detain her vesture's hem,
Nor the palest rose she flung
From her summer diadem.

Though thou loved her as thyself,
As a self of purer clay,
Though her parting dims the day,
Stealing grace from all alive;
Heartily know
When half-gods go,
The gods arrive.

First dances are important: What will you wear; how will you look; are you really popular? The anxieties and questions are universal. That delightful commentator on the human emotions Hildegard Dolson always approaches such feelings with high good humor. Somehow or other, she makes the traditional first prom—which is the hardest—also the funniest, as you will find in the pages that follow.

THE FIRST PROM'S
THE HARDEST

HILDEGARDE DOLSON

There seems to be a popular theory that little girls who have brothers learn very early to adopt an easy, bantering manner toward members of the opposite sex. In my own case, this theory held water like a sieve. It's true that in a rough game of croquet I could banter as well as the next one, or even bawl the daylights out of one of Bobby's friends. But when it came to social presence, I had none.

Every Saturday afternoon for several years, twenty-nine other little girls and I had sat on one side of the room at Miss Steele's dancing school and heard Miss Steele say, "Now choose your partners." At this, most of the boys would charge across the room as one man—but not at me. When the mists cleared away, and the belles of the place had more partners than they knew what to do with, Miss Steele stepped in. After spotting those of us who were leftovers, she'd rush up reinforcements by the napes of their necks, before they could escape to the hall. On the days when there weren't enough boys to go around, somehow I was always one of the girls who danced with a girl. As a wallflower, I was rapidly going to seed. My one respite came during the Paul Jones, when, as Miss Steele blew her whistle, every boy was honor-bound to dance with the lady on his right. I must say that the whistle blew some really good dancers my way. They may have acted sullen, but at least they kept time.

Until I was fifteen, my social activities were confined largely to these gay Saturday afternoon dancing school whirls. I was now a sophomore in high school, and much more concerned over the fact that Mother wouldn't let me wear high heels than that I was undoubtedly about to flunk geometry. Even more acute than the high heels was the throbbing fear that I wouldn't be asked to the Junior Prom. I had a grim conviction that now was the test of whether I was to face the future as a withered old maid or a prom trotter.

Unfortunately, a freshman in short pants named Freddie Perkins settled the matter five days before the prom, by edging up to me at the end of Study Hall and requesting my company on May 29th. I think his actual words were, "My mother was talking to your mother and she said you hadn't been asked to the prom, so do you want to go?"

Somehow it had never occurred to me that it was possible to be asked to a prom by the wrong man—especially a man in short pants —and the stark horror in my face must have frightened even Freddie, because he backed away several paces and stood waiting for my answer. He had nondescript hair parted in the middle above goggle-rim glasses, and the whole effect was profoundly depressing. "I have to stay home and study geometry that night," I finally said sullenly. Freddie pointed out in a dogged manner that I could study all day Saturday.

I began concocting an elaborate excuse about going to Meadville to visit an aunt, when a nasty thought struck me. "Does your mother know for sure you were going to ask me?"

"Of course," Freddie said, obviously surprised that I could think him capable of such folly on his own hook. "She told me to."

The thought of what would happen when Mrs. Perkins cross-questioned Freddie and phoned my mother stopped me short. Frantically I tried to decide whether to take my chances on the prom-in-short-pants, or go home and face Mother's wrath. Quailing at the thought of her stern conviction that "Freddie is a nice little boy and his mother belongs to our church," I muttered something which the waiting Freddie took to mean consent. He trotted off without another word, and I went glumly down to gym class, brooding over the way Fate had gummed up my first big chance at Society.

While we were struggling into our middies in the locker room, Ellie May Matthews, a sharp-nosed girl I disliked with abandon, said maybe I could get my kid brother to take me to the prom. With that, I yanked up my bloomers and prepared to defend my honor. "I'm going with somebody else," I said haughtily. Looking her straight in the eye, I unblushingly added that as a matter of fact I'd had two invitations, but Mother had made me turn down the best one.

"Then who are you going with?" she persisted.

It was one of those moments when I'd gladly have traded my present set-up for a desert island and a geometry teacher. "Freddie Perkins," I said.

The ensuing silence was hideous, with the thought of Freddie's pants hanging unmentionably in the air. Even Ellie May was too taken aback to speak. "The family made me," I added hopelessly. My friend Betty Evans did her loyal best for a lost cause by saying that Freddie was awfully bright. "He's on the Honor Roll every month." As we filed onto the gym floor, she said delicately that maybe the Perkinses would buy Freddie a new suit.

For five days I silently implored Heaven to get Freddie out of short pants, and argued with Mother about my own costume for the prom. She was lengthening my pink organdy dress by adding a ruffle around the knees, and she listened unmoved to my wild-eyed descriptions of what the other girls were wearing. "I don't know what their mothers can be thinking of," she'd say firmly, making it clear that my chances of getting a pleated red crepe and high-heeled satin slippers dyed to match were as remote as Judgment Day. She was equally adamant about dangly earrings from Woolworth's, but she finally promised that if it were a nice warm night, I could wear her Spanish shawl, at present decorating the piano.

Cheered by a mental image of myself tossing a shawl about with Castilian grace and a rose in my hair, I concentrated on coaxing for a boyish bob. Always before I'd had my hair neatly cut and clippered up the back of the neck by the same barber who did my brothers'. The one Ladies' Hairdresser in town was a man who charged seventy-five cents and often vanished for a week at a time. Mother disapproved of him sharply, but worn down by my bulldog tenacity, she finally consented, on the afternoon of the prom, to my getting a stylish boyish bob by Mister Leo.

I think I must have caught Mister Leo in an off moment, because he whacked off my hair in what struck even me as a somewhat impetuous manner. Mother let out an involuntary shriek when I trotted home proudly to display my coiffure, and at dinner Bobby referred to me somewhat crudely as "Ratface," until Father threatened to send him from the table.

After dinner Mother got to work on me with a curling iron, and the Spanish shawl was dragged from the piano for my further adornment. Sally, whose bedtime had been postponed to allow her to watch this gilding process, was big-eyed with envy. What made her envious was not the fact that I was going to a prom, but that I was going to stay up late. If I'd been going out with a hoot owl, the effect, in my sister's mind, would have been equally impressive. "Will you stay up past ten o'clock?" she kept asking. I said Pooh, ten o'clock was early, and intimated that if there were a creak on the stairs toward morning, it would be Hildegarde Coming Home.

Mother, who was now brandishing the iron on my shortest back wisps, said amiably that twelve o'clock was late enough for a little girl of fifteen. However, she agreed that as long as I was with Freddie she wouldn't worry. In a way, I could see what she meant.

By 8:15 I was dressed to the teeth, and Sally had gone storming off to bed with the taunt of "Just wait till I'm as old as Hildegarde. You'll see." As I stood before the downstairs hall mirror, trying the Spanish shawl at every possible angle, the sound of the doorbell froze me in my tracks. Would Freddie have new pants or wouldn't he?

I opened the door, took one look at Freddie's legs, and experienced a primitive urge to push him off the porch. The fact that he was not only in short pants but carrying an umbrella filled me with sullen rage. "It's going to rain," he said. "You'd better wear your rubbers."

Rather impulsively I shut the door in his face, knowing that if Mother saw Freddie's rain outfit I'd never get out of the house without my rubbers. Grabbing up the shawl, I dashed into the living room to say good-bye. "Can't Freddie come in, dear?" Mother asked.

"No, he says we're late. Some other kids are waiting at the corner." Then I turned and bolted, with her "Have a good time" following me as I went out the door to my doom.

Freddie got up off the railing and stood patiently while I hitched the Spanish shawl up over one shoulder and anchored it at the left hip with my elbow. "What's that?" he asked.

"It's an evening wrap," I said fiercely.

In silence we started out for the high school. About halfway down the first block, Freddie asked me what I got in Latin last month. He also checked up on my marks in English, history and geometry, and then mentioned smugly that he'd had all A's. About that time it began to rain, and he hoisted the umbrella with the righteous air of a man who's always right. "It's a good thing I brought this," he said. I believe it was at this point that I remarked pleasantly I'd rather die of pneumonia than be seen carrying an umbrella.

We walked the rest of the way in damp silence, while I wished passionately that one of us would fall and break a leg—preferably Freddie. In those days, my vocabulary didn't contain the word "Dope," but we had other standards to judge by. A boy who wore a yellow slicker with everybody's nickname written on the back was *smooth*. A boy who got all A's and carried an umbrella was *dumb*. The fact that Freddie also wore short pants put him in some horrible category beyond description.

I felt this even more despairingly as we walked into the high school gym, past laughing groups of couples, all of whom I suspected darkly of laughing at Freddie's pants and my Spanish shawl. The gym was a brilliant glare, with Japanese lanterns strung along the walls for exotic atmosphere, and the five-piece orchestra a dazzling spectacle on a platform at one end of the room. Somebody handed Freddie a dance program with a dangling little pencil attached, and my heart went down into my damp white shoes as I looked at it. Ten dances to fill out. All around me were boys in white flannels and dark-blue serge coats, but I was doomed to dance all evening with a pair of short pants. In panic, I fled to the girls' dressing room. It was crowded with the same girls I sat with in classes, but now that they were all dressed up and laughing shrilly together, I felt stiff with loneliness. While I stood miserably in one corner, trying to decide where to put my shawl, Betty Evans came in. She admired my new boyish bob with heartening coos, and then turned all around so that I could get the full effect of her lavender crepe with lace panels. When we went back to the gym, I hung on her arm trustingly, because she'd been to three dances in the last year, and it reassured me to be seen with such a sophisticate.

Our escorts were nowhere in sight, but that didn't abash Betty in the least. She hailed one of the boys, a senior I viewed with awe because he played halfback on the football team. "Ooooooo, Stevie," she called gaily. "What I don't know about you."

Stevie promptly came over. "Yeah, what?"

"Oh, I couldn't tell for anything. You'd die if you knew."

This went on for several minutes, until Stevie insisted he'd get the second dance with Betty and make her tell. "Don't you dare," she squealed after him. I'd been listening in alarmed fascination, wondering what dark secret Betty had discovered, and as soon as Stevie had gone off to look for Betty's escort, I asked, "What *did* you hear about him?"

"Nothing," she said. "It's just a line. Boys always like you better if you hand them a line." I stared at her in shocked admiration, as her partner came to claim the first dance. Suddenly I felt nakedly young, with no line to guide me.

The next two hours still come back to me in nightmares. Freddie had exchanged dances with five members of the Freshman Debating Team and with Mr. Higgins, the Latin teacher, who was there with his wife as chaperon. To say that neither Freddie, his fellow debaters, nor Mr. Higgins were good dancers is to wallow in understatement. Freddie went on the principle that a dogged walk from one end of the dance floor to the other was good enough for any girl. Plowing back and forth with him until my legs ached, I tried desperately to look as if I'd never seen him before and was coolly amused at the mistake which had brought us together. Then I was passed on to the other dancing debaters, including one called Roscoe who jerked, and a youth who embarrassed me hideously by shouting above the music to give me his views on States' Rights. After him came Mr. Higgins, who did a sort of leaping quadrille and regained his lost youth by running around me in a spirited Highland Fling. As far as I was concerned, being made conspicuous by Mr. Higgins was a fate infinitely worse than death. After that dance, even plodding up and down the floor with Freddie had a certain restful monotony.

It was while we were plodding through the next-to-last dance that I heard somebody say, "Hi, Fred, mind if I cut in?" To my utter astonishment, ten seconds later I was gliding down the floor with a tall, handsome boy in a gray suit, while Freddie gaped after us like a surprised goldfish. "I'm Fred's cousin," the boy said. He mentioned something about stopping overnight on his way home from Allegheny College, but if he'd told me he'd just slain fifty dragons, I'd have accepted his story just as unquestioningly. "Aunt Helen sent me over here to see Fred," he added. We smiled at each other, and in a daze of emotions, I stumbled all over his feet. I apologized frenziedly, seized with the awful fear that he'd give me back to Freddie. "That was my fault," he said. "I was trying a new step they do down at school called the Charleston. See, it's kick to the side and then forward."

From then on I drifted along in a rosy haze, kicking to the side and forward. I think he had brown eyes and brown hair, but the important thing was that he was *smooth*, and he actually went to college. We exchanged names—his was Donald—and he told me he was coming back later in the summer to visit. "Now that I have a good reason," he said, tenderly squeezing my hand. At this, I was so overcome that I kicked in the wrong direction and landed a mean one on his shin. Even that didn't seem to discourage my dream prince. "Do you date Freddie very often?" he asked.

I shook my head violently and proceeded to make it very clear that Freddie had little part in my gay, prom-trotting existence. "The family made me come with him tonight and I was furious." Then, remembering that Freddie was his cousin, I added hastily that he was a very nice boy. "But I'd really rather date older men," I concluded brightly. My conscience gave a startled lurch as I said it, but it seemed to have a devastating effect on Donald, because he immediately invited me up for a football game the next fall. Somehow I managed to accept without swooning. We both forgot Freddie completely after that, until he turned up at the tag end of "Home Sweet Home." "Hel-*lo*, where've you been?" I said roguishly. Donald apologized like a gentleman for taking the last dance—a gesture which Freddie dismissed by saying his shoes hurt. They exchanged a few cousinly remarks, and then Donald asked where we were going to eat.

Freddie just stared, while I said glibly that everybody always went to Chacona's Ice Cream Parlor. It was not for nothing that I'd listened to Betty Evans. "We're off to Chacona's," Donald announced, taking my arm. Freddie pointed out that it was after twelve o'clock. He also said baldly that his mother had only given him enough money for the prom tickets. "She didn't say anything about eating."

Donald assured him masterfully that he'd take care of everything, and I went off to collect my shawl. In the dressing room I was surprised and gratified when at least ten girls greeted me fondly and told me I looked awfully cute. I was even more overcome when the most popular girl in the senior class came up to say that she simply adored my dress. She herself wore a short red taffeta evening wrap, and I was almost blinded by her glory.

"Who were you dancing the last two dances with?" she asked. All the girls crowded around to listen, and suddenly I knew, with belated feminine instinct, why they'd admired my dress. Instead of resenting it, my lungs nearly burst with pride. "Oh, that's a college man I know," I said. "He's invited me up for a football game next fall."

In the midst of a rustling, respectful silence, I flung the piano shawl grandly over my last year's organdy. "He has a marvelous line," I said. Then I swept out the door to meet Donald.

The tide had turned and I had found my sea-legs.

In the next two years our living room began to fill up with a modest number of men, or what Mother, in an unguarded moment, once referred to as "callow youths."

"Dear, do we know his family?" she often asked doubtfully.

To me, this was entirely beside the point. If they wore long pants and liked Guy Lombardo, then what was she fussing about? Jimmy and Sally had other standards to judge by. Any boy who brought me candy was their idea of a good, substantial Romeo, and even a stick of gum was better than nothing. When I received my first corsage, my younger brother and sister were honestly puzzled by my pleasure. After all, who wants to eat rosebuds?

Have you heard of some ghostly apparition that haunts an individual's imagination—the shadow of a ghost, perhaps, that one can see while others cannot—a phantom who seems to have a special significance for the person who can see him?

Can you be enchanted and enthralled, held in perpetual suspense by a figure you see in a window? Can you? Well, you certainly can if he appears in the major but little-known story by one of the best suspense writers of all times, Mrs. Oliphant.

THE LIBRARY WINDOW

MRS. OLIPHANT

I

I was not aware at first of the many discussions which had gone on about that window. It was almost opposite one of the windows of the large, old-fashioned drawing-room of the house in which I spent that summer, which was of so much importance in my life. Our house and the library were on opposite sides of the broad High Street of St. Rule's, which is a fine street, wide and ample, and very quiet, as strangers think who come from noisier places; but in a summer evening there is much coming and going, and the stillness is full of sound—the sound of footsteps and pleasant voices, softened by the summer air.

There are even exceptional moments when it is noisy: the time of the fair, and on Saturday night sometimes, and when there are excursion trains. Then even the softest sunny air of the evening will not smooth the harsh tones and the stumbling steps; but at these unlovely moments we shut the windows, and even I, who am so fond of that deep recess where I can take refuge from all that is going on inside, and make myself a spectator of all the varied story out of doors, withdraw from my watch-tower. To tell the truth, there never was very much going on inside.

The house belonged to my aunt, to whom (she says, "Thank God!") nothing ever happens. I believe that many things have happened to her in her time; but that was all over at the period of which I am speaking, and she was old, and very quiet. Her life went on in a routine never broken. She got up at the same hour every day, and did the same things in the same rotation, day by day the same. She said that this was the greatest support in the world, and that routine is a kind of salvation. It may be so; but it is a very dull salvation, and I used to feel that I would rather have incident, whatever kind of incident it might be. But then at that time I was not old, which makes all the difference.

At the time of which I speak the deep recess of the drawing-room window was a great comfort to me. Though she was an old lady (perhaps because she was so old) she was very tolerant, and had a kind of feeling for me. She never said a word, but often gave me a smile when she saw how I had built myself up, with my books and my basket of work.

I did very little work, I fear—now and then a few stitches when the spirit moved me, or when I had got well afloat in a dream, and was more tempted to follow it out than to read my books, as sometimes happened. At other times, and if the book were interesting, I used to get through volume after volume sitting there, paying no attention to anybody. And yet I did pay a kind of attention. Aunt Mary's old ladies came in to call, and I heard them talk, though I very seldom listened; but for all that, if they had anything to say that was interesting, it is curious how I found it in my mind afterwards, as if the air had blown it to me. They came and went, and I had the sensation of their old bonnets gliding in and out and their dresses rustling; and now and then had to jump up and shake hands with someone who knew me and asked after my papa and mamma. Then Aunt Mary would give me a little smile again, and I slipped back to my window. She never seemed to mind.

My mother would not have let me do it, I know. She would have remembered dozens of things there were to do. She would have sent me upstairs to fetch something which I was quite sure she did not

want, or downstairs to carry some quite unnecessary message to the housemaid. She liked to keep me running about. Perhaps that was one reason why I was so fond of Aunt Mary's drawing-room, and the deep recess of the window, and the curtain that fell half over it, and the broad window-seat where one could collect so many things without being found fault with for untidiness. Whenever we had anything the matter with us in these days, we were sent to St. Rule's to get up our strength. And this was my case at the time of which I am going to speak.

Everybody had said, since ever I learned to speak, that I was fantastic and fanciful and dreamy, and all the other words with which a girl who may happen to like poetry, and to be fond of thinking, is so often made uncomfortable. People don't know what they mean when they say fantastic. It wounds like Madge Wildfire, or something of that sort. My mother thought I should always be busy, to keep nonsense out of my head. But really I was not at all fond of nonsense. I was rather serious than otherwise. I would have been no trouble to anybody if I had been left to myself. It was only that I had a sort of second sight and was conscious of things to which I paid no attention.

Even when reading the most interesting book, the things that were being talked about blew in to me; and I heard what the people were saying in the streets as they passed under the window. Aunt Mary always said I could do two or indeed three things at once —both read and listen and see. I am sure that I did not listen much, and seldom looked out—of set purpose—as some people do who notice what bonnets the ladies in the street have on. But I did hear what I couldn't help hearing, even when I was reading my book, and I did see all sorts of things, though often for a whole half-hour I might never lift my eyes.

This does not explain what I said at the beginning, that there were many discussions about that window. It was, and still is, the last window in the row of the College Library, which is opposite my aunt's house in the High Street. Yet it is not exactly opposite, but a little to the west, so that I could see it best from the left side of my recess, I took it calmly for granted that it was a window like any other till I first heard the talk about it which was going on in the drawing-room. "Have you never made up your mind, Mrs. Balcarres," said old Mr. Pitmilly, "whether that window opposite is a window or no?" He said Mistress Balcarres—and he was always called Mr. Pitmilly Morton: which was the name of his place.

"I am never sure of it, to tell the truth," said Aunt Mary, "all these years."

"Bless me!" said one of the old ladies. "And what window may that be?"

Mr. Pitmilly had a way of laughing as he spoke, which did not please me; but it was true that he was not perhaps desirous of pleasing me. He said: "Oh, just the window opposite," with his laugh running through his words; "our friend can never make up her mind about it, though she has been living opposite it since——"

"You need never mind the date," said another; "the leebrary window! Dear me, what should it be but a window? Up at that height it could not be a door."

"The question is," said my aunt, "if it is a real window with glass in it, or if it is merely painted, or if it once was a window and has been built up. And the oftener people look at it, the less they are able to say."

"Let me see this window," said old Lady Carnbee, who was very active and strong-minded; and then they all came crowding upon me —three or four old ladies, very eager, and Mr. Pitmilly's white hair appearing over their heads, and my aunt sitting quiet and smiling behind.

"I mind the window very well," said Lady Carnbee; "ay, and so do more than me. But in its present appearance it is just like any other window; but has not been cleaned, I should say, in the memory of man."

"I see what ye mean," said one of the others. "It is just a very dead thing without any reflection in it; but I've seen as bad before."

"Ay, it's dead enough," said another, "but that's no rule; for these huzzies of women-servants in this ill age——"

"Nay, the women are well enough," said the softest voice of all, which was Aunt Mary's. "I will never let them risk their lives cleaning the outside of mine. And there are no women-servants in the old library: there is maybe something more in it than that."

They were all pressing into my recess, pressing upon me, a row of old faces, peering into something they could not understand. I had a sense in my mind how curious it was, the wall of old ladies in their old satin gowns all glazed with age, Lady Carnbee with her lace about her head. Nobody was looking at me or thinking of me; but I felt unconsciously the contrast of my youngness to their oldness, and stared at them as they stared over my head at the library window. I had given it no attention up to this time. I was more taken up with the old ladies than with the thing they were looking at.

"The framework is all right at least, I can see that, and pented black——"

"And the panes are pented black too. It's no window, Mrs. Balcarres. It has been filled in, in the days of the window duties: you will mind, Leddy Carnbee."

"Mind!" said that oldest lady. "I mind when your mother was marriet, Jeanie: and that's neither the day nor yesterday. But as for the window, it's just a delusion; and that is my opinion of the matter, if you ask me."

"There's a great want of light in that muckle room at the college," said another. "If it was a window, the leebrary would have more light."

"One thing is clear," said one of the younger ones: "it cannot be a window to see through. It may be filled in or it may be built up, but it is not a window to give light."

"And whoever heard of a window that was no' to see through?" Lady Carnbee said. I was fascinated by the look on her face, which was a curious, scornful look as of one who knew more than she chose to say; and then my wandering fancy was caught by her hand as she held it up, throwing back the lace that drooped over it. Lady Carnbee's lace was the chief thing about her—heavy, black, Spanish lace with large flowers. Everything she wore was trimmed with it. A large veil of it hung over her old bonnet. But her hand coming out of this heavy lace was a curious thing to see.

She had very long fingers, very taper, which had been much admired in her youth; and her hand was very white, or rather more than white: pale, bleached, and bloodless, with large blue veins standing up upon the back; and she wore some fine rings, among others a big diamond in an ugly old claw setting. They were too big for her, and were wound round and round with yellow silk to make them keep on: and this little cushion of silk, turned brown with long wearing, had twisted round so that it was more conspicuous than the jewels; while the big diamond blazed underneath in the hollow of her hand, like some dangerous thing hiding and sending out darts of light. The hand, which seemed to come almost to a point, with this strange ornament underneath, clutched at my half-terrified imagination. It too seemed to mean far more than was said. I felt as if it might clutch me with sharp claws, and the lurking, dazzling creature bite—with a sting that would go to the heart.

Presently, however, the circle of the old faces broke up, the old ladies returned to their seats, and Mr. Pitmilly, small but very erect, stood up in the midst of them, talking with mild authority like a little oracle among the ladies. Only Lady Carnbee always contradicted the neat, little old gentleman. She gesticulated when she talked, like a Frenchwoman, and darted forth that hand of hers with the lace hanging over it, so that I always caught a glimpse of the lurking diamond. I thought she looked like a witch among the comfortable little group which gave such attention to everything Mr. Pitmilly said.

"For my part, it is my opinion there is no window there at all," he said. "It's very like the thing that's called in scienteefic language an optical illusion. It arises generally, if I may use such a word in the presence of ladies, from a liver that is not just in the perfitt order and balance that organ demands—and then you will see things—a blue dog, I remember, was the thing in one case, and in another——"

"The man has gane gyte," said Lady Carnbee; "I mind the windows in the auld leebrary as long as I mind anything. Is the leebrary itself an optical illusion too?"

"Na, na," and "No, no," said the old ladies. "A blue dogue would be a strange vagary; but the library we have all kent from our youth," said one. "And I mind when the Assemblies were held there one year when the Town Hall was building," another said.

"It is just a great divert to me," said Aunt Mary; but what was strange was that she paused there, and said in a low tone, "now," and then went on again, "For whoever comes to my house, there are aye discussions about that window. I have never just made up my mind about it myself. Sometimes I think it's a case of these wicked window duties, as you said, Miss Jeanie, when half the windows in our houses were blocked up to save the tax. And then I think it may be due to that blank kind of building like the great new buildings on the Earthen Mound in Edinburgh, where the windows are just ornaments. And then wiles I am sure I can see the glass shining when the sun catches it in the afternoon."

"You could so easily satisfy yourself, Mrs. Balcarres, if you were to ____"

"Give a laddie a penny to cast a stone, and see what happens," said Lady Carnbee.

"But I am not sure that I have any desire to satisfy myself," Aunt Mary said. And then there was a stir in the room, and I had to come out from my recess and open the door for the old ladies and see them downstairs as they all went away following one another. Mr. Pitmilly gave his arm to Lady Carnbee, though she was always contradicting him; and so the tea-party dispersed. Aunt Mary came to the head of the stairs with her guests in an old-fashioned gracious way, while I went down with them to see that the maid was ready at the door. When I came back Aunt Mary was still standing in the recess looking out. Returning to my seat she said, with a kind of wistful look, "Well, honey, and what is your opinion?"

"I have no opinion. I was reading my book all the time," I said.

"And so you were, honey, and no' very civil; but all the same I ken well you heard every word we said."

II

It was a night in June; dinner was long over, and had it been winter the maids would have been shutting up the house, and my Aunt

Mary preparing to go upstairs to her room. But it was still clear daylight, that daylight out of which the sun has been long gone, and which has no longer any rose reflections, but all has sunk into a pearly, neutral tint—a light which is daylight yet is not day. We had taken a turn in the garden after dinner, and now we had returned to what we called our usual occupations. My aunt was reading. The English post had come in, and she had got her *Times*, which was her great diversion. The *Scotsman* was her morning reading, but she liked her *Times* at night.

As for me, I too was at my usual occupation, which at that time was doing nothing. I had a book as usual, and was absorbed in it; but I was conscious of all that was going on all the same. The people strolled along the broad pavement, making remarks as they passed under the open window which came up into my story or my dream and sometimes made me laugh. The tone and the faint singsong, or rather chant, of the accent, which was "a wee Fifish," was novel to me and associated with holiday, and pleasant; and sometimes they said to each other something that was amusing, and often something that suggested a whole story; but presently they began to drop off; the footsteps slackened; the voices died away. It was getting late, though the clear, soft daylight went on and on.

All through the lingering evening, which seemed to consist of interminable hours, long but not weary, drawn out as if the spell of the light and the outdoor life might never end, I had now and then, quite unawares, cast a glance at the mysterious window which my aunt and her friends had discussed, as I felt, though I dared not say it even to myself, rather foolishly. It caught my eye without any intention on my part, as I paused, as it were, to take breath, in the flowing and current of undistinguishable thoughts and things from without and within which carried me along.

First it occurred to me, with a little sensation of discovery, how absurd to say it was not a window, a living window, one to see through! Why, then, had they never *seen* it, these old folk? I saw as I looked up suddenly the faint grayness as of visible space within—a room behind, certainly—dim, as it was natural a room should be on the other side of the street—quite indefinite; yet so clear that if someone were to come to the window there would be nothing surprising in it. For certainly there was a feeling of space behind the panes which these old half-blind ladies had disputed about whether they were glass or only fictitious panes marked on the wall. How silly, when eyes that could see could make it out in a minute! It was only a grayness at present, but it was unmistakable: a space that went back into gloom, as every room does when you look into it across a street.

There were no curtains to show whether it was inhabited or not; but a room—oh, as distinctly as ever room was! I was pleased with myself, but said nothing while Aunt Mary rustled her paper, waiting for a favorable moment to announce a discovery which settled her problem at once. Then I was carried away upon the stream again and forgot the window, till somebody threw, unawares, a word from the outer world, "I'm goin' hame; it'll soon be dark." Dark! what was the fool thinking of? it never would be dark if one waited out, wandering in the soft air for hours longer; and then my eyes, acquiring easily that new habit, looked across the way again.

Ah, now! nobody indeed had come to the window; and no light had been lighted, seeing it was still beautiful to read by—a still, clear, colorless light; but the room inside had certainly widened. I could see the gray space and air a little deeper, and a sort of vision, very dim, of a wall, and something against it—something dark, with the blackness that a solid article, however indistinctly seen, takes in the lighter darkness that is only space: a large, black, dark thing coming out into the gray. I looked more intently, and made sure it was a piece of furniture, either a writing-table or perhaps a large bookcase. No doubt it must be the last, since this was part of the old library. I never visited the old College Library, but I had seen such places before, and I could well imagine it to myself. How curious that for all the time these old people had looked at it they had never seen this before!

It was more silent now, and my eyes, I suppose, had grown dim with gazing, doing my best to make it out, when suddenly Aunt Mary said: "Will you ring the bell, my dear? I must have my lamp."

"Your lamp?" I cried, "when it is still daylight." But then I gave another look at my window, and perceived with a start that the light had indeed changed: for now I saw nothing. It was still light, but there was so much change in the light that my room, with the gray space and the large shadowy bookcase, had gone out, and I saw them no more; for even a Scotch night in June, though it looks as if it would never end, does darken at the last. I had almost cried out, but checked myself and rang the bell for Aunt Mary and made up my mind I would say nothing till next morning, when, to be sure, naturally, it would be more clear.

Next morning I rather think I forgot all about it, or was busy, or was more idle than usual—the two things meant nearly the same. At all events I thought no more of the window, though I still sat in my own, opposite to it, but occupied with some other fancy. Aunt Mary's visitors came as usual in the afternoon; but their talk was of other things, and for a day or two nothing at all happened to bring back my thoughts into this channel.

It might be nearly a week before the subject came back, and once more it was old Lady Carnbee who set me thinking. Not that she said anything upon that particular theme, but she was the last of my aunt's afternoon guests to go away, and when she rose to leave she threw up her hands, with those lively gesticulations which so many old Scotch ladies have. "My faith!" said she, "there is that bairn there still like a dream. Is the creature bewitched, Mary Balcarres? and is she bound to sit there by night and by day for the rest of her days? You should mind that there's things about, uncanny for women of our blood."

I was too much startled at first to recognize that it was of me she was speaking. She was like a figure in a picture, with her pale face the colour of ashes, and the big pattern of the Spanish lace hanging half over it, and her hand held up, with the big diamond blazing at me from the inside of her uplifted palm. It was held up in surprise, but it looked as if it were raised in malediction; and the diamond threw out darts of light and glared and twinkled at me. If it had been in its right place it would not have mattered; but there, in the open of the hand! I started up, half in terror, half in wrath. And then the old lady laughed, and her hand dropped.

"I've wakened you to life and broke the spell," she said, nodding her old head at me, while the large black silk flowers of the lace waved and threatened. And she took my arm to go downstairs, laughing and bidding me be steady, and no' tremble and shake like a broken reed. "You should be as steady as a rock at your age. I was like a young tree," she said, leaning so heavily that my willowy girlish frame quivered. "I was a support to virtue, like Pamela, in my time."

"Aunt Mary, Lady Carnbee is a witch!" I cried, when I came back.

"Is that what you think, honey? well, maybe she once was," said Aunt Mary, whom nothing surprised.

And it was that night once more after dinner, and after the post came in, and *The Times*, that I suddenly saw the library window again. I had seen it every day—and noticed nothing; but tonight, still in a little tumult of mind over Lady Carnbee and her wicked diamond which wished me harm, and her lace which waved threats and warnings at me, I looked across the street, and there I saw quite plainly the room opposite, far more clear than before.

I saw dimly that it must be a large room, and that the big piece of furniture against the wall was a writing-desk. That in a moment, when first my eyes rested upon it, was quite clear: a large, old-fashioned escritoire, standing out into the room: and I knew by the shape of it that it had a great many pigeon-holes and little drawers in the back, and a large table for writing. There was one just like it in my father's library at home. It was such a surprise to see it all so clearly that I closed my eyes, for the moment almost giddy, wondering how papa's desk could have come here—and then when I reminded myself that this was nonsense and that there were many such writing-tables besides papa's, and looked again—lo! it had all become quite vague and indistinct as it was at first; and I saw nothing but the blank window of which the old ladies could never be certain whether it was filled up to avoid the window-tax, or whether it had ever been a window at all.

This occupied my mind very much, and yet I did not say anything to Aunt Mary. For one thing, I rarely saw anything at all in the early part of the day; but, then, that is natural: you can never see into a place from outside, whether it is an empty room or a looking-glass or people's eyes or anything else that is mysterious, in the day. It has, I suppose, something to do with the light. But in the evening in June in Scotland—then is the time to see. For it is daylight, yet it is not day, and there is a quality in it which I cannot describe, it is so clear, as if every object was a reflection of itself.

I used to see more and more of the room as the days went on. The large escritoire stood out more and more into the space: with sometimes white glimmering things, which looked like papers, lying on it: and once or twice I was sure I saw a pile of books on the floor close to the writing-table, as if they had gilding upon them in broken specks, like old books. It was always about the time when the lads in the street began to call to one another that they were going home, and sometimes a shriller voice would come from one of the doors, bidding somebody to "cry upon the laddies" to come back to their suppers. That was always the time I saw best, though it was close upon the moment when the veil seemed to fall and the clear radiance became less living, and all the sounds died out of the street, and Aunt Mary said in her soft voice, "Honey, will you ring for the lamp?" She said honey as people say darling; and I think it is a prettier word.

Then, finally, while I sat one evening with my book in my hand, looking straight across the street, not distracted by anything, I saw a little movement within. It was not anyone visible—but everybody must know what it is to see the stir in the air, the little disturbance —you cannot tell what it is, but that it indicates someone there, even though you can see no one. Perhaps it is a shadow making just one flicker in the still place. You may look at an empty room and the furniture in it for hours, and then suddenly there will be the flicker, and you know that something has come into it. It might only be a dog or a cat; it might be, if that were possible, a bird flying across; but it is someone, something living, which is so different, so completely different, in a moment from the things that are not living. It seemed to strike right through me, and I gave a little cry. Then Aunt Mary stirred a little, and put down the huge newspaper that almost covered her from sight, and said, "What is it, honey?"

I cried, "Nothing," with a little gasp, quickly, for I did not want to be disturbed just at this moment when somebody was coming! But I suppose she was not satisfied, for she got up and stood behind to see what it was, putting her hand on my shoulder. It was the softest touch in the world, but I could have flung it off angrily: for that moment everything was still again, and the place grew gray and I saw no more.

"Nothing," I repeated, but I was so vexed I could have cried. "I told you it was nothing, Aunt Mary. Don't you believe me, that you come to look—and spoil it all!"

I did not mean, of course, to say these last words; they were forced out of me. I was so much annoyed to see it all melt away like a dream: for it was no dream, but as real as—as real as—myself or anything I ever saw.

She gave my shoulder a little pat with her hand. "Honey," she said, "were you looking at something? Is't that? is't that?"

"Is it what?" I wanted to say, shaking off her hand, but something in me stopped me: for I said nothing at all and she went quietly back to her place. I suppose she must have rung the bell herself, for immediately I felt the soft flood of the light behind me, and the evening outside dimmed down, as it did every night, and I saw nothing more.

It was next day, I think, in the afternoon, that I spoke. It was brought on by something she said about her fine work. "I get a mist before my eyes," she said; "you will have to learn my old lace stitches, honey, for I soon will not see to draw the threads."

"Oh, I hope you will keep your sight," I cried, without thinking what I was saying. I was then young and very matter of fact. I had not found out that one may mean something, yet not half or a hundredth part of what one seems to mean: and even then probably hoping to be contradicted if it is anyhow against one's self.

"My sight!" she said, looking up at me with a look that was almost angry; "there is no question of losing my sight—on the contrary, my eyes are very strong. I may not see to draw fine threads, but I see at a distance as well as ever I did—as well as you do."

"I did not mean any harm, Aunt Mary," I said. "I thought you said —But how can your sight be as good as ever when you are in doubt about that window? I can see into the library room as clear as—" My voice wavered, for I had just looked up and across the street, and I could have sworn that there was no window at all, but only a false image of one painted on the wall.

"Ah!" she said, with a little tone of keenness and of surprise; and she half rose up, throwing down her work hastily, as if she meant to come to me. Then, perhaps seeing the bewildered look on my face, she paused and hesitated. "Ay, honey!" she said, "have you got so far ben as that?"

What did she mean? Of course I knew all the Scotch phrases as well as I knew myself; but it is a comfort to take refuge in a little ignorance, and I know I pretended not to understand whenever I was put out. "I don't know what you mean by 'far ben,'" I cried out, very impatient. I don't know what might have followed, but someone just then came to call, and she could only give me a look before she went forward, putting out her hand to her visitor. It was a very soft look, but anxious, and as if she did not know what to do: and she shook her head a very little, and I thought, though there was a smile on her face, there was something wet about her eyes. I retired into my recess, and nothing more was said.

But it was very tantalizing that it should fluctuate so; for sometimes I saw that room quite plain and clear—quite as clear as I could see papa's library, for example, when I shut my eyes. I compared it naturally to my father's study, because of the shape of the writing-table, which, as I tell you, was the same as his. At times I saw the papers on the table quite plain, just as I had seen his papers many a day. And the little pile of books on the floor at the foot—not ranged regularly in order, but put down one above the other, with all their angles going different ways, and a speck of the old gilding shining here and there. And then again at other times I saw nothing, absolutely nothing, and was no better than the old ladies who had peered over my head, drawing their eyelids together, and arguing that the window had been shut up because of the old, long-abolished window tax, or else that it had never been a window at all. It annoyed me very much at those dull moments to feel that I too puckered up my eyelids and saw no better than they.

Aunt Mary's old ladies came and went day after day while June went on. I was to go back in July, and I felt that I should be very unwilling indeed to leave until I had quite cleared up—as I was indeed in the way of doing—the mystery of that window which changed so strangely and appeared quite a different thing, not only to different people, but to the same eyes at different times. "Of course," I said to myself, "it must simply be an effect of the light." And yet I did not quite like that explanation, either, but would have been better pleased to make out to myself that it was some superiority in me which made it so clear to me, if it were only the great superiority of young eyes over old—though that was not quite enough to satisfy me, seeing it was a superiority which I shared with every little lass and lad in the street. I rather wanted, I believe, to think that there was some particular insight in me which gave clearness to my sight— which was a most impertinent assumption but really did not mean half the harm it seems to mean when it is put down here in black and white. I had several times again, however, seen the room quite plain, and made out that it was a large room, with a great picture in a dim gilded frame hanging on the farther wall, and many other pieces of solid furniture making a blackness here and there, besides the great escritoire against the wall, which had evidently been placed near the window for the sake of the light. One thing became visible to me after another, till I almost thought I should end by being able to read the old lettering on one of the big volumes which projected from the others and caught the light; but this was all preliminary to the great event which happened about Midsummer Day—the day of St. John, which was once so much thought of as a festival but now means nothing at all in Scotland any more than any other of the saints' days: which I shall always think a great pity and loss to Scotland, whatever Aunt Mary may say.

III

It was about midsummer, I cannot say exactly to a day when, but near that time, when the great event happened. I had grown very well acquainted by this time with that large, dim room. Not only the escritoire, which was very plain to me now, with the papers upon it, and the books at its foot, but the great picture that hung against the farther wall, and various other shadowy pieces of furniture, especially a chair which one evening I saw had been moved into the space before the escritoire—a little change which made my heart beat, for it spoke so distinctly of someone who must have been there, the someone who had already made me start, two or three times before, by some vague shadow of him or thrill of him which made a sort of movement in the silent space: a movement which made me sure that next minute I must see something or hear something which would explain the whole—if it were not that something always happened outside to stop it, at the very moment of its accomplishment.

I had no warning this time of movement or shadow. I had been looking into the room very attentively a little while before, and had made out everything almost clearer than ever; and then had bent my attention again on my book, and read a chapter or two at a most exciting period of the story: and consequently had quite left St. Rule's, and the High Street, and the College Library, and was really in a South American forest, almost throttled by the flowery creepers, and treading softly lest I should put my foot on a scorpion or a dangerous snake. At this moment something suddenly called my attention to the outside. I looked across, and then, with a start, sprang up, for I could not contain myself. I don't know what I said, but enough to startle the people in the room, one of whom was old Mr. Pitmilly. They all looked round upon me to ask what was the matter. And when I gave my usual answer of "Nothing," sitting down again, shamefaced but very much excited, Mr. Pitmilly got up and came forward, and looked out, apparently to see what was the cause. He saw nothing, for he went back again, and I could hear him telling Aunt Mary not to be alarmed, for Missy had fallen into a doze with the heat, and had startled herself waking up, at which they all laughed: another time I could have killed him for his impertinence, but my mind was too much taken up now to pay any attention. My head was throbbing and my heart beating. I was in such high excitement, however, that to restrain myself completely, to be perfectly silent, was more easy to me then than at any other time of my life. I waited until the old gentleman had taken his seat again, and then I looked back. Yes, there he was. I had not been deceived. I knew then, when I looked across, that this was what I had been looking for all the time—that I had known he was there, and had been waiting for him, every time there was that flicker of movement in the room—him and no one else. And there at last, just as I had expected, he was. I don't know that in reality I ever had expected him, or anyone: but this was what I felt when, suddenly looking into that curious dim room, I saw him there.

He was sitting in the chair, which he must have placed for himself, or which someone else in the dead of night when nobody was looking must have set for him, in front of the escritoire—with the back of his head towards me—writing. The light fell upon him from the left hand, and therefore upon his shoulders and the side of his head, which, however, was too much turned away to show anything of his face. Oh, how strange that there should be someone staring at him as I was doing, and he never to turn his head, to make a movement! If anyone stood and looked at me, were I in the soundest sleep that ever was, I would wake, I would jump up, I would feel it through everything. But there he sat and never moved. You are not to suppose, though I said the light fell upon him from the left hand, that there was very much light. There never is in a room you are looking into like that across the street; but there was enough to see him by—the outline of his figure, dark and solid, seated in the chair, and the fairness of his head visible faintly, a clear spot against the dimness. I saw this outline against the dim gilding of the frame of the large picture which hung on the farther wall.

I sat, all the time the visitors were there, in a sort of rapture, gazing at this figure. I knew no reason why I should be so much moved. In an ordinary way, to see a student at an opposite window quietly doing his work might have interested me a little, but certainly it would not have moved me in any such way. It is always interesting to have a glimpse like this of an unknown life—to see so much and yet know so little, and to wonder, perhaps, what the man is doing, and why he never turns his head. One would go to the window—but not too close, lest he should see you and think you were spying upon him—and one would ask, "Is he still there? Is he writing, writing always? I wonder what he is writing!" And it would be a great amusement: but no more. This was not my feeling at all in the present case. It was a sort of breathless watch, an absorption. I did not feel that I had eyes for anything else, or any room in my mind for another thought. I no longer heard, as I generally did, the stories and the wise remarks (or foolish) of Aunt Mary's old ladies or Mr. Pitmilly. I heard only a murmur behind me, the interchange of voices, one softer, one sharper; but it was not as in the time when I sat reading and heard every word, till the story in my book and the stories they were telling (what they said almost always shaped into stories) were all mingled into one another, and the hero in the novel became somehow the hero (or more likely heroine) of them all. But I took no notice of what they were saying now. And it was not that there was anything very interesting to look at, except the fact that he was there. He did nothing to keep up the absorption of my thoughts. He moved just so much as a man will do when he is very busily writing, thinking of nothing else.

There was a faint turn of his head as he went from one side to another of the page he was writing; but it appeared to be a long, long page which never wanted turning. Just a little outward, inclination when he was at the end of the line, and then a little inclination inward when he began the next. That was little enough to keep one gazing. But I suppose it was the gradual course of events leading up to this, the finding out of one thing after another as the eyes got accustomed to the vague light: first the room itself, and then the writing-table, and then the other furniture, and last of all the human inhabitant who gave it all meaning. This was all so interesting that it was like a country which one had discovered. And then the extraordinary blindness of the other people who disputed among themselves whether it was a window at all! I did not, I am sure, wish to be disrespectful, and I was very fond of my Aunt Mary, and I liked Mr. Pitmilly well enough, and I was afraid of Lady Carnbee. But yet to think of the—I know I ought not to say stupidity—the blindness of them, the foolishness, the insensibility! discussing it as if a thing that your eyes could see was a thing to discuss! It would have been unkind to think it was because they were old and their faculties dimmed. It is so sad to think that the faculties grow dim, that such a woman as my Aunt Mary should fail in seeing, or hearing, or feeling, that I would not have dwelt on it for a moment, it would have seemed so cruel! And then such a clever old lady as Lady Carnbee— who could see through a millstone, people said—and Mr. Pitmilly, such an old man of the world. It did indeed bring tears to my eyes to think that all those clever people, solely by reason of being no longer young as I was, should have the simplest things shut out from them; and for all their wisdom and their knowledge be unable to see what a girl like me could see so easily. I was too much grieved for them to dwell upon that thought, and half ashamed, though perhaps half proud too, to be so much better off than they.

All those thoughts flitted through my mind as I sat and gazed across the street. And I felt there was so much going on in that room across the street! He was so absorbed in his writing, never looked up, never paused for a word, never turned round in his chair, or got up and walked about the room as my father did. Papa is a great writer, everybody says: but he would have come to the window and looked out, he would have drummed with his fingers on the pane, he would have watched a fly and helped it over a difficulty, and played with the fringe of the curtain, and done a dozen other nice, pleasant, foolish things, till the next sentence took shape.

"My dear, I am waiting for a word," he would say to my mother when she looked at him with a question why he was so idle in her eyes; and then he would laugh and go back again to his writing-table. But He over there never stopped at all. It was like a fascination. I could not take my eyes from him and that little scarcely perceptible movement he made, turning his head. I trembled with impatience to see him turn the page or perhaps throw down his finished sheet on the floor, as somebody looking into a window like me once saw Sir Walter do, sheet after sheet.

I should have cried out if this Unknown had done that. I should not have been able to help myself, whoever had been present; and gradually I got into such a state of suspense waiting for it to be done that my head grew hot and my hands cold. And then, just when there was a little movement of his elbow, as if he were about to do this, to be called away by Aunt Mary to see Lady Carnbee to the door! I believe I did not hear her till she had called me three times, and then I stumbled up, all flushed and hot, and nearly crying. When I came out from the recess to give the old lady my arm (Mr. Pitmilly had gone away some time before) she put up her hand and stroked my cheek. "What ails the bairn?" she said; "she's fevered. You must not let her sit her lane in the window, Mary Balcarres. You and me know what comes of that." Her old fingers had a strange touch, cold like something not living, and I felt that dreadful diamond sting me on the cheek.

I do not say that this was not just a part of my excitement and suspense; and I know it is enough to make anyone laugh when the excitement was all about an unknown man writing in a room on the other side of the way, and my impatience because he never came to an end of the page. If you think I was not quite as well aware of this as anyone could be! But the worst was that this dreadful old lady felt my heart beating against her arm that was within mine. "You are just in a dream," she said to me, with her old voice close at my ear as we went downstairs. "I don't know who it is about, but it's bound to be some man that is not worth it. If you were wise you would think of him no more."

"I am thinking of no man!" I said, half crying. "It is very unkind and dreadful of you to say so, Lady Carnbee. I never thought of—any man, in all my life!" I cried in a passion of indignation. The old lady clung tighter to my arm, and pressed it to her, not unkindly.

"Poor little bird," she said, "how it's strugglin' and flutterin'! I'm not saying but what it's more dangerous when it's all for a dream."

She was not at all unkind; but I was very angry and excited and would scarcely shake that old pale hand which she put out to me from her carriage window when I had helped her in. I was angry with her, and I was afraid of the diamond, which looked up from under her finger as if it saw through and through me; and whether you believe me or not, I am certain that it stung me again—a sharp, malignant prick, oh, full of meaning! She never wore gloves, but only black lace mittens, through which that horrible diamond gleamed. I ran upstairs—she had been the last to go—and Aunt Mary too had gone to get ready for dinner, for it was late. I hurried to my place, and looked across, with my heart beating more than ever. I made quite sure I should see the finished sheet lying white upon the floor. But what I gazed at was only the dim blank of that window which they said was no window.

The light had changed in some wonderful way during that five minutes I had been gone, and there was nothing, nothing, not a reflection, not a glimmer. It looked exactly as they all said, the blank form of a window painted on the wall. It was too much: I sat down in my excitement and cried as if my heart would break. I felt that they had done something to it, that it was not natural, that I could not bear their unkindness—even Aunt Mary. They thought it not good for me! not good for me! and they had done something— even Aunt Mary herself—and that wicked diamond that hid itself in Lady Carnbee's hand.

Of course I knew all this was ridiculous as well as you could tell me; but I was exasperated by the disappointment and the sudden stop to all my excited feelings, and I could not bear it. It was more strong than I.

I was late for dinner, and naturally there were some traces in my eyes that I had been crying when I came into the full light in the dining-room, where Aunt Mary could look at me at her pleasure and I could not run away. She said, "Honey, you have been shedding tears. I'm loth, loth that a bairn of your mother's should be made to shed tears in my house."

"I have not been made to shed tears," cried I; and then, to save myself another fit of crying, I burst out laughing and said, "I am afraid of that dreadful diamond on old Lady Carnbee's hand. It bites—I am sure it bites! Aunt Mary, look here."

"You foolish lassie," Aunt Mary said; but she looked at my cheek under the light of the lamp, and then she gave it a little pat with her soft hand. "Go away with you, you silly bairn. There is no bite; but a flushed cheek, my honey, and a wet eye. You must read out my paper to me after dinner when the post is in; and we'll have no more thinking and no more dreaming for tonight."

"Yes, Aunt Mary," said I. But I knew what would happen; for when she opens up her *Times,* all full of the news of the world, and the speeches and things which she takes an interest in—though I cannot tell why—she forgets. And as I kept very quiet and made not a sound, she forgot tonight what she had said, and the curtain hung a little more over me than usual, and I sat down in my recess as if I had been a hundred miles away.

And my heart gave a great jump, as if it would have come out of my breast; for he was there. But not as he had been in the morning —I suppose the light, perhaps, was not good enough to go on with his work without a lamp or candles—for he had turned away from the table and was fronting the window, sitting leaning back in his chair, and turning his head to me. Not to me—he knew nothing about me. I thought he was not looking at anything; but with his face turned my way.

My heart was in my mouth: it was so unexpected, so strange! Though why it should have seemed strange I know not, for there was no communication between him and me that it should have moved me; and what could be more natural than that a man, wearied of his work, and feeling the want, perhaps, of more light, and yet that it was not dark enough to light a lamp, should turn round in his own chair, and rest a little, and think—perhaps of nothing at all? Papa always says he is thinking of nothing at all. He says things blow through his mind as if the doors were open, and he has no responsibility. What sort of things were blowing through this man's mind? Or was he thinking, still thinking, of what he had been writing and going on with it still?

The thing that troubled me most was that I could not make out his face. It's is very difficult to do so when you see a person only through two windows, your own and his. I wanted very much to recognize him afterwards if I should chance to meet him in the street. If he had only stood up and moved about the room I should have made out the rest of his figure, and then I should have known him again; or if he had only come to the window (as Papa always did), then I should have seen his face clearly enough to have recognized him.

But to be sure, he did not see any need to do anything in order that I might recognize him, for he did not know I existed; and probably if he had known I was watching him, he would have been annoyed and gone away.

But he was as immovable there, facing the window, as he had been seated at the desk. Sometimes he made a little faint stir with a hand or a foot, and I held my breath, hoping he was about to rise from his chair—but he never did it. And with all the efforts I made I could not be sure of his face. I puckered my eyelids together, as old Miss Jeanie did who was short-sighted, and I put my hands on each side of my face to concentrate the light on him: but it was all in vain. Either the face changed as I sat staring, or else it was the light that was not good enough, or I don't know what it was.

His hair seemed to me light—certainly there was no dark line about his head, as there would have been had it been very dark—and I saw, where it came across the old gilt frame on the wall behind, that it must be fair: and I am almost sure he had no beard. Indeed I am sure that he had no beard, for the outline of his face was distinct enough; and the daylight was still quite clear out of doors, so that I recognized perfectly a baker's boy who was on the pavement opposite, and whom I should have known again whenever I had met him: as if it were of the least importance to recognize a baker's boy!

There was one thing, however, rather curious about this boy. He had been throwing stones at something or somebody. In St. Rule's they have a great way of throwing stones at one another, and I suppose there had been a battle. I suppose also that he had one stone in his hand left over from the battle, and his roving eye took in all the incidents of the street to judge where he could throw it with most effect and mischief. But apparently he found nothing worthy of it in the street, for he suddenly turned round with a flick under his leg to show his cleverness, and aimed it straight at the window.

I remarked without remarking that it struck with a hard sound and without any breaking of glass, and fell straight down on the pavement. But I took no notice of this even in my mind, so intently was I watching the figure within, which moved not nor took the slightest notice, and remained just as dimly clear, as perfectly seen, yet as undistinguishable, as before. And then the light began to fail a little, not diminishing the prospect within, but making it still less distinct than it had been.

Then I jumped up, feeling Aunt Mary's hand upon my shoulder. "Honey," she said, "I asked you twice to ring the bell; but you did not hear me."

"Oh, Aunt Mary!" I cried in great penitence, but turned again to the window in spite of myself.

"You must come away from there; you must come away from there," she said, almost as if she were angry: and then her soft voice grew softer, and she gave me a kiss. "Never mind about the lamp, honey; I have rung myself, and it is coming; but, silly bairn, you must not aye be dreaming—your little head will turn."

All the answer I made, for I could scarcely speak, was to give a little wave with my hand to the window on the other side of the street.

She stood there patting me softly on the shoulder for a whole minute or more, murmuring something that sounded like, "She must go away, she must go away." Then she said, always with her hand soft on my shoulder, "Like a dream when one awaketh." And when I looked again I saw the blank of an opaque surface and nothing more.

Aunt Mary asked me no more questions. She made me come into the room and sit in the light and read something to her. But I did not know what I was reading, for there suddenly came into my mind and took possession of it, the thud of the stone upon the window, and its descent straight down, as if from some hard substance that threw it off: though I had myself seen it strike upon the glass of the panes across the way.

IV

I am afraid I continued in a state of great exaltation and commotion of mind for some time. I used to hurry through the day till the evening came, when I could watch my neighbor through the window opposite. I did not talk much to anyone, and I never said a word about my own questions and wonderings. I wondered who he was, what he was doing, and why he never came till the evening (or very rarely); and I also wondered much to what house the room belonged in which he sat. It seemed to form a portion of the old College Library, as I have often said.

The window was one of the line of windows which, I understood, lighted the large hall; but whether this room belonged to the library itself, or how its occupant gained access to it, I could not tell. I made up my mind that it must open out of the hall, and that the gentleman must be the librarian or one of his assistants, perhaps kept busy all the day in his official duties, and only able to get to his desk and do his own private work in the evening. One had heard of so many things like that—a man who had to take up some other kind of work for his living, and then when his leisure time came, gave it all up to something he really loved—some study or some book he was writing.

My father himself at one time had been like that. He had been in the Treasury all day, and then in the evening wrote his books, which made him famous. His daughter, however little she might know of other things, could not but know that! But it discouraged me very much when somebody pointed out to me one day in the street an old gentleman who wore a wig and took a great deal of snuff, and said, "That's the librarian of the old college." It gave me a great shock for a moment; but then I remembered that an old gentleman has generally assistants, and that it must be one of them.

Gradually I became quite sure of this. There was another small window above, which twinkled very much when the sun shone, and looked a very kindly, bright little window, above that dullness of the other which hid so much. I made up my mind this was the window of his other room, and that these two chambers at the end of the beautiful hall were really beautiful for him to live in, so near all the books, and so retired and quiet, that nobody knew of them. What a fine thing for him! and you could see what use he made of his good fortune as he sat there, so constant at his writing for hours together.

Was it a book he was writing, or could it be perhaps poems? This was a thought which made my heart beat; but I concluded with much regret that it could not be poems, because no one could possibly write poems like that, straight off, without pausing for a word or a rhyme. Had they been poems he must have risen up, he must have paced about the room or come to the window as Papa did—not that Papa wrote poems: he always said, "I am not worthy even to speak of such prevailing mysteries," shaking his head—which gave me a wonderful admiration and almost awe of a poet, who was thus much greater even than Papa.

But I could not believe that a poet could have kept still for hours and hours like that. What could it be, then? Perhaps it was history; that is a great thing to work at, but you would not, perhaps, need to move nor to stride up and down, or look out upon the sky and the wonderful light.

He did move now and then, however, though he never came to the window. Sometimes, as I have said, he would turn round in his chair and turn his face towards it and sit there for a long time musing, when the light had begun to fail and the world was full of that strange day which was night, that light without color, in which everything was so clearly visible and there were no shadows. "It was between the night and the day, when the fairy folk have power." This was the after-light of the wonderful, long, long summer evening, the light without shadows. It had a spell in it, and sometimes it made me afraid: and all manner of strange thoughts seemed to come in, and I always felt that if only we had a little more vision in our eyes we might see beautiful folk walking about in it, who were not of our world. I thought most likely he saw them, from the way he sat there looking out: and this made my heart expand with the most curious sensation, as if of pride that, though I could not see, he did, and did not even require to come to the window, as I did, sitting close in the depth of the recess, with my eyes upon him, and almost seeing things through his eyes.

I was so much absorbed in these thoughts and in watching him every evening—for now he never missed an evening, but was always there—that people began to remark that I was looking pale and that I could not be well, for I paid no attention when they talked to me, and did not care to go out, nor to join the other girls for their tennis, nor to do anything that others did. And some said to Aunt Mary that I was quickly losing all the ground I had gained, and that she could never send me back to my mother with a white face like that.

Aunt Mary had begun to look at me anxiously for some time before that, and, I am sure, held secret consultations over me, sometimes with the doctor, and sometimes with her old ladies, who thought they knew more about young girls than even the doctors. And I could hear them saying to her that I wanted diversion, that I must be diverted, and that she must take me out more, and give a party, and that when the summer visitors began to come there would perhaps be a ball or two, or Lady Carnbee would get up a picnic.

"And there's my young lord coming home," said the old lady whom they called Miss Jeanie, "and I never knew the young lassie yet that would not cock up her bonnet at the sight of a young lord."

But Aunt Mary shook her head. "I would not lippen much to the young lord," she said. "His mother is sore set upon siller for him; and my poor bit honey has no fortune to speak of. No, we must not fly so high as the young lord; but I will gladly take her about the country to see the old castles and towers. It will perhaps rouse her up a little."

"And if that does not answer we must think of something else," the old lady said.

I heard them, perhaps, that day because they were talking of me, which is always so effective a way of making you hear—for latterly I had not been paying any attention to what they were saying; and I thought to myself how little they knew, and how little I cared about even the old castles and curious houses, having something else in my mind. But just about that time Mr. Pitmilly came in, who was always a friend to me, and, when he heard them talking, he managed to stop them and turn the conversation into another channel.

And after a while, when the ladies were gone away, he came up to my recess, and gave a glance right over my head. And then he asked my Aunt Mary if ever she had settled her question about the window opposite "that you thought was a window sometimes, and then not a window, and many curious things," the old gentleman said.

My Aunt Mary gave me another very wistful look; and then she said, "Indeed, Mr. Pitmilly, we are just where we were, and I am quite as unsettled as ever; and I think my niece she has taken up my views, for I see her many a time looking across and wondering, and I am not clear now what her opinion is."

"My opinion!" I said. "Aunt Mary!" I could not help being a little scornful, as one is when one is very young. "I have no opinion. There is not only a window but there is a room, and I could show you——" I was going to say, "show you the gentleman who sits and writes in it," but I stopped, not knowing what they might say, and looked from one to another. "I could tell you—all the furniture that is in it," I said. And then I felt something like a flame that went over my face, and that all at once my cheeks were burning. I thought they gave a little glance at one another, but that may have been folly. "There is a great picture, in a big dim frame," I said, feeling a little breathless, "on the wall opposite the window——"

"Is there so?" said Mr. Pitmilly, with a little laugh. And he said, "Now I will tell you what we'll do. You know that there is a conversation party, or whatever they call it, in the big room tonight, and it will be all open and lighted up. And it is a handsome room, and two-three things well worth looking at. I will just step along after we have all got our dinner, and take you over to the pairty, madam— Missy and you——"

"Dear me!" said Aunt Mary. "I have not gone to a pairty for more years than I would like to say—and never once to the Library Hall." Then she gave a little shiver, and said quite low, "I could not go there."

"Then you will just begin again tonight, madam," said Mr. Pitmilly, taking no notice of this, "and a proud man will I be leading in Mistress Balcarres that was once the pride of the ball."

"Ah, once!" said Aunt Mary, with a low little laugh and then a sigh. "And we'll not say how long ago," and after that she made a pause, looking always at me: and then she said, "I accept your offer, and we'll put on our braws; and I hope you will have no occasion to think shame of us. But why not take your dinner here?"

That was how it was settled, and the old gentleman went away to dress, looking quite pleased. But I came to Aunt Mary as soon as he was gone, and besought her not to make me go. "I like the long bonnie night and the light that lasts so long. And I cannot bear to dress up and go out, wasting it all in a stupid party. I hate parties, Aunt Mary!" I cried, "and I would far rather stay here."

"My honey," she said, taking both my hands, "I know it will maybe be a blow to you—but it's better so."

"How could it be a blow to me?" I cried; "but I would far rather not go."

"You'll just go with me, honey, just this once: it is not often I go out. You will go with me this one night, just this one night, my honey sweet."

I am sure there were tears in Aunt Mary's eyes, and she kissed me between the words. There was nothing more that I could say; but how I grudged the evening! A mere party, a conversazione (when all the college was away, too, and nobody to make conversation!), instead of my enchanted hour at my window and the soft, strange light, and the dim face looking out, which kept me wondering and wondering what was he thinking of, what was he looking for, who was he? all one wonder and mystery and question, through the long, long, slowly fading night.

It occurred to me, however, when I was dressing—though I was so sure that he would prefer his solitude to everything—that he might perhaps, it was just possible, be there. And when I thought of that, I took out my white frock—though Janet had laid out my blue one—and my little pearl necklace which I had thought was too good to wear. They were not very large pearls, but they were real pearls, and very even and lustrous though they were small; and though I did not think much of my appearance then, there must have been something about me—pale as I was but apt to color in a moment, with my dress so white, and my pearls so white, and my hair all shadowy —perhaps, that was pleasant to look at: for even old Mr. Pitmilly had a strange look in his eyes, as if he was not only pleased but sorry too, perhaps thinking me a creature that would have troubles in this life, though I was so young and knew them not.

And when Aunt Mary looked at me, there was a little quiver about her mouth. She herself had on her pretty lace and her white hair very nicely done, and looking her best. As for Mr. Pitmilly, he had a beautiful fine French cambric frill to his shirt, plaited in the most minute plaits, and with a diamond pin in it which sparkled as much as Lady Carnbee's ring; but this was a fine, frank, kindly stone that looked you straight in the face and sparkled, with the light dancing in it as if it were pleased to see you, and to be shining on that old gentleman's honest and faithful breast: for he had been one of Aunt Mary's lovers in their early days and still thought there was nobody like her in the world.

I had got into quite a happy commotion of mind by the time we set out across the street in the soft light of the evening to the Library Hall. Perhaps, after all, I should see him, and see the room which I was so well acquainted with, and find out why he sat there so constantly and never was seen abroad. I thought I might even hear what he was working at, which would be such a pleasant thing to tell Papa when I went home. A friend of mine at St. Rule's—oh, far, far more busy than you ever were, Papa!—and then my father would laugh, as he always did, and say he was but an idler and never busy at all.

The room was all light and bright, flowers wherever flowers could be, and the long lines of the books that went along the walls on each side, lighting up wherever there was a line of gilding or an ornament, with a little response. It dazzled me at first, all that light; but I was very eager, though I kept very quiet, looking round to see if perhaps in any corner, in the middle of any group, he would be there. I did not expect to see him among the ladies. He would not be with them—he was too studious, too silent: but perhaps among that circle of gray heads at the upper end of the room—perhaps——

No; I am not sure that it was not half a pleasure to me to make quite sure that there was not one whom I could take for him, who was at all like my vague image of him. No: it was absurd to think that he would be here, amid all that sound of voices, under the glare of that light. I felt a little proud to think that he was in his room as usual, doing his work, or thinking so deeply over it, as when he turned round in his chair with his face to the light.

I was thus getting a little composed and quiet in my mind—for now that the expectation of seeing him was over, though it was a disappointment it was a satisfaction too—when Mr. Pitmilly came up to me, holding out his arm. "Now," he said, "I am going to take you to see the curiosities." I thought to myself that after I had seen them and spoken to everybody I knew, Aunt Mary would let me go home, so I went very willingly, though I did not care for the curiosities. Something, however, struck me strangely as we walked up the room. It was the air, rather fresh and strong, from an open window at the east end of the hall. How should there be a window there? I hardly saw what it meant for the first moment, but it blew in my face as if there was some meaning in it, and I felt very uneasy without seeing why.

Then there was another thing that startled me. On that side of the wall which was to the street there seemed no windows at all. A long line of bookcases filled it from end to end. I could not see what that meant either, but it confused me. I was altogether confused. I felt as if I was in a strange country, not knowing where I was going, not knowing what I might find out next. If there were no windows on the wall to the street where was my window? My heart, which had been jumping up and calming down again all the time, gave a great leap at this, as if it would have come out of me— but I did not know what it could mean.

Then we stopped before a glass case, and Mr. Pitmilly showed me some things in it. I could not pay much attention to them. My head was going round and round. I heard his voice going on, and then myself speaking with a queer sound that was hollow in my ears; but I did not know what I was saying or what he was saying.

Then he took me to the very end of the room, the east end, saying something I caught—that I was pale, that the air would do me good. The air was blowing full on me, lifting the lace of my dress, lifting my hair, almost chilly. The window opened into the pale daylight, into the little lane that ran by the end of the building. Mr. Pitmilly went on talking, but I could not make out a word he said. Then I heard my own voice speaking through it, though I did not seem to be aware that I was speaking. "Where is my window?— where, then, is my window?" I seemed to be saying, and I turned right round, dragging him with me, still holding his arm. As I did this my eyes fell upon something at last which I knew. It was a large picture in a broad frame, hanging against the farther wall.

What did it mean? Oh, what did it mean? I turned round again to the open window at the east end, and to the daylight, the strange light without any shadow that was all round about this lighted hall, holding it like a bubble that would burst, like something that was not real. The real place was the room I knew, in which that picture was hanging, where the writing-table was, and where he sat with his face to the light. But where was the light and the window through which it came? I think my senses must have left me. I went up to the picture which I knew, and then I walked straight across the room, always dragging Mr. Pitmilly, whose face was pale, but who did not struggle but allowed me to lead him, straight across to where the window was—where the window was not—where there was no sign of it. "Where is my window? where is my window?" I said. And all the time I was sure that I was in a dream, and these lights were all some theatrical illusion, and the people talking; and nothing real but the pale, pale, watching, lingering day standing by to wait until that foolish bubble should burst.

"My dear," said Mr. Pitmilly, "my dear! Mind that you are in public. Mind where you are. You must not make an outcry and frighten your Aunt Mary. Come away with me. Come away, my dear young lady, and you'll take a seat for a minute or two and compose yourself; and I'll get you an ice or a little wine." He kept patting my hand, which was on his arm, and looking at me very anxiously. "Bless me! bless me! I never thought it would have this effect," he said.

But I would not allow him to take me away in that direction. I went to the picture again and looked at it without seeing it: and then I went across the room again, with some kind of wild thought that if I insisted I should find it. "My window, my window!" I said.

There was one of the professors standing there, and he heard me. "The window!" said he. "Ah, you've been taken in with what appears outside. It was put there to be in uniformity with the window on the stair. But it never was a real window. It is just behind that bookcase. Many people are taken in by it," he said.

His voice seemed to sound from somewhere far away, and as if it would go on forever; and the hall swam in a dazzle of shining and of noises round me; and the daylight through the open window grew grayer, waiting till it should be over, and the bubble burst.

V

It was Mr. Pitmilly who took me home: or rather it was I who took him, pushing him on a little in front of me, holding fast by his arm, not waiting for Aunt Mary or anyone. We came out into the daylight again outside, I, without even a cloak or a shawl, with my bare arms, and uncovered head, and the pearls round my neck. There was a rush of the people about, and a baker's boy, that baker's boy, stood right in my way and cried, "Here's a braw ane!" shouting to the others: the words struck me somehow, as his stone had struck the window, without any reason. But I did not mind the people staring, and hurried across the street, with Mr. Pitmilly half a step in advance.

The door was open, and Janet standing at it, looking out to see what she could see of the ladies in their grand dresses. She gave a shriek when she saw me hurrying across the street; but I brushed past her, and pushed Mr. Pitmilly up the stairs, and took him breathless to the recess, where I threw myself down on the seat, feeling as if I could not have gone another step farther, and waved my hand across to the window. "There! there!" I cried. Ah! there it was— not that senseless mob—not the theatre and the gas, and the people all in a murmur and clang of talking. Never in all these days had I see that room so clearly.

There was a faint tone of light behind, as if it might have been a reflection from some of those vulgar lights in the hall, and he sat against it, calm, wrapped in his thoughts, with his face to the window. Nobody but must have seen him. Janet could have seen him had I called her upstairs. It was like a picture, all the things I knew, and the same attitude, and the atmosphere, full of quietness, not disturbed by anything. I pulled Mr. Pitmilly's arm before I let him go. "You see, you see!" I cried. He gave me the most bewildered look, as if he would have liked to cry. He saw nothing! I was sure of that from his eyes. He was an old man, and there was no vision in him. If I had called up Janet, she would have seen it all. "My dear!" he said. "My dear!" waving his hands in a helpless way.

"He has been there all these nights," I cried, "and I thought you could tell me who he was and what he was doing; and that he might have taken me in to that room, and showed me, that I might tell Papa. Papa would understand, he would like to hear. Oh, can't you tell me what work he is doing, Mr. Pitmilly? He never lifts his head as long as the light throws a shadow, and then when it is like this he turns round and thinks, and takes a rest!"

Mr. Pitmilly was trembling, whether it was with cold or I know not what. He said, with a shake in his voice, "My dear young lady, my dear——" and then stopped and looked at me as if he were going to cry. "It's peetiful, it's peetiful," he said; and then in another voice, "I'm going across there again to bring your Aunt Mary home; do you understand, my poor little thing, my—— I am going to bring her home—you will be better when she is here."

I was glad when he went away, as he could not see anything: and I sat alone in the dark, which was not dark but quite clear light —a light like nothing I ever saw. How clear it was in that room! Not glaring like the gas and the voices, but so quiet, everything so visible, as if it were in another world. I heard a little rustle behind me, and there was Janet, standing staring at me with two big eyes wide open. She was only a little older than I was. I called to her, "Janet, come here, come here, and you will see him—come here and see him!" impatient that she should be so shy and keep behind. "Oh, my bonnie young leddy!" she said, and burst out crying. I stamped my foot at her, in my indignation that she would not come, and she fled before me with a rustle and swing of haste, as if she were afraid.

None of them, none of them! not even a girl like myself, with the sight in her eyes, would understand. I turned back again, and held out my hands to him sitting there, who was the only one that knew. "Oh," I said, "say something to me! I don't know who you are, or what you are: but you're lonely and so am I; and I only—feel for you. Say something to me!" I neither hoped that he would hear, nor expected any answer. How could he hear, with the street between us, and his window shut, and all the murmuring of the voices and the people standing about? But for one moment it seemed to me that there was only him and me in the whole world.

But I gasped with my breath, that had almost gone from me, when I saw him move in his chair! He had heard me, though I knew not how. He rose up, and I rose too, speechless, incapable of anything but this mechanical movement. He seemed to draw me as if I were a puppet moved by his will. He came forward to the window, and stood looking across at me. I was sure that he looked at me. At last he had seen me: at last he had found out that somebody, though only a girl, was watching him, looking for him, believing in him.

I was in such trouble and commotion of mind and trembling, that I could not keep on my feet, but dropped kneeling on the window-seat, supporting myself against the window, feeling as if my heart were being drawn out of me. I cannot describe his face. It was all dim, yet there was a light on it: I think it must have been a smile; and as closely as I looked at him he looked at me. His hair was fair, and there was a little quiver about his lips. Then he put his hands upon the window to open it. It was stiff and hard to move; but at last he forced it open with a sound that echoed all along the street. I saw that the people heard it, and several looked up.

As for me, I put my hands together, leaning with my face against the glass, drawn to him as if I could have gone out of myself, my heart out of my bosom, my eyes out of my head. He opened the window with a noise that was heard from the West Port to the Abbey. Could anyone doubt that?

And then he leaned forward out of the window, looking out. There was not one in the street but must have seen him. He looked at me first, with a little wave of his hand, as if it were a salutation —yet not exactly that either, for I thought he waved me away; and then he looked up and down in the dim shining of the ending day, first to the east, to the old Abbey towers, and then to the west, along the broad line of the street where so many people were coming and going, but so little noise, all like enchanted folk in an enchanted place.

I watched him with such a melting heart, with such a deep satisfaction as words could not say; for nobody could tell me now that he was not there—nobody could say I was dreaming any more. I watched him as if I could not breathe—my heart in my throat, my eyes upon him. He looked up and down, and then he looked back to me. I was the first, and I was the last, though it was not for long: he did know, he did see, who it was that had recognized him and sympathized with him all the time. I was in a kind of rapture, yet stupor too; my look went with his look, following it as if I were his shadow; and then suddenly he was gone, and I saw him no more.

I dropped back again upon my seat, seeking something to support me, something to lean upon. He had lifted his hand and waved it once again to me. How he went I cannot tell, nor where he went I cannot tell; but in a moment he was away, and the windows standing open, and the room fading into stillness and dimness, yet so clear, with all its space, and the great picture in its gilded frame upon the wall.

It gave me no pain to see him go away. My heart was so content, and I was so worn out and satisfied—for what doubt or question could there be about him now? As I was lying back as weak as water, Aunt Mary came in behind me and flew to me with a little rustle as if she had come on wings, and put her arms round me, and drew my head on to her breast. I had begun to cry a little, with sobs like a child. "You saw him, you saw him!" I said.

To lean upon her, and feel her so soft, so kind, gave me a pleasure I cannot describe, and her arms round me, and her voice saying "Honey, my honey!" as if she were nearly crying too. Lying there I came back to myself, quite sweetly, glad of everything. But I wanted some assurance from them that they had seen him too.

I waved my hand to the window that was still standing open, and the room that was stealing away into the faint dark. "This time you saw it all!" I said, getting more eager.

"My honey!" said Aunt Mary, giving me a kiss; and Mr. Pitmilly began to walk about the room with short little steps behind, as if he were out of patience.

I sat straight up and put away Aunt Mary's arms. "You cannot be so blind, so blind!" I cried. "Oh, not tonight, at least not tonight!" But neither the one nor the other made any reply.

I shook myself quite free, and raised myself up. And there, in the middle of the street, stood the baker's boy like a statue, staring up at the open window, with his mouth open and his face full of wonder—breathless, as if he could not believe what he saw. I darted forward, calling to him, and beckoned him to come to me. "Oh, bring him up! bring him, bring him to me!" I cried.

Mr. Pitmilly went out directly, and got the boy by the shoulder. He did not want to come. It was strange to see the little old gentleman, with his beautiful frill and his diamond pin, standing out in the street, with his hand upon the boy's shoulder, and the other boys round, all in a little crowd. And presently they came towards the house, the others all following, gaping and wondering. He came in unwilling, almost resisting, looking as if we meant him some harm.

"Come away, my laddie, come and speak to the young lady," Mr. Pitmilly was saying. And Aunt Mary took my hands to keep me back. But I would not be kept back.

"Boy," I cried, "you saw it too, you saw it, tell them you saw it! It is that I want, and no more."

He looked at me as they all did, as if he thought I were mad. "What's she wantin' wi' me?" he said; and then, "I did nae harm, even if I did throw a big stane at it—and it's nae sin to throw a stane."

"You rascal!" said Mr. Pitmilly, giving him a shake; "have you been throwing stones? You'll kill somebody one of these days with your stones." The old gentleman was confused and troubled, for he did not understand what I wanted, nor anything that had happened. And then Aunt Mary, holding my hands and drawing me close to her, spoke.

"Laddie," she said, "answer the young lady, like a good lad. There's no intention of finding fault with you. Answer her, my man, and then Janet will give ye your supper before you go."

"Oh, speak, speak!" I cried, "answer them and tell them! you saw that window opened, and the gentleman look out and wave his hand?"

"I saw nae gentleman," he said, with his head down, "except this wee gentleman here."

"Listen, laddie," said Aunt Mary. "I saw ye standing in the middle of the street staring. What were ye looking at?"

"It was naething to make a wark about. It was just yon windy yonder in the library that is nae windy. And it was open—as sure's death. You may laugh if you like. Is that a' she's wantin' wi' me?"

"You are telling a pack of lies, laddie," Mr. Pitmilly said.

"I'm tellin' nae lees—it was standin' open just like ony ither windy. It's as sure's death. I couldna believe it mysel'; but it's true."

"And there it is," I cried, turning round and pointing it out to them with great triumph in my heart. But the light was all gray; it had faded; it had changed. The window was just as it had always been, a sombre break upon the wall.

I was treated like an invalid all that evening, and taken upstairs to bed, and Aunt Mary sat up in my room the whole night through. Whenever I opened my eyes she was always sitting there close to me, watching. And there never was in all my life so strange a night. When I would talk in my excitement, she kissed me and hushed me like a child. "Oh, honey, you are not the only one!" she said. "Oh, whisht, whisht, bairn! I should never have let you be there!"

"Aunt Mary, Aunt Mary, you have seen him too?"

"Oh, whisht, whisht, honey!" Aunt Mary said; her eyes were shining—there were tears in them. "Oh, whisht, whisht! Put it out of your mind, and try to sleep. I will not speak another word," she cried.

But I had my arms round her, and my mouth at her ear. "Who is he there? Tell me that and I will ask no more——"

"Oh, honey, rest, and try to sleep! It is just—how can I tell you?

—a dream, a dream! Did you not hear what Lady Carnbee said?—the women of our blood——"

"What? What? Aunt Mary, oh, Aunt Mary——"

"I canna tell you," she cried in her agitation, "I canna tell you! how can I tell you, when I know just what you know and no more? It is a longing all your life after—it is a looking—for what never comes."

"He will come," I cried. "I shall see him tomorrow—that I know, I know!"

She kissed me and cried over me, her cheek hot and wet like mine. "My honey, try if you can sleep—try if you can sleep: and we'll wait to see what tomorrow brings."

"I have no fear," said I. And then, I suppose, though it is strange to think of, I must have fallen asleep—I was so worn out, and young, and not used to lying in my bed awake. From time to time I opened my eyes, and sometimes jumped up remembering everything; but Aunt Mary was always there to soothe me, and I lay down again in her shelter like a bird in its nest.

But I would not let them keep me in bed next day. I was in a kind of fever, not knowing what I did. The window was quite opaque, without the least glimmer in it, flat and blank like a piece of wood. Never from the first day had I seen it so little like a window.

"It cannot be wondered at," I said to myself, "that seeing it like that, and with eyes that are old, not so clear as mine, they should think what they do." And then I smiled to myself to think of the evening and the long light, and whether he would look out again, or only give me a signal with his hand. I decided I would like that best: not that he should take the trouble to come forward and open it again, but just a turn of his head and a wave of his hand. It would be more friendly, and show more confidence—not as if I wanted that kind of demonstration every night.

I did not come down in the afternoon, but kept at my own window upstairs alone, till the tea-party should be over. I could hear them making a great talk; and I was sure they were all in the recess staring at the window, and laughing at the silly lassie. Let them laugh! I felt above all that now.

At dinner I was very reckless, hurrying to get it over; and I think Aunt Mary was restless too. I doubt whether she read her *Times* when it came; she opened it up, so as to shield her, and watched from a corner. And I settled myself in the recess, with my heart full of expectation. I wanted nothing more than to see him writing at his table, and to turn his head and give me a little wave of his hand, just to show that he knew I was there. I sat from half past seven o'clock to ten o'clock; and the daylight grew softer and softer, till at last it was as if it was shining through a pearl, and not a shadow to be seen. But the window all the time was as black as night, and there was nothing, nothing there.

Well: but other nights it had been like that; he would not be there every night only to please me. There are other things in a man's life, a great learned man like that. I said to myself I was not disappointed. Why should I be disappointed? There had been other nights when he was not there. Aunt Mary watched me, every movement I made, her eyes shining, often wet, with a pity in them that almost made me cry: but I felt as if I were more sorry for her than for myself. And then I flung myself upon her, and asked her, again and again, what it was, and who it was, imploring her to tell me if she knew? and when she had seen him, and what had happened? and what it meant about the women of our blood?

She told me that how it was she could not tell, nor when: it was just at the time it had to be; and that we all saw him in our time. "That is," she said, "the ones that are like you and me." What was it that made her and me different from the rest? but she only shook her head and would not tell me.

"They say," she said, and then stopped short. "Oh, honey, try to forget all about it—if I had but known you were of that kind! They say—that once there was one that was a scholar, and liked his books more than any lady's love. Honey, do not look at me like that. To think I should have brought all this on you!"

"He was a scholar?" I cried.

"And one of us, that must have been a light woman, not like you and me—— But may be it was just in innocence; for who can tell? She waved to him and waved to him to come over: and yon ring was the token: but he would not come. But still she sat at her window and waved and waved—till at last her brothers heard of it, that were stirring men; and then—— Oh, my honey, let us speak of it no more!"

"They killed him!" I cried, carried away. And then I grasped her with my hands, and gave her a shake, and flung away from her. "You tell me that to throw dust in my eyes—when I saw him only last night: and he as living as I am, and as young!"

"My honey, my honey!" Aunt Mary said.

After that I would not speak to her for a long time; but she kept close to me, never leaving me when she could help it, and always with that pity in her eyes. For the next night it was the same; and the third night. That third night I thought I could not bear it any longer. I would have to do something—if only I knew what to do! If it would ever get dark, quite dark, there might be something to be done. I had wild dreams of stealing out of the house and getting a ladder, and mounting up to try if I could not open that window in the middle of the night—if perhaps I could get the baker's boy to help me; and then my mind got into a whirl, and it was as if I had done it; and I could almost see the boy put the ladder to the window, and hear him cry out that there was nothing there.

Oh, how slow it was, the night! and how light it was, and everything so clear—no darkness to cover you, no shadow, whether on one side of the street or on the other side. I could not sleep, though I was forced to go to bed. And in the deep midnight, when it is dark, dark in every other place, I slipped very softly downstairs, though there was one board on the landing-place that creaked—and opened the door and stepped out.

There was not a soul to be seen, up or down, from the Abbey to the West Port: and the trees stood like ghosts, and the silence was terrible, and everything as clear as day. You don't know what silence is till you find it in the light like that, not morning but night, no sun rising, no shadow, but everything as clear as the day.

It did not make any difference as the slow minutes went on: one o'clock, two o'clock. How strange it was to hear the clocks striking in that dead light when there was nobody to hear them! But it made no difference. The window was quite blank; even the marking of the panes seemed to have melted away. I stole up again, cold and trembling, after a long time, through the silent house, in the clear light with despair in my heart.

I am sure Aunt Mary must have watched and seen me coming back, for after a while I heard faint sounds in the house, and very early, when there had come a little sunshine into the air, she came to my bedside with a cup of tea in her hand; and she, too, was looking like a ghost. "Are you warm, honey—are you comfortable?" she said. "It doesn't matter," said I. I did not feel as if anything mattered; unless if one could get into the dark somewhere—the soft, deep dark that would cover you over and hide you—but I could not tell from what. The dreadful thing was that there was nothing, nothing to look for, nothing to hide from—only the silence and the light.

That day my mother came and took me home. I had not heard she was coming; she arrived quite unexpectedly, and said she had no time to stay but must start the same evening so as to be in London next day, Papa having settled to go abroad. At first I had a wild thought I would not go. But how can a girl say I will not, when her mother has come for her, and there is no reason, no reason in the world, to resist, and no right. I had to go, whatever I might wish or anyone might say. Aunt Mary's dear eyes were wet; she went about the house drying them quietly with her handkerchief, but she always said, "It is the best thing for you, honey, the best thing for you!" Oh, how I hated to hear it said that it was the best thing, as if anything mattered, one more than another!

The old ladies were all there in the afternoon, Lady Carnbee looking at me from under her black lace, and the diamond lurking, sending out darts from under her finger. She patted me on the shoulder, and told me to be a good bairn. "And never lippen to what you see from the window," she said. "The eye is deceitful as well as the heart." She kept patting me on the shoulder, and I felt again as if that sharp, wicked stone stung me. Was that what Aunt Mary meant when she said yon ring was the token? I thought afterwards I saw the mark on my shoulder. You will say why? How can I tell why? If I had known, I should have been contented, and it would not have mattered any more.

I never went back to St. Rule's, and for years of my life I never again looked out of a window when any other window was in sight. You ask me did I ever see him again? I cannot tell: the imagination is a great deceiver, as Lady Carnbee said: and if he stayed there so long, only to punish the race that had wronged him, why should I ever have seen him again? for I had received my share. But who can tell what happens in a heart that often, often, and so long as that, comes back to do its errand? If it was he whom I have seen again, the anger is gone from him, and he means good and no longer harm to the house of the woman who loved him.

I have seen his face looking at me from a crowd. There was one time when I came home a widow from India, very sad, with my little children: I am certain I saw him there among all the people coming to welcome their friends. There was nobody to welcome me—for I was not expected: and very sad was I, without a face I knew: when all at once I saw him, and he waved his hand to me. My heart leaped up again: I had forgotten who he was, but only that it was a face I knew, and I landed almost cheerfully, thinking here was someone who would help me. But he had disappeared, as he did from the window, with that one wave of his hand.

And again I was reminded of it all when old Lady Carnbee died —an old, old woman—and it was found in her will that she had left me that diamond ring. I am afraid of it still. It is locked up in an old sandalwood box in the lumber-room in the little old country house which belongs to me, but where I never live. If anyone would steal it, it would be a relief to my mind. Yet I never knew what Aunt Mary meant when she said: "Yon ring was the token," nor what it could have to do with that strange window in the old College Library of St. Rule's.

Throughout history young lovers have been building up an elaborate ritual about love. There are special holidays appropriate to lovers, special charms, special foods—and even special flowers.

Since classical times lovers and gardeners have evolved what is known as the language of flowers. Even up into the last century a gift of a flower had a very special significance if one knew the story behind each bloom. Here is such an alphabet of love.

THE FLOWER ALPHABET OF LOVE

SUSAN BELCHER AND SEON MANLEY

Anemone

One legend of ancient Greece says that the beautiful and fragile anemone sprang from the tears of Venus, but most old storytellers say that it emerged from the blood of the great god Adonis. In the language of flowers it means "go away (but not too far)," an interpretation that occurred probably because the opening and shutting of the petals depend on the capriciousness of the wind. If you pick the first anemone that you see in the year saying, "I gather thee for a remedy against disease," you will, according to the old lore, never grow ill.

Bachelor's Button

The bachelor's button tells its story by its very name. When a young man wore one in his buttonhole, he told the world he was a bachelor. It was the custom in years gone by to carry the flower in your pocket, for you could tell how lucky in love you would be by whether the blossom lost or retained its freshness.

Crocus

In Greek mythology Crocus was a handsome youth who fell in love with the nymph Smilex. Impatient and impetuous, he was turned into the golden flower we know today, remaining forever young. In the language of flowers the crocus means, "We are glad to be young together, and we are strongly attached."

Daisy

Traditionally English milkmaids hung their shoes out of the windows and placed daisies' roots under their pillows. They would then go to sleep and dream of their lovers. Everyone knows the common charm that we use today in the United States, "He loves me, he loves me not," as one picks off the leaflets. The older French charm had a variation:

> *Does he love me,*
> *Does he love me little,*
> *Does he love me much,*
> *Does he love me passionately,*
> *Does he love me not at all?*

In Victorian times daisies signified innocence; today they signify faithfulness.

Evening Primrose

The evening primrose, which opens only at night and closes with morning, is too inconstant to give to a loved one. It means "I find you very fickle." In Greek mythology Paralisos, the son of Flora and Priapus, stricken unto death because he lost his betrothed, was transformed by his parents into a primrose.

Fern

The fern has always been associated with magic. At one time it was thought that a fern seed was invisible and that it could be obtained only on certain nights, for example at midnight on July 8. In the language of flowers it means "You fascinate me."

Geranium

The geranium was created, so says ancient lore, when the prophet Mohammed threw his shirt upon a mallow plant. The flower was

associated with the great adventurer Robin Hood, but nonetheless it is a poor plant to give to a man. In the language of flowers it means "You are childish."

Holly

The holly, leaf and blossom, was used as the daisy still is for divination. You plucked the berries to see if your love was reciprocated. It has always had religious significance from the times of the martyred Christians, who believed the Cross itself was made from holly wood and witches did not come near it. Some of that old fear was transferred into the language of flowers, and to give a gift of holly meant "I do not dare come near you."

Iris

The iris signifies "I send you a message of love." It was the flower chosen by Louis VII, King of France, as he set out for his crusade to the Holy Land. The purple iris became the flower of Louis and eventually the fleur-de-lys, still a symbol of France.

Jonquil

The jonquil says, "Have pity on my passion," an interpretation that the famous woman traveler Lady Mary Wortley Montague brought back from Turkey. Lady Mary explained how you could send an entire letter just in flowers:

"There is no color, no flower, no weed, no fruit, herb, pebble or feather that has not a verse belonging to it, and you may quarrel, reproach, or send letters of passion, friendship or civility, or even of news, without even inking your fingers."

Kiss-Me-Quick

Kiss-me-quick is an old country name for saxifrage, the wild rock-loving bush and flower. It means just what it says, including the variations, "Kiss me, love, at the garden gate," and "Meet me, love, behind the garden gate."

Lilac

The lilac, perhaps because it is such a symbol of spring, is the flower that represents young love. In Devon, England, it used to be called the May flower, but it has also had less romantic names—duck's bills, for example, and even oysters—both far removed from the Persian civilization that gave it the name lilac and where the plant originated.

Marigold

In ancient Greece marigolds were referred to as the gold flower, a tradition carried on in nineteenth century riddles: "What flower is that which bears the Virgin's name/The richest metal joined with the same?" The answer, of course, was Mary-gold. The flower has always been associated with magic. If dipped in the water, a drop on the eye allows you to see the spirit world. In the language of flowers it means "I am jealous."

Narcissus

The story of the young Narcissus, who so loved himself that he drowned in a pool that reflected his image, is one of the most popular of all myths. The narcissus has always had deep meaning in Greece, where it was hung in the temples and formed crowns for the goddesses. Naturally, a gift of the narcissus means "You mean more to yourself than others can ever mean to you."

Orange Blossom

Traditional to weddings, the orange blossom has bedecked brides since the time of the ancient Saracens. Supposedly the orange was the "golden apple" that was guarded by a dragon and the three daughters of Hesperus, which Hercules had to obtain in one of his labors. It was given by Jupiter to Juno on her wedding day. In the language of flowers it means "Your purity equals your loveliness."

Pansy

A pansy is the flower that Puck put on the eyes of Titania so that when she awakened she fell in love with the first object she saw. Alas, for Titania, her love had the head of an ass. In folklore, pansy means "I am thinking of you." The word itself comes from the French *pensées*, meaning thoughts, and in France the flower means *Pensez a moi*, "think of me." Shakespeare used this reference when he said, "And there is Pansies—that's for thoughts."

Quince

The quince blossom means "I am tempted." However, in early Greece every bride ate a quince before she married. The name is a corruption of one of the ancient cities of Crete where it was indigenous. It was a blossom sacred to Venus. To dream of quince is to dream of successful love.

Rose

Of all the flowers in the world the rose is most frequently the symbol of love. Often in years gone by a young girl would send her lover a rose to show that she reciprocated his emotion. The rose is also sacred to the goddess of beauty. The red rose, says mythology, was created when Venus ran through the woods in despair at the loss of Adonis and pierced her foot with a thorn. The blood that flowed from the wound gave the rose its red color, while the white rose was created from the tears that she shed. A yellow rose means "I am jealous." A rose leaf means "There is still hope for us." A half-blown rose means "My love is young." The gift of a full-blown rose means "We are engaged forever." The ancient Greeks and Romans always planted roses on the graves of lovers.

Shamrock

The shamrock means "You are my lighthearted love." Known to all of us because of its appearance on Saint Patrick's Day, it was sacred to that saint because its three leaves on one stalk were used by him to explain the doctrine of the Trinity. It may be put under the pillow, as might the four-leafed clover, to bring dreams of a beloved.

Tulip

The tulip, dearly beloved in the Orient, has always been the symbol of love and affection. A young Persian gave red tulips to his girl to convey the idea that his face was as red as the blossom, and the black stamen showed that his heart had been reduced to coal.

Unshoe-The-Horse

The moonwort, long known as a magic herb, was popularly known as Unshoe-the-Horse, because if a horse stepped upon it he lost his shoe. It was also famous for opening locked doors. It was used as an ingredient in witches' brews. Ben Jonson also names others for such a brew: "I have been plucking (plants among) Hemlock, Henbane, Adder's Tongue, Nightshade, Moonwort, Sheppard's-bane." Naturally, moonwort means bad luck in the language of flowers.

Violet

The violet is a flower long in use for festive occasions. It is unlucky, however, to carry a single violet into the house when it first comes into season. The violet was known as the flower of Napoleon. When he was deported to Elba he promised to return in "violet time," and violets became the secret symbol of his followers. The violet was so sacred to the Greeks that a single yellow violet was one of the rewards of their ancient games. The violet says, "I return your love."

Willow

In Shakespeare's time it was the custom to weave willow garlands for those who had been jilted in love. A popular rhyme of his time says.

> Come all you forsaken and sit down by me,
> He that complaineth of his false love,
>   mine's falser than she;
> The willow wreath weare I, since my love did fleet,
> A garland for lovers forsaken must meet.

The willow still means disappointed love.

Xeranthemum

The flower of eternity, according to the ancients, meant "My love is immortal."

Yggdrosil

The "tree of the universe," as it was called, was probably the oak. In many mythologies man was said to have sprung from such a tree, most popularly thought to be the oak. A gift of its leaves meant "I am brave for your sake."

Zinnia

The bright zinnia of the summer is an appropriate gift to send to an absent friend. It means "I think of you."

Love has many aspects: sometimes it is all retreat, sometimes it is all acceptance. It is like a pendulum, swinging from one side to another. One swing knows despair; a moment later there is complete and utter joy. Katherine Mansfield, the magnificent English short story writer, was able to capture fleeting emotions the way others might capture a moment in a photograph. In "The Singing Lesson" the pain and then the joy of love strike just the right note.

THE SINGING LESSON

KATHERINE MANSFIELD

With despair—cold, sharp despair—buried deep in her heart like a wicked knife, Miss Meadows, in cap and gown and carrying a little baton, trod the cold corridors that led to the music hall. Girls of all ages, rosy from the air, and bubbling over with that gleeful excitement that comes from running to school on a fine autumn morning, hurried, skipped, fluttered by; from the hollow classrooms came a quick drumming of voices; a bell rang; a voice like a bird cried, "Muriel." And then there came from the staircase a tremendous knock-knock-knocking. Some one had dropped her dumbbells.

The Science Mistress stopped Miss Meadows.

"Good mor-ning," she cried, in her sweet, affected drawl. "Isn't it cold? It might be win-ter."

Miss Meadows, hugging the knife, stared in hatred at the Science Mistress. Everything about her was sweet, pale, like honey. You would not have been surprised to see a bee caught in the tangles of that yellow hair.

"It is rather sharp," said Miss Meadows, grimly.

The other smiled her sugary smile.

"You look fro-zen," she said. Her blue eyes opened wide; there came a mocking light in them. (Had she noticed anything?)

"Oh, not quite as bad as that," said Miss Meadows, and she gave the Science Mistress, in exchange for her smile, a quick grimace and passed on. . . .

Forms Four, Five, and Six were assembled in the music hall. The noise was deafening. On the platform, by the piano, stood Mary Beazley, Miss Meadows' favorite, who played accompaniments. She was turning the music stool. When she saw Miss Meadows she gave a loud, warning "Sh-sh! girls!" and Miss Meadows, her hands thrust in her sleeves, the baton under her arm, strode down the centre aisle, mounted the steps, turned sharply, seized the brass music stand, planted it in front of her, and gave two sharp taps with her baton for silence.

"Silence, please! Immediately!" and, looking at nobody, her glance swept over that sea of colored flannel blouses, with bobbing pink faces and hands, quivering butterfly hair-bows, and music-books outspread. She knew perfectly well what they were thinking. "Meady is in a wax." Well, let them think it! Her eyelids quivered; she tossed her head, defying them. What could the thoughts of those creatures matter to some one who stood there bleeding to death, pierced to the heart, to the heart, by such a letter——

. . . "I feel more and more strongly that our marriage would be a mistake. Not that I do not love you. I love you as much as it is possible for me to love any woman, but, truth to tell, I have come to the conclusion that I am not a marrying man, and the idea of settling down fills me with nothing but—" and the word "disgust" was scratched out lightly and "regret" written over the top.

Basil! Miss Meadows stalked over to the piano. And Mary Beazley, who was waiting for this moment, bent forward; her curls fell over her cheeks while she breathed, "Good morning, Miss Meadows," and she motioned towards rather than handed to her mistress a beautiful yellow chrysanthemum. This little ritual of the flower had been gone through for ages and ages, quite a term and a half. It was as much part of the lesson as opening the piano. But this morning, instead of taking it up, instead of tucking it into her belt while she leant over Mary and said, "Thank you, Mary. How very nice! Turn to page thirty-two," what was Mary's horror when Miss Meadows totally ignored the chrysanthemum, made no reply to her greeting, but said in a voice of ice, "Page fourteen, please, and mark the accents well."

Staggering moment! Mary blushed until the tears stood in her eyes, but Miss Meadows was gone back to the music stand; her voice rang through the music hall.

"Page fourteen. We will begin with page fourteen. 'A Lament.' Now, girls, you ought to know it by this time. We shall take it all together; not in parts, all together. And without expression. Sing it, though, quite simply, beating time with the left hand."

She raised the baton; she tapped the music stand twice. Down came Mary on the opening chord; down came all those left hands, beating the air, and in chimed those young, mournful voices:

> Fast! Ah, too Fast Fade the Ro-o-ses of Pleasure;
> Soon Autumn yields unto Wi-i-nter Drear.
> Fleetly! Ah, Fleetly Mu-u-sic's Gay Measure
> Passes away from the Listening Ear.

Good Heavens, what could be more tragic than that lament! Every note was a sigh, a sob, a groan of awful mournfulness. Miss Meadows lifted her arms in the wide gown and began conducting with both hands. ". . . I feel more and more strongly that our marriage would be a mistake. . . ." she beat. And the voices cried: *Fleetly! Ah, Fleetly*. What could have possessed him to write such a letter! What could have led up to it! It came out of nothing. His last letter had been all about a fumed-oak bookcase he had bought for "our" books, and a "natty little hall-stand" he had seen, "a very neat affair with a carved owl on a bracket, holding three hat-brushes in its claws." How she had smiled at that! So like a man to think one needed three hat-brushes! *From the Listening Ear*, sang the voices.

"Once again," said Miss Meadows. "But this time in parts. Still without expression." *Fast! Ah, too Fast*. With the gloom of the contraltos added, one could scarcely help shuddering. *Fade the Roses of Pleasure*. Last time he had come to see her, Basil had worn a rose in his buttonhole. How handsome he had looked in that bright blue suit, with that dark red rose! And he knew it, too. He couldn't help knowing it. First he stroked his hair, then his moustache; his teeth gleamed when he smiled.

"The headmaster's wife keeps on asking me to dinner. It's a perfect nuisance. I never get an evening to myself in that place."

"But can't you refuse?"

"Oh, well, it doesn't do for a man in my position to be unpopular."

Music's Gay Measure, wailed the voices. The willow trees, outside the high, narrow windows, waved in the wind. They had lost half their leaves. The tiny ones that clung wriggled like fishes caught on a line. ". . . I am not a marrying man. . . ." The voices were silent; the piano waited.

"Quite good," said Miss Meadows, but still in such a strange, stony tone that the younger girls began to feel positively frightened. "But now that we know it, we shall take it with expression. As much expression as you can put into it. Think of the words, girls. Use your imaginations. *Fast! Ah too Fast,*" cried Miss Meadows. "That ought to break out—a loud, strong *forte*—a lament. And then in the second line, *Winter Drear,* make that *Drear* sound as if a cold wind were blowing through it. *Dr-ear!*" said she so awfully that Mary Beazley, on the music stool, wriggled her spine. "The third line should be one crescendo. *Fleetly! Ah, Fleetly Music's Gay Measure.* Breaking on the first word of the last line, *Passes.* And then on the word, *Away,* you must begin to die . . . to fade . . . until *The Listening Ear* is nothing more than a faint whisper. . . . You can slow down as much as you like almost on the last line. Now, please."

Again the two light taps; she lifted her arms again. *Fast! Ah, too Fast.* ". . . and the idea of settling down fills me with nothing but disgust—" Disgust was what he had written. That was as good as to say their engagement was definitely broken off. Broken off! Their engagement! People had been surprised enough that she had got engaged. The Science Mistress would not believe it at first. But nobody had been as surprised as she. She was thirty. Basil was twenty-five. It had been a miracle, simply a miracle, to hear him say, as they walked home from church that very dark night, "You know, somehow or other, I've got fond of you." And he had taken hold of the end of her ostrich feather boa. *Passes away from the Listening Ear.*

"Repeat! Repeat!" said Miss Meadows. "More expression, girls! Once more!"

Fast! Ah, too Fast. The older girls were crimson; some of the younger ones began to cry. Big spots of rain blew against the windows, and one could hear the willows whispering, ". . . not that I do not love you. . . ."

"But, my darling, if you love me," thought Miss Meadows, "I don't mind how much it is. Love me as little as you like." But she knew he didn't love her. Not to have cared enough to scratch out that word "disgust," so that she couldn't read it! *Soon Autumn yields unto Winter Drear.* She would have to leave the school, too. She could never face the Science Mistress or the girls after it got known. She would have to disappear somewhere. *Passes away.* The voices began to die, to fade, to whisper . . . to vanish. . . .

Suddenly the door opened. A little girl in blue walked fussily up the aisle, hanging her head, biting her lips, and twisting the silver bangle on her red little wrist. She came up the steps and stood before Miss Meadows.

"Well, Monica, what is it?"

"Oh, if you please, Miss Meadows," said the little girl, gasping, "Miss Wyatt wants to see you in the mistress's room."

"Very well," said Miss Meadows. And she called to the girls, "I shall put you on your honor to talk quietly while I am away." But they were too subdued to do anything else. Most of them were blowing their noses.

The corridors were silent and cold; they echoed to Miss Meadows' steps. The head mistress sat at her desk. For a moment she did not look up. She was as usual disentangling her eye-glasses, which had got caught in her lace tie. "Sit down, Miss Meadows," she said very kindly. And then she picked up a pink envelope from the blotting-pad. "I sent for you just now because this telegram has come for you."

"A telegram for me, Miss Wyatt?"

Basil! He had committed suicide, decided Miss Meadows. Her hand flew out, but Miss Wyatt held the telegram back a moment. "I hope it's not bad news," she said, so more than kindly. And Miss Meadows tore it open.

"Pay no attention to letter, must have been mad, bought hat-stand to-day—Basil," she read. She couldn't take her eyes off the telegram.

"I do hope it's nothing very serious," said Miss Wyatt, leaning forward.

"Oh, no, thank you, Miss Wyatt," blushed Miss Meadows. "It's nothing bad at all. It's"—and she gave an apologetic little laugh—"it's from my *fiancé* saying that . . . saying that—" There was a pause. "I *see*," said Miss Wyatt. And another pause. Then—"You've fifteen minutes more of your class, Miss Meadows, haven't you?"

"Yes, Miss Wyatt." She got up. She half ran towards the door.

"Oh, just one minute, Miss Meadows," said Miss Wyatt. "I must say I don't approve of my teachers having telegrams sent to them in

174 ⮬ *The Singing Lesson*

school hours, unless in case of very bad news, such as death," explained Miss Wyatt, "or a very serious accident, or something to that effect. Good news, Miss Meadows, will always keep, you know."

On the wings of hope, of love, of joy, Miss Meadows sped back to the music hall, up the aisle, up the steps, over to the piano.

"Page thirty-two, Mary," she said, "page thirty-two," and, picking up the yellow chrysanthemum, she held it to her lips to hide her smile. Then she turned to the girls, rapped with her baton: "Page thirty-two, girls. Page thirty-two."

> *We come here To-day with Flowers o'erladen,*
> *With Baskets of Fruit and Ribbons to boot,*
> *To-oo Congratulate. . . .*

"Stop! Stop!" cried Miss Meadows. "This is awful. This is dreadful." And she beamed at her girls. "What's the matter with you all? Think, girls, think of what you're singing. Use your imaginations. *With Flowers o'erladen. Baskets of Fruit and Ribbons to boot.* And *Congratulate.*" Miss Meadows broke off. "Don't look so doleful, girls. It ought to sound warm, joyful, eager. *Congratulate.* Once more. Quickly. All together. Now then!"

And this time Miss Meadows' voice sounded over all the other voices—full, deep, glowing with expression.

The great pages of love do not mention how meaningful and how dear nonhuman experiences can sometimes be to us. There is love, for example, between a man and his dog, or a girl and her dog. In this enchanting story William Saroyan has captured a little aside in a rounded portrait of love.

LADY DAISY AND
HER CRAZY DOG

WILLIAM SAROYAN

"*One* thing about cats," a little girl named Daisy Hamilcar said to her mother. "They don't go jumping up on your new dress with muddy paws the minute they see you again."

"No, they don't," Daisy's mother said. "But they do go sneaking around. Fido loves you."

"Well, I hate him," Daisy said. "This isn't the first new dress he's muddied up with his stupid love. It's the second. I don't want Fido any more. I want a cat."

"Look at the poor fellow," Daisy's mother said. "He's all crushed by your rudeness."

"My rudeness?" Daisy said. "Mother, I don't believe I've ever known such a stupid dog."

"Fido's breed is famous for its intelligence," Mrs. Hamilcar said.

"They're notorious, I'd say, for barking when there isn't a thief for miles around, for muddying people's dresses and for whimpering with all their hearts and souls when they think everybody they know isn't madly in love with them. I am looking at the silly fellow, and I may say the silly fellow's looking at me."

"As he has been ever since you rejected his pure, steadfast, indestructible love," Mrs. Hamilcar said. "They broke the mold when they made Fido. He's a big dog with a soft heart. Red hair. A man's head, rather than a dog's. Eyes that any calf would be proud to look at wildflowers with. Ears as alert as any hare's. Tail as long as a pony's, as vibrant as a lion's. A posture like a lord's. A stance like a statue's. A walk like a boulevardier's."

"What the devil's a boulevardier?"

"Did you pick up that kind of language at camp?

"Oh, no. They'd never let us speak intelligently there. I got it from father, of course. What is a boulevardier?"

"A boulevardier is a man who wears spats, carries a stick and always has a rosebud in his lapel. If he has a mustache, he waxes it and keeps the ends twisted up."

"I don't believe I've ever seen one of those."

"Most likely not. They do the better part of their boulevardiering in Paris."

"France?"

"Well, not Paris, Texas."

"But I was born there."

"Yes, but you were moved to New York, and then to California, when you were still very little."

"How little?"

"One year."

"That's not so little."

"Too little to enjoy watching a boulevardier walk down the Rue de la Paix."

"Why there?"

"Well, we lived on the Rue de la Paix while your father worked for the *Herald Tribune,* and you and I often sat at the window and watched the people in the street, including the boulevardiers."

"And you think Fido walks the way they do?"

"Exactly. I've never seen anything like it. I think you ought to know, Daisy, that you picked a great entity from the Pacific Palisades Pound when you picked Fido."

"What's an entity?"

"A whole being."

"Every dog's that."

"Not by a long shot, and I wouldn't care to think of Fido as merely a dog, because you and I know he's a good deal more. Kiss and make up."

"I will not."

"You're breaking his heart."

"I don't care if I am."

"But what's a little mud on a dress?"

"Mother, that dress was given to me last year on my eighth birthday by Miss Quillercape. Out of all of the girls of Oh-Ho Hill, Miss Quillercape gave only me a dress. What did she give the other girls on their birthdays? Little things. Little Spanish fans. Little bracelets and necklaces of Indian beads. Little handkerchiefs. But when it was my birthday, she gave me that dress, handmade by Miss Quillercape herself, bright yellow, with all kinds of little flowers sewed in."

"The dress will be as good as new just as soon as Margie comes on Thursday and does the laundry."

"My plan was to walk up to Miss Quillercape's as soon as I got home—in the dress she gave me, as I promised I would."

Mrs. Hamilcar stopped reading the galleys of her husband's third novel in order to have a good look at her daughter, for, if the truth were told—and why shouldn't it be?—she was jealous of Miss Quillercape, a little old woman of seventy who had captured the affection and admiration of every little girl in Oh-Ho Hill from the age of two to twelve. After twelve, the little girls became young women and got themselves uncaptured, only to become captured by the boys of the neighborhood who had suddenly become young men.

"As you promised you would?" Mrs. Hamilcar said.

"Yes, mother. Miss Quillercape and I are the best friends we have ever had or ever will. Why, there is no place in the whole world like her house, and no lady like Miss Quillercape."

"Well, now, I begin to understand why you're so annoyed with Fido. Perhaps we ought to have him destroyed."

"Mother, I wish you wouldn't be so insensitive and—well, vulgar!"

"I'm a little hurt," Mrs. Hamilcar said, "and when I'm hurt I'm always a little insensitive and vulgar."

"Why should you be hurt? I haven't blamed you. I've blamed Fido.

"I'm a little hurt that somebody else—another woman, at that— could mean so much to you. Why, you haven't even given me a hug since the bus let you off at the corner fifteen minutes ago."

"I didn't get a chance," Daisy said. "Wasn't Fido all over me with his big stupid muddy paws?"

"Well?" Mrs. Hamilcar said.

"Well, what?"

"Well, what's the matter with right now?"

"Golly," Daisy said. "Sometimes I'm absolutely impossible. Just get me a little mad and I think I wouldn't recognize my own mother." She ran to her mother, and they hugged and kissed.

"But I'm still mad at Fido," she said. "And I want a cat."

"Look in your closet for a nice dress, and go on up the hill to Miss Quillercape's."

"I will not."

"Why not?"

"I couldn't pay her a visit unless I had on the dress she gave me. I would be the worst manners in the world between friends like us. Oh, she wouldn't notice, of course. She'd be thrilled to see me, and we'd have hot chocolate and Scotch scones and butter and jam, and we'd talk about everything under the sun, but it wouldn't be the same, and I'd know. I'd know, and I'd die of shame because she'd know I knew, and neither of us would speak of it. We're both ladies that way all the time, and the strain of it would be more than I could bear, that's all. After two long, unbearable weeks at that goody-goody camp."

"Well, we can talk about the camp later. One thing at a time, and first things first. You promised Miss Quillercape to visit her the minute you got home from camp?"

"Yes."

"Wearing the dress she gave you?"

"That wasn't part of the promise, but, of course, I myself had planned it that way, as an expression of my gratitude and appreciation. That's why I put the dress on at camp this morning, and went to so much trouble to keep it clean all the way home—three hours of weary travel! First, we marched from the camp to where a bus was waiting. Then we got on the bus and rode to where the boat was. Then we got on the boat and sailed from Catalina to San Pedro. Then we marched again to where another bus was waiting. Then we got on that bus, and it took us to where the last bus was waiting. Then we got on that bus, and it started and stopped, letting off girls at their houses all over the whole world. And wouldn't I be the last to get off?"

"I'm sorry," Mrs. Hamilcar said.

She got up suddenly and went to the washing machine just beyond the kitchen, her daughter walking behind her, Fido lying in front of the fireplace where Mrs. Hamilcar had ordered him to lie, and stay! A request—a demand—that was now driving the dog mad with curiosity.

He had followed the conversation with anxiety and fascination, waiting desperately for the hardness to leave Daisy's voice—his Daisy, his wonderful Daisy, his beautiful Daisy, his Daisy who had been gone from Oh-Ho Hill for so long, his Daisy he had searched for everywhere, coming suddenly upon all manner of creatures, day and night, creatures he had never before even known existed—that skunk, for instance, standing stock-still and just looking at him, with its tail straight up; and that possum that waddled slowly away, stopping now and then to look back, neither a friend nor an enemy, neither scared nor eager for friendship or a fight; that garter snake that tumbled away, in and out of the tall grass, in a kind of frantic running he couldn't understand, but just had to see more of, until the poor snake was exhausted and couldn't run any more and just stopped and waited for the worst, which Fido was astonished to discover the poor fellow expected, since all Fido had been after was to study that kind of running. He went up close and looked into the little eyes, and then at the colors—why, the poor fellow was beautiful, that's what he was.

And all the little girls he'd found, instead of Daisy—the dozens he had seen from a distance and had hoped and prayed would turn out to be Daisy, but never were, some of them running into houses and hiding, others urging him on and then stroking his head and talking to him, and even asking him in to meet their people.

Well, now, here was Daisy home at last—from the other end of the world, most likely. After great trials and tribulations, great dangers, great escapes, so naturally he'd been beside himself with surprise and gratitude to heaven for bringing Daisy safely home. How was he to have remembered that his feet were muddy at a time like that?

He wanted to get up and follow them. He wanted to, but he didn't. He just stayed where his best friend in the world of adults had ordered him to stay. He just stayed and waited, and tried to go on hearing them, waiting for the hardness to leave Daisy's voice.

Mrs. Hamilcar lifted the lid of the washing machine and brought out Daisy's muddied dress, but, of course, Fido didn't see it happen, didn't, in fact, know what was happening, or why, and that was what was so difficult.

Well, now, when were they going to start talking again? He heard water running out of a faucet into a sink, but still no talk. He heard the sound of soap being rubbed into cloth, and then he heard sloshing, but still no talk. What were they up to?

At last Daisy spoke, "What are you doing, mother?"

"What am I doing?" Fido heard Mrs. Hamilcar say. Her voice was gentle and kind; but then, it always was. It always had a touch of merry laughter in it, too, but that touch wasn't in it now. Something was going on. Something more. Something different.

"I'm trying," Fido heard Mrs. Hamilcar say, "to be your friend."

"Oh, mother, you're my mother. Mothers don't have to be friends too."

"Yes, they do," Mrs. Hamilcar said. "I almost think I'd rather be your friend than your mother. You know, you're just about all your father and I have that we really care about. You are all of our kids. All the daughters we were going to have, and all the sons too. We swore there were going to be six of each. All young husbands and wives swear the same thing, I suppose, but I think Morley really meant it, and I know I did. Well, things happen, and one of them happened to me, of all people. And so that was all for us—you. Well, you're nine now, and we know we aren't going to have very much more of you! What little time we have left, I want us to be—well, friends. Forever."

"Mother," Fido heard Daisy say, "am I going to die or are you?"

"Neither of us," Mrs. Hamilcar laughed, "except the little I die every time I notice how much more you've grown—which I'm always thrilled to notice too."

"Mother, what are you doing? Just tell me that, please."

"I'm laundering the dress Miss Quillercape gave you on your eighth birthday. After I launder it, I'm going to iron it. Then, you're going to put it on and walk up the hill and keep your promise."

"But why, mother?"

"Because I love you. Because I love your father. Because I love Miss Quillercape. Because I love everybody you know. Because I love Fido."

Fido almost sat up at the mention of his name, but not quite. This was a time for lying still, for listening, for waiting, for watching—if they'd only come back into the living room so he could watch, though.

"I'm sorry I said all those awful things about Fido."

Lady Daisy and Her Crazy Dog   ৺ৡ

"I knew you would be."

"I don't want a cat at all."

"You can have a cat, too, if you want one."

"Cat?" Fido thought. "Just bring a cat into this house and——"
But he cut the thought short. Suppose they did? Suppose they actually brought a cat into the house? Any kind of a cat. Not necessarily
the kind he couldn't even bear to see. Not one of those serene, snooty
Angoras. Any kind at all. They'd expect him to get along, of course.
They'd expect him even to like the cat—or at any rate to pretend to
—and he'd probably try, because of love of Daisy, but it would be
criminal.

Fido prayed. "Please," he said. "Please help them to decide they don't
want a cat at all. I'm not saying cats aren't all right. They probably
are, but I don't like to have them around. I don't hate them, maybe.
I'm willing to live and let live, but I don't love them, either. I've
gone to a lot of trouble not to chase them, because Mr. and Mrs.
Hamilcar and Daisy have asked me not to, but it's never been easy,
and the cats misunderstand my control. I've actually had them walk
right up to my nose, and it's been fairly frightening, on the whole. I
don't know whether they think they're dogs or I'm a cat, and I don't
like not knowing about a thing like that, because I know they're cats
and I'm a dog. Please help them to decide for themselves that we
don't want a cat around here. There's not one mouse in the whole
house. There's several crickets, but we're all devoted to them.
Amen."

As if in answer to the prayer, Fido heard Daisy say, "But I don't
want a cat. I just said I did because I was angry."

Fido breathed easier.

"Cats and dogs get along fine these days," Mrs. Hamilcar said.

"Oh, no," Fido groaned. "Please don't say that, Mrs. Hamilcar.
Please don't believe that. Believe me, they don't get along at all. Even
when it looks as if they do, they don't. And it's always the dog who
has to do the hard work. The cat never tries to meet the dog halfway. A cat is always a cat. But a dog, he tries to keep peace and harmony in the house. He pretends and pretends. Pretty soon it makes
him a little queer. I know three dogs in Oh-Ho Hill who have been
getting along with cats for years, and every one of them is a little
queer. They're confused. They don't know what happened to them.

They know something did, but they're not sure what. Dogs are gentlemen. Cats may be ladies, or something like them, or something like some of them, but they aren't ladies enough. They'll watch a dog go out of his way to be courteous, but they won't go even a little out of their way to make it a little easier for a dog to go on being courteous. And that's what does the damage. Pretty soon a dog is a little off the beam. Please don't believe cats and dogs get along, Mrs. Hamilcar. It's always dogs alone putting up with cats, the same as people, if you ask me. Live and let live and all that, but a cat is a cat, and you bring one into the house and you'll soon have a different kind of place entirely—silence, silence, silence, as if they were thinking something. Well, they're thinking nothing. That's only the way they are. They walk around and look and don't say anything. They're phony, all of them, and that's what dogs hate about them. Please don't believe cats and dogs get along, Mrs. Hamilcar."

"Oh, I know cats and dogs get along fine," Fido heard Daisy say, "but what about me? I don't get along with cats."

"Bravo, Daisy!"

"I love Fido," Daisy said, "and I don't want to have any other friend from the animal world—not even another dog."

"Double bravo, Daisy!"

"Well," Mrs. Hamilcar said, "I don't like cats, either. As a matter of fact, I can't have them around."

"Triple bravo, Mrs. Hamilcar!"

Fido relaxed and listened. They talked about everything, and the laughter came back into Mrs. Hamilcar's voice and the love into Daisy's. Fido fell asleep.

He woke up when Mrs. Hamilcar called out from the kitchen, "Stay right where you are, Fido. Don't even stand."

Fido half opened his eyes. He saw them come out of the kitchen into the living room, and they were good to see. Good to smell too. The good old Hamilcar smell of health, harmony, humor and love. Daisy was in the bright-yellow dress again, and she looked brand-new and different. Bigger, brighter and wiser.

"Don't move, Fido," Mrs. Hamilcar said. "Just look." Fido opened his eyes wider, as if to ask, "Like this?"

"Daisy's going to call on Miss Quillercape, as she promised she would."

"Don't I know?" Fido thought. Hadn't he gone along with Daisy

Lady Daisy and Her Crazy Dog   ⤐ 183

time after time to the very door of Miss Quillercape's little house and stretched out on the little patch of lawn there, with the blossoming rose trees all around, and the lilac trees, and the honeysuckle vines all entwined around the porch railings and posts? Hadn't he waited there, breathing the perfume, until Daisy had come out?

"Fido?" Daisy said. "I apologize for being so mean. Will you walk with me to Miss Quillercape's, please?"

"Will I?" Fido thought, and almost leaped to his feet. He manage to stay put, though, waiting for the good word to come from Mrs. Hamilcar.

"Do you really want him to tag along?" Mrs. Hamilcar said.

"Mother," Daisy said, "I haven't seen poor old Fido in two long weeks. Of course I want him to come along."

"All right, Fido," Mrs. Hamilcar said. "Up, now—but take it easy."

Fido sat up slowly, and waited. Daisy went to him. She knelt and looked into his eyes. She smiled, and then she put her face alongside of his, and then she kissed him. But Fido didn't stir. Oh, it wasn't that he wasn't gone, away out there, in heaven itself. It was just that he didn't want to make any more blunders for some time to come.

Daisy stood up, embraced Mrs. Hamilcar, and then she said, "You're my best friend, mamma. My very best friend. Good-by, I'm going to visit Miss Quillercape now. Come on, Fido."

Daisy walked to the front door. Fido walked slowly and carefully behind her, aware for the first time in years that he had four feet— or was it five? Daisy walked out of the house, and Fido followed. Daisy turned and Fido turned. Mrs. Hamilcar stood in the doorway. Daisy waved, and Fido watched. Mrs. Hamilcar smiled, and then all of a sudden Fido saw tears in her eyes.

Now, what the devil were they for? Would he ever understand people? He stood as if stuck in soft tar. He wanted to hurry to Mrs. Hamilcar, but he wasn't sure he should. Then he heard Daisy say, "All right, Fido, run! Run ahead!" Fido turned quickly. He was about to bound off when he just had to have another look at Mrs. Hamilcar. Some of the tears were rolling down her cheeks now. Now, what should a dog do about a thing like that?

"Go on, Fido," Mrs. Hamilcar said. "Run! Run ahead!" And there was actually merry laughter in her voice.

"I don't get it," Fido thought.

He turned quickly and bounded away. As he ran he heard them both laugh gaily. He would have laughed, too, if he weren't sure there must be still something more to people than he had ever before noticed. What the devil was it? Probably something human.

Love, of course, is of all times. It radiates from a giving person with all the warmth of the sun's rays. There is love between man and woman, between friends, between parents and children. Some persons are made to love and be always disappointed, but they love on in any case with a simple, tireless devotion. In "A Simple Heart," Gustave Flaubert, the master in exploring the diversity of emotion—and frequently the diversity of love itself—has written a simple story of enormous sensitivity.

A SIMPLE HEART

GUSTAVE FLAUBERT

For fifty years the good ladies of Pont-L'Évêque had longed for Madame Aubin's servant Félicité.

She received four pounds a year. For this she did the cooking and the general housework, the sewing, the washing, and the ironing. She could bridle a horse, fatten poultry, and churn butter, and she was ever faithful to her mistress, who was far from amiable.

Madame Aubin had married a light-hearted young bachelor without any money who died at the beginning of 1809, leaving her with two small children and a mass of debts. She then sold all her property except the farms of Toucques and Geffosses, which brought her in five thousand francs a year at most, and she left her house in Saint-Me-laine for a less costly one, that had belonged to her ancestors and was situated behind the market.

This house had a slate roof and stood between an archway and a narrow lane which went down to the river. There was an unevenness in the level of the floors which made you stumble. A narrow front hall divided the kitchen from the sitting room in which Madame Aubin sat all day long in a wicker armchair beside the window. Eight mahogany chairs stood in a row against the white-painted panels. On an old piano that stood under a barometer were heaped wooden and cardboard boxes like a pyramid. A stuffed armchair was placed on either side of the yellow marble Louis Quinze chimney-piece, which had a clock in the middle in the shape of a Temple of Vesta. The whole room was rather musty, because the floor was below the garden level.

"Madame's" room was on the first floor. It was very large, with a faded flowery wallpaper and a portrait of "Monsieur" dressed up as a dandy of the period. It let into a smaller room, which had two cots without mattresses. Next to it was the drawing room, which was always shut up and filled with furniture covered with dustsheets. A corridor led to a study. Books and odd papers filled the shelves of a large bookcase, and inside its three wings was a wide writing table of dark wood. The two panels at the end of the room were covered with pen and ink drawings, landscapes in water colors, and engravings by Audran, relics of better days and departed glory. On the second floor a dormer window, which looked out over the fields, let light into Félicité's attic.

She rose at dawn, so as not to be late for Mass, and worked until evening without stopping. Then, when dinner was over, the plates and dishes were put away, and the door was tightly fastened, she thrust a log in the dying embers and went to sleep in front of the hearth with her rosary in her hand. She was the most obstinate bargainer in the town, and as for cleanliness, the shine on her pots and pans was the despair of other servants. Thrifty in everything, she ate slowly, gathering up from the table the crumbs of her loaf, a twelve-pound loaf specially baked for her, which lasted three weeks. From year's end to year's end she wore a print cotton handkerchief, fastened with a pin behind, a bonnet that concealed her hair, gray stockings, a red skirt, and a bibbed apron, such as hospital nurses wear, over her jacket. Her voice was harsh and her face was thin. At twenty-five she looked forty. After fifty she looked any age. Silent, straight, and wasting no gestures, she was like a wooden woman who went by clockwork.

II

She had had her love story like others.

Her father. a mason, was killed by falling off a scaffold. Then her

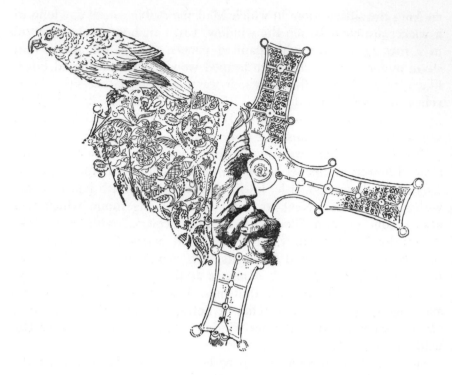

mother died, her sisters went off here and there, and a farmer took her in while she was a little girl and gave her charge of the cows in his fields. She was ragged and shivered; she lay flat on the ground and lapped water up from the pools; she was beaten for nothing; and finally she was turned out of the house for stealing thirty sous that she hadn't stolen. She went to another farm and looked after the hens; and because her employers liked her, the others were jealous.

One evening in August—she was then eighteen—they took her to a feast at Colleville. She was dazed and bewildered by the stir of the fiddlers, the lamps in the trees, the laces and gold crosses in the dresses, and the crowd of folk all dancing together. She was standing aside shyly when a comfortable looking young chap, who was leaning on the shaft of a cart and smoking his pipe, came up to her and asked her to dance. He treated her to cider, coffee, and cakes and bought her a silk handkerchief, and imagining that she understood what he wanted, offered to see her home. When they came to a cornfield, he threw her down roughly. She was terrified and cried out for help. And he got out of the way.

One evening after this, she was on the Beaumont road, and a great haycart was moving along slowly in front of her. She wanted to pass it, and as she brushed by the wheel she recognized Théodore. He spoke to her quite coolly, telling her that she must forgive him, because it was all the fault of the drink. She could not think what to say and longed to run away.

He began at once to talk about the crops and the important people of the commune, saying that his father had left Colleville for his farm at Les Ecots, so now they were neighbors. "Well, well!" she said. He added that his people wanted him to settle down, but he was in no hurry and would please himself in finding a wife. She dropped her eyes. Then he asked her if she thought of getting married. She answered with a smile that it wasn't fair to make fun of her.

"But I'm not, I swear it!" And he passed his left arm round her waist. She walked on, supported by his clasp, and their pace slackened. The wind was soft, the stars twinkled, the huge haycart swung on in front of them, and the four weary horses raised the dust with their dragging feet. Then, without a word from Théodore they turned to the right. He embraced her once more, and she disappeared in the night.

Next week she consented to meet him sometimes.

They used to meet in farmyards, behind a wall, or under some solitary tree. She was not innocent as young ladies are—the ways of animals had taught her something—but her good sense and the instinct of her honor saved her from falling. Her resistance inflamed Théodore's passion so much that, to satisfy it, or perhaps for more innocent reasons, he proposed marriage to her. She hesitated to believe him, but he swore ardent oaths of faithfulness.

Presently he confessed that he had something awkward to tell her. A year ago his parents had bought him a substitute for the army, but he might be taken again any day now, and the idea of military service terrified him. His cowardice seemed to Félicité a proof of his affection, and it redoubled hers. She stole off at night to meet him, and when she came to him Théodore worried her with his fears and entreaties.

At last he told her that he would go himself to the Prefecture to find out, and that he would let her know the result between eleven and twelve on the following Sunday night.

She hurried to meet him at the appointed hour. She found one of his friends instead at the meeting place.

He told her that she must not see Théodore any more. To save himself from conscription, he had married Madame Lehoussais, a wealthy old woman of Toucques.

There was a wild outburst of grief. She flung herself down on the ground, screamed and appealed to Almighty God, and lay moaning all alone in the field till daybreak. Then she returned to the farm and told them she was leaving at the end of the month. She received her wages, tied up all her little belongings in a handkerchief, and went to Pont-L'Évêque.

In front of the inn there, she asked questions of a woman in a widow's cap, who, as luck would have it, was looking for a cook. The girl had no experience, but she seemed so willing and modest in her demands that Madame Aubin ended by saying: "Very well, I will engage you."

A quarter of an hour later Félicité took up her quarters in this woman's house.

At first she lived there in terror at "the style of the house" and the memory of "Monsieur" hovering over it all. Paul and Virginie, the former seven and the latter just four, seemed to her creatures of a precious substance. She carried them pick-a-back, and it distressed her that Madame Aubin ordered her not to kiss them every minute. However, she was happy there. Her sorrow thawed in the pleasantness of her surroundings.

Every Thursday some regular visitors came in for a game of boston, and Félicité laid out the cards and foot-warmers beforehand. They arrived sharply on the stroke of eight and left before the clock struck eleven.

Every Monday morning the old scrap dealer, who lived under the archway, spread out his iron. Then the town buzzed with voices, horses neighed, lambs bleated, pigs grunted, and carts rattled sharply on the pavement.

About noon, when the market had got thoroughly busy, you would see a tall, hook-nosed old farmer with his cap on the back of his head come to the door. It was Robelin, the farmer of Geffosses. Soon afterward came Lièbard, the farmer of Toucques, short, flushed and podgy, in a gray jacket and spurred gaiters.

Both had chickens or cheeses to offer their landlady. Félicité was always up to their tricks, and they would go away filled with respect for her.

At uncertain intervals Madame Aubin would have a call from one of her uncles, the Marquis de Gremanville, who had ruined himself by hard living and now lived on the last scrap of his land at Falaise. He always came at lunchtime with a nasty poodle whose paws left dirty marks all over the furniture. In spite of all his efforts to seem a gentleman—he even went so far as to lift his hat every time he said "my late father"—habit got the better of him. He would pour out glass after glass and indulge in pothouse conversation. Félicité used to coax him out of the house. "You've had enough, Monsieur de Gremanville! That's enough till next time!" And she shut the door on him.

She would open it with pleasure for Monsieur Bourais, a retired lawyer. His bald head, white stock, frilled shirt front, and loose brown coat, his way of curving his arm when he took snuff, his whole personality, in fact, gave you that special feeling we have whenever we see an extraordinary man.

As he looked after "Madame's" property, he would stay shut up with her for hours in "Monsieur's" study, though all the time he was afraid of being compromised. He had great respect for the law and claimed to know Latin.

To join instruction and pleasure, he gave the children a geography full of pictures. They showed scenes in all parts of the world: cannibals with feathers in their hair, a monkey carrying off a young lady, Bedouins in the desert, harpooning a whale, and so on. Paul would explain these pictures to Félicité, and that was all the education she ever had. The children's education was undertaken by Guyot, a humble creature employed in the town hall, who was well known for his beautiful handwriting and used to sharpen his penknife on his boots.

When the weather was fine, the household used to start off early sometimes for a day at the Geffosses farm.

Its courtyard was on a slope, with the farmhouse in the middle, and the sea looked like a far-off gray streak on the horizon.

Félicité would take slices of cold meat out of her basket, and they would have lunch in a room beside the dairy. It was the last relic of a country house which was no more. The wallpaper was in tatters and rattled in a draught. Madame Aubin would sit with bowed head, overcome by her memories of the past. The children were afraid to speak. "Why don't you go off and play?" she would say, and they would hurry off.

Paul climbed up into the barn, caught birds, played ducks and drakes on the pond, or hammered with his stick on the great casks, which echoed like drums. Virginie fed the rabbits or ran off to pick cornflowers, her scampering legs showing her little embroidered drawers.

One autumn evening they went home by the fields. The moon was in its first quarter and lit up part of the sky. A mist floated like a scarf over the winding Toucques. Cattle, lying out in the meadow, looked placidly at these four as they passed by. In the third meadow some of them got up and made a half circle in front of them. "There's nothing to be afraid of," said Félicité, stroking the back of the nearest animal while she crooned softly. He wheeled round and the others did the same. But as they crossed the next field, they heard a dreadful bellow. It was a bull, which was hidden by the mist. Madame Aubin started to run. "No! no! don't go so fast!" They hurried on, all the same, hearing a loud breathing behind them which kept coming nearer and nearer. His hoofs thudded on the turf like hammerstrokes. Now he was galloping! Félicité turned round and tore up some clods, which she threw into his eyes with both hands. The bull lowered his muzzle, shook his horns, and bellowed with fury terribly. Madame Aubin, who had reached the end of the field with her two children, was looking distractedly for a place to climb over the high bank. Félicité kept retreating, always facing the bull, showering clods at his face which blinded him, and crying out, "Be quick! be quick!"

Madame Aubin got down into the ditch, pushed Virginie first and then Paul, fell several times trying to climb the steep bank, and finally managed it with a courageous effort.

The bull had driven Félicité back against a fence, his slaver was blowing in her face, and in an instant he would have gored her. She had just time to slip between the rails, and the hulking brute stopped short in amazement.

This adventure was discussed in Pont-L'Évêque for many a year. Félicité took no special pride in what she had done, and it never occurred to her for an instant that she had been heroic.

Virginie was her sole object of care, for, as a result of her fright, the child had become very nervous, and Monsieur Paupart, the doctor, advised sea bathing at Trouville. The place had few visitors in those days. Madame Aubin gathered information, consulted Bourais, and prepared as if she were going on a long journey.

She sent off her luggage in Lièbard's cart the day before. Next day he brought round two horses, one of which had a lady's saddle with a velvet back, while on the back of the other he had made a kind of pillion out of a rolled-up coat. Madame Aubin rode on this horse behind the farmer, while Félicité took care of Virginie, and Paul rode on Monsieur Lechaptois' ass, which had been lent on condition that great care was taken of it.

The road was so bad that it took them two hours to go five miles. The horses sank in the mud up to their pasterns, and their rumps floundered about as they tried to get out. Sometimes they stumbled in the ruts, or else had to jump. In some places Lièbard's mare stopped dead. He waited patiently until she went on again, talking about the people who owned property along the road, and adding moral reflections to their stories. And so, when they were in the middle of Toucques, as they passed by some windows smothered with nasturtiums, he shrugged his shoulders and said: "Madame Lehoussais lives there. Instead of taking a young man, she . . ." Félicité did not hear the rest. The horses trotted on and the donkey galloped. They all turned down a side lane. A gate swung open, two boys appeared, and they all dismounted in front of a manure heap just outside the farmhouse door.

When Madame Lièbard saw her mistress, her generosity expressed her joy. She served them a lunch with a sirloin of beef, tripe, black pudding, a fricassee of chicken, sparkling cider, fruit pie and brandied plums, seasoning it with compliments to Madame, who seemed in better health; to Mademoiselle, who was now "splendid"; and to Monsieur Paul, who "was filling out wonderfully." Nor did she forget their departed grandparents, whom the Lièbards had known well, as they had been in the family's service for several generations. The farm, like them, had the hallmark of antiquity. The beams on the ceiling were worm-eaten, the walls black with smoke, the window panes gray with dust. All sorts of useful objects were set out on an oak dresser—jugs, plates, pewter bowls, wolf-traps, sheep-shears, and a huge syringe that made the children laugh. Every tree in the three courtyards had mushrooms growing at the foot of it and a sprig of mistletoe in its branches. Several of them had been thrown down by the wind and had taken root again in the middle. All were bending under their wealth of apples. The thatched roofs, like brown velvet and varying in thickness, withstood the heaviest gales, but the cart shed was tumbling down. Madame Aubin said that she would see about it and ordered the animals to be saddled again.

After another half hour they reached Trouville. The little troop dismounted to pass Ecores, an overhanging cliff with boats on the sea beneath it, and three minutes later they reached the end of the quay and entered the courtyard of the Golden Lamb, kept by worthy Madame David.

From the first day of their stay, Virginie began to grow stronger, thanks to the change of air and the sea baths. These she took in her chemise for want of a bathing suit, and Félicité used to dress her afterwards in a coastguard's cabin that was used by the bathers.

In the afternoons they used to take the donkey and wander off beyond the black rocks beyond Hennequeville. At first the path went up hill and down dale through a green sward like a park. Then it came out on a plateau, where green fields and arable land were lying side by side. Holly rose stiffly out of masses of briar at the side of the road, and here and there the branches of a great withered tree zigzagged against the blue sky.

They nearly always rested in a meadow, with Deauville on their left, Havre on their right, and the open sea in front of them. It gleamed in the sunshine, smooth as a mirror, and it was so still that its murmur could scarcely be heard. Hidden sparrows chirped, and the great sky arched over all. Madame Aubin would do needlework, Virginie plaited rushes beside her, Félicité gathered lavender, and Paul was bored and wanted to go home.

On other days they crossed the Toucques in a boat and hunted for shells. When the tide had gone out, sea-urchins, starfish, and jelly fish were left stranded, and the children scurried after the flakes of foam which scudded along the wind. The sleepy waves broke on the sand and rolled all along the beach, which stretched far out of sight, bounded on the land by the dunes between it and the Marsh, a broad meadow shaped like an arena. As they came home that way, Trouville, on the hill behind, grew larger at every step, and its varied huddle of houses seemed to break into bright disorder.

When the weather was too hot, they did not leave their room. Bars of light from the dazzling outside fell through the lattices. There was no sound in the village, and not a soul on the pavement outside. This silence made the quiet profound. In the distance, men were caulking, and you could hear the tap of their hammers as they plugged the hulls of their boats, and a heavy breeze wafted up the smell of tar.

The chief amusement was watching the return of the fishing boats. They began to tack as soon as they had passed the buoys. The sails were lowered on two of the three masts, and they glided along through the ripple of the waves, with the foresails bellying out like balloons, till they reached the middle of the harbor, when they suddenly dropped anchor. Then the boats were drawn up against the quay, and the fishermen began to throw their quivering fish over the side. A line of carts was waiting, and women in cotton bonnets darted out to take the baskets and kiss their men.

One of these women came up to Félicité one day, and she went home a little later in a state of happiness. She had found a sister. Nastasie Barette, "Leroux's wife," showed up behind her, with a baby at her breast and another child in her right hand, and on her left walked a little cabin boy with arms akimbo and his cap on one ear.

After a quarter of an hour Madame Aubin sent them away, but they were always to be seen around the kitchen, or met whenever they went for a walk. The husband never appeared.

Félicité grew very fond of them. She bought them a blanket, some shirts, and a stove. Evidently they were doing quite well out of her. Madame Aubin was annoyed by this weakness, and she did not like the nephew's familiarity when he said "thee" and "thou" to Paul. And so, as Virginie was coughing and the weather had broken, they returned to Pont-L'Évêque.

Monsieur Bourais gave her advice about a boys' school. Caen was supposed to be the best, and so Paul was sent there. He said goodbye bravely, glad enough to go and live where he would have playmates.

Madame Aubin resigned herself to the boy's absence. It had to be. Virginie soon forgot all about it. Félicité missed his noisiness about the house. But she found an occupation to distract her. After Christmas she took the little girl to catechism every day.

III

After making a genuflection at the door she walked up between the double row of chairs in the lofty nave, opened Madame Aubin's pew, sat down, and began to look around. The choir stalls were filled with boys on the right and girls at the left, and the curé stood at the lectern. From a stained glass window in the apse the Holy Ghost looked down at the Blessed Virgin. In another window she was kneeling before the Infant Jesus, and behind the shrine on the altar a carved wooden group showed St. Michael overcoming the dragon.

The priest began with an outline of sacred history. The Garden of Eden, the Flood, the Tower of Babel, cities in flames, dying nations, idols overthrown, passed in a vision before her eyes, and the bewildering dream left her clinging reverently to the Most High in fear of

His wrath. Then she wept at the story of the Passion. Why had they crucified Him, He who loved children, fed the multitudes, healed the blind, and had chosen, in His meekness, to be born among the poor on the dungheap of a stable? The sowings, the harvests, the wine-presses, all the familiar things of which the Gospels speak, were an ordinary part of her life. God's passing had made them holy, and she loved the lambs more tenderly for her love of the Lamb, and the doves because of the Holy Ghost.

She could hardly imagine Him in person, for not only was He a bird, but He was a flame as well, and even a breath some times. Perhaps it is His Light, she would think, which flits over the edge of the marshes at night, His Breath which makes the clouds run across the sky, His Voice which gives clear music to the bells; and she would sit lost in adoration, enjoying the coolness and stillness of the church.

Of dogma she understood nothing, and made no effort to understand it. The curé discoursed, the children said their lessons, and finally she went to sleep, waking up startled by their wooden shoes clattering on the flagstones as they went out of the church.

So Félicité, whose religious education had been neglected in her youth, learned her catechism by being obliged to listen to it. From that day she imitated Virginie in all her religious practices, fasting when she fasted and going to confession when she did. On the feast of Corpus Christi they made a repository together.

Virginie's first communion lay anxiously before her. Félicité worried over her shoes, her rosary, her book, and her gloves. And how she trembled as she helped the little girl's mother to dress her up for the occasion!

All through Mass she was feverish with anxiety. Monsieur Bourais hid one side of the choir from her, but straight in front was the flock of maidens, with their white crowns above their drooping veils, making a field of snow; and she knew her dear little one at a distance by her dainty neck and reverent air. The bell tinkled. All heads bowed, and there was silence. The organ pealed, and choir and congregation joined in the *Agnus Dei*. Then the procession of the boys began, and the girls rose after them. Step by step, with their hands clasped in prayer, they drew near the lighted altar, knelt on the first step, each received the Blessed Sacrament in turn, and they came back to their seats in the same order. When Virginie's turn came, Félicité leaned forward to see her; and with the imagination of tender affection it seemed to her as if she were that child. Virginie's face became hers. She was wearing the child's crown, the little girl's heart beat in her breast. When it was time to open her mouth, she closed her eyes and nearly fainted. Next morning she went to the sacristy to receive Communion from Monsieur the Curé. She received it with devotion, but did not feel the same delight.

Madame Aubin was anxious to give her daughter the best education possible, and as Guyot could not teach her music or English, decided to put her in the Ursuline Convent at Honfleur as a boarder. The child made no complaint. Félicité sighed and thought that Madame was hard-hearted. Then she considered that no doubt her mistress was right. These affairs were beyond her.

So one day an old cart drew up at the door, and a nun stepped out of it who was come to fetch the young lady. Félicité set the luggage on top of the cart, gave special orders to the driver, and placed six pots of jam, a dozen pears, and a bunch of violets under the child's seat.

At the last moment Virginie sobbed bitterly, and threw her arms round the neck of her mother, who kissed her on the forehead and kept saying: "Come now, be brave! be really brave!" The steps were raised and the cart drove off.

Then Madame Aubin's strength broke down. In the evening all her friends, the Lormeaus, Madame Lechaptois, the Rochefeuille girls, Monsieur de Houppeville, and Bourais, came in to comfort her.

At first life was very painful to her without her daughter, but she heard from her three times a week, wrote to her on the other days, walked in her garden, and so passed the weary time away.

Félicité went into Virginie's room in the morning as usual and stared at the walls. It was dull for her not to have the child's hair to comb, her boots to lace, and her body to tuck into bed, not to see her dear face all the time and to hold her hand when they went out together. To fill up her idleness she tried to make lace, but her fingers were too clumsy and she kept breaking the threads. She could not settle down to anything, lost sleep, and, as she said, was "ruined."

To amuse herself, she asked permission for her nephew Victor to visit her.

He would come on Sundays after Mass with rosy cheeks and bare chest, and country air all about him from his walk. She set the table for him promptly and they lunched together face to face. She ate as little as possible herself to save money, but she would stuff him till he fell asleep. When the bell first sounded for Vespers, she would wake him up, brush his trousers, fasten his tie, and set off for church leaning on his arm with a mother's pride.

His parents always told Victor to get something out of her, a damp packet of sugar, perhaps, or a cake of soap, some brandy, or even money now and then. He brought her his clothes to mend, and she gladly undertook this task, grateful for anything that would bring him back to her.

In August his father took him away for a sea trip along the coast. It was holiday time for the children, and their arrival consoled her. But Paul was getting selfish and Virginie too old to say "thee" and "thou" to her any longer. This made things stiff and created a barrier between them.

Victor went to Morlaix, Dunkirk, and Brighton in succession, and brought Félicité a present after each trip. First he brought her a box made out of shells, then a coffee cup, and finally a big gingerbread man. He was growing handsome with his fine figure, his hint of a moustache, his honest clear eyes, and a little leather cap clinging to the back of his head like a pilot's. He amused her with stories adorned with nautical terms.

It was on a Monday, the 14th of July, 1819 (she never forgot that date), that he told her how he had signed on for a long voyage and two nights later was to go on board the boat for Honfleur, where he was to join his schooner, which was weighing anchor shortly from Havre. He might be gone two years.

The thought of this long absence plunged Félicité in distress. She must say goodbye once more, and so, on Wednesday evening after Madame had finished her dinner, she put on her wooden shoes and soon covered the twelve miles between Pont-L'Évêque and Honfleur.

When she came to the Calvary, she turned to the right instead of the left, went astray in the timber yard, and had to retrace her steps. Some people to whom she spoke told her to hurry. She went all round the harbor, which was full of shipping, and kept tripping over hawsers. Then the ground fell away, lights flashed across each other, and she thought she was losing her wits, for she saw horses way up in the sky. Others were neighing beside the quay afraid of the sea. They were hoisted up with tackle and lowered in a boat, in which passengers were bumping into each other amid cider casks, hampers of cheese, and sacks of corn. Hens were cackling, the captain swore, and a cabin boy was leaning over the bow, indifferent to it all. Félicité, who had not recognised him, cried "Victor!" He raised his head. Just as she was rushing forward, the gangway was pulled back.

The Honfleur packet, with women singing as they hauled, went out of the harbor, its ribs creaking and heavy waves slapping against the bows. The sails swung round, and no one could be seen now on board. The boat was a black speck on the sea which shimmered with silver in the moonlight. It faded away little by little, dipped, and was gone.

As Félicité passed the Calvary, she had an impulse to commend to God what she cherished most, and she stood praying for a long time with her face bathed in tears and her eyes staring at the clouds. The town was asleep, coastguards were walking to and fro, and water poured incessantly through the holes in the sluice with the noise of a torrent. The clocks struck two.

The convent parlor would not be open before dawn. If Félicité were late, Madame would be sure to be annoyed. In spite of her wish to kiss the other child, she went home. The maids at the inn were just waking up when she came home to Pont-L'Évêque.

So the poor little chap was going to be tossed for months and months at sea! His previous voyages had not alarmed her. You were sure to come back safely from England or Brittany, but America, the Colonies and the Islands were lost in a faint cloudy region on the other side of the world.

From that day Félicité thought only of her nephew. On sunny days she was troubled by thinking of his thirst; when it was stormy, she was afraid of the lightning lest it should strike him. As she listened to the wind moaning in the chimney or stripping off the slates, she saw him bruised by that same tempest at the top of a shattered mast, with his body thrown back under a sheet of foam; or (remembering the illustrated geography) he was being devoured by savages, captured by monkeys in the forest, or dying on some desert shore. She never spoke of her anxiety.

Madame Aubin had anxieties of her own about her daughter. The good nuns considered her an affectionate but delicate child. The least emotion unnerved her. She had to give up the piano.

Her mother insisted on hearing regularly from the Convent. One morning, when the letter-carrier did not come, she lost patience, and walked up and down the parlor from her chair to the window. It was astonishing. No news for four days!

To console Madame Aubin by her own example, Félicité said: "It is six months since I had a letter!"

"From whom?"

"Why, from my nephew," answered the servant gently.

"Oh! your nephew!" And Madame Aubin resumed her walk and shrugged her shoulders, as much as to say: "I wasn't thinking about him, and besides what does a mere scamp of a cabin boy matter? Now my daughter . . . why, think of it!"

Félicité, though she had been brought up roughly enough, was indignant with Madame and then forgot all about it. It seemed natural enough to her to lose your head over the little girl. For her, the two children were equally important. They were united in her heart by the same bond, and their destinies must be the same.

The chemist informed her that Victor's ship had reached Havana. He had read the news in a paper.

Cigars made her picture Havana as a place where no one did anything but smoke, and she could see Victor moving about among Negroes in a cloud of tobacco. Could a man, she wondered, "in case he had to," come home by land? How far was it from Pont-L'-Évêque? She asked Monsieur Bourais questions to find out.

He took down his atlas and began to explain the longitudes. Félicité's confusion aroused a broad pedantic smile. At last he marked with his pencil a tiny black spot in an oval place on the map, and said, "Here it is." She stooped over the map. The network of colored lines tired her eyes without conveying anything to her. When Bourais asked her to tell him what was the matter, she begged him to show her the house in which Victor lived. Bourais threw up his hands, sneezed, and went into peals of laughter. Her simplicity delighted him. And Félicité could not understand why! How could she, when she expected, no doubt, actually to see a picture of her nephew, her mind was so simple!

A fortnight later Lièbard came into the kitchen at market time as usual, and gave her a letter from her brother-in-law. As neither could read, she carried it to her mistress.

Madame Aubin, who was counting the stitches in her knitting, set down her work and broke the seal of the letter. She started and murmured with a meaning look: "It's bad news . . . that they have to tell you. . . . Your nephew . . ."

He was dead. The letter said no more

Félicité fell on a chair with her head leaning against the wall. She closed her eyelids, which suddenly went pink. Then, with bent forehead, hands hanging down, and rigid eyes, she kept saying at intervals: "Poor little fellow! Poor little fellow!"

Lièbard watched her and sighed. Madame Aubin trembled a little.

She suggested that Félicité ought to go and see her sister at Trouville. Félicité replied with a gesture that it was no use.

There was a silence. The worthy Lièbard thought it was time to withdraw.

Then Félicité said:

"They don't care, they don't!"

Her head drooped again, and now and then she picked up mechanically the long needles on her work table.

Some women went through the yard with a barrow of dripping linen.

As she saw them through the window, she remembered her washing. She had put it to soak yesterday. Today she must wring it out. She left the room.

Her plank and tub were at the edge of the Toucques. She threw a heap of linen on the bank and rolled up her sleeves, and, taking her wooden beater, she dealt such blows that they could be heard in the neighboring gardens. The fields were empty. The river stirred faintly in the wind. Below, long grasses waved like the hair of corpses floating on the water. She mastered her grief and was very brave until the evening, but once in her room she gave way to it entirely, lying stretched out on the mattress with her face buried in the pillow and her hands clenched against her temples.

Much later she heard the circumstances of Victor's end from the captain himself. They had bled him too much for yellow fever at the hospital. Four doctors were holding him at once. He had died instantly and the chief had said: "Bah! that's another one gone!"

His parents had always been cruel to him. She preferred not to see them again, and they made no advances, either because they had forgotten all about her or because they were hardened in their desperate poverty.

Virginie began to grow weaker.

Constriction in the chest, coughing, chronic fever, and the marble veins on her cheek bones betrayed some deep-seated ailment. Monsieur Poupart advised a stay in Provence. Madame Aubin decided on it and would have brought home her daughter at once had it not been for the climate of Pont-L'Évêque.

She contracted with a job-master who drove her to the Convent every Tuesday. There is a terrace in the garden which overlooks the Seine. Virginie walked there over the fallen vine leaves on her mother's arm. A beam of sunlight through the clouds sometimes made her blink, as she gazed at the sails in the distance and the wide horizon from the Château de Tancarville to the lighthouses of Havre. Afterwards they would rest in the harbor. Her mother had procured a small cask of excellent Malaga; and Virginie, laughing at the idea of getting tipsy, used to drink a thimbleful of it, but no more.

You could see her strength coming back. The autumn glided by softly. Félicité reassured Madame Aubin, but one evening, when she had been out on an errand in the neighborhood, she found Monsieur Poupart's gig at the door. He was in the hall and Madame Aubin was tying her bonnet.

"Give me my foot-warmer, and my purse and gloves! Hurry, be quick about it!"

Virginie had inflammation of the lungs. It might be hopeless.

"Not yet!" said the doctor, and they both got into the carriage in a whirl of snowflakes. Night was coming on, and it was very cold.

Félicité rushed into the church to light a candle. Then she ran after the gig, caught up with it in an hour, jumped in lightly behind, and hung on to the fringes. Suddenly she thought: "The courtyard has not been shut up! Suppose thieves break in!" And she jumped down.

At dawn next day she was at the doctor's door. He had come in and started off for the country again. Then she waited in the inn, thinking that a letter would come by somebody or other. Finally, when it was growing dark, she took the Lisieux coach.

The Convent was at the end of a steep lane. When she was half way up, she heard strange sounds, a passing-bell was tolling. "It's for someone else," thought Félicité, and she struck the knocker violently.

After some minutes, there was a sound of shuffling slippers, the door opened partly, and a nun appeared.

The good sister, with an air of compunction, said that "she had just passed away." At that moment the bell of St. Leonard's tolled harder than ever.

Félicité went up to the second floor. From the doorway she saw Virginie stretched out on her back with clasped hands, open mouth, and her head thrown back under a black crucifix which leaned towards her, between curtains hanging stiffly, less pale than her face.

Madame Aubin, at the foot of the bed which she was clasping with her arms, was choking with agonized sobs. The Mother Superior was standing on the right. Three candlesticks on the chest of drawers made red spots, and a white fog came seeping in through the windows. Some nuns came and led Madame Aubin away.

For two nights Félicité never left the dead child. She kept repeating the same prayers, sprinkled holy water on the sheets, came and sat down again, and watched her. At the end of her first vigil, she noticed that the face had become yellow, the lips had turned blue, the nose was sharper, and the eyes had sunk in. She kissed them several times and would not have been very much surprised if Virginie had opened them again. To minds like hers the supernatural is perfectly simple. She made the girl's toilet, wrapped her in her shroud, lifted her into the coffin, laid a wreath on her head, and spread out her hair. It was fair and surprisingly long for her age. Félicité cut off a big lock of it, and slipped half of it into her bosom, determined never to part with it.

The body was brought back to Pont-L'Évêque, in accordance with the wish of Madame Aubin, who followed the hearse in a closed carriage.

It took another three-quarters of an hour after the Mass to reach the cemetery. Paul walked in front, sobbing. Monsieur Bourais followed, and then came the principal citizens of Pont-L'Évêque, the women in black mantles, and Félicité. She thought of her nephew, and since she had been unable to pay him these honors, her grief was doubled, as if the one were being buried with the other.

Madame Aubin's despair was unbounded. At first she rebelled against God, deeming it unjust for Him to have taken her daughter from her, who had never done any harm and whose conscience was clear! Ah! no! she ought to have taken Virginie to the South! Other doctors would have saved her. Now she accused herself, longed to join her child, and cried out in distress in the middle of her dreams. One dream especially haunted her. Her husband, dressed as a sailor, came back from a long voyage, and shed tears as he told her that he was ordered to carry Virginie away. Then they consulted how to hide her somewhere.

Once she came in from the garden quite upset. Just now—and she pointed out the spot—father and daughter had appeared to her, standing side by side. They did nothing, but looked at her.

For several months after this she stayed passively in her room. Félicité lectured her gently. She must live for her son, and for the other, in remembrance of "her."

"Her?" answered Madame Aubin, as though just rousing from slumber. "Ah, yes! . . . yes! . . . you do not forget her!" This was an allusion to the cemetery, to which she was strictly forbidden to go.

Félicité went there every day.

On the stroke of four she would skirt the houses, climb the hill, open the gate, and come to Virginie's grave. It was a little pillar of pink marble with a stone underneath and a garden plot enclosed by chains. The beds were hidden under a carpet of flowers. She watered their leaves, freshened up the gravel, and knelt down to soften the earth better. Whenever Madame Aubin was able to come there, she felt relieved and somehow consoled.

The years slipped by, one much like another, marked only by the great feast days as they recurred—Easter, the Assumption, All Saints' Day. Household happenings marked dates that were mentioned afterwards. In 1825, for example, two glaziers whitewashed the hall. In 1827, a piece of the roof fell into the courtyard and nearly killed a man. In the summer of 1828, it was Madame's turn to offer the blessed bread. About this time, Bourais went away mysteriously. One by one the old acquaintances died: Guyot, Lièbard, Madame Lechaptois, Robelin, and Uncle de Gremanville, who had been paralyzed for a long time.

One night the driver of the mail coach announced in Pont-L'-Évêque the Revolution of July. A new sub-Prefect was appointed a few days later. It was Baron de Larsonnière, who had been a Consul in America, and he brought with him, besides his wife, his sister-in-law and three grown-up young ladies. They were to be seen on the lawn in loose drapery, and they had a Negro and a parrot. They called on Madame Aubin, and she did not fail to return the call. As soon as they were seen in the distance, Félicité ran and told her mistress. But only one thing could really move her—letters from her son.

He lived in taverns and could follow no career. She used to pay his debts and he made new ones. Madame Aubin's sighs, as she sat knitting by the window, reached Félicité spinning in the kitchen.

They used to walk together along the espaliered wall, always talking of Virginie and wondering if this or that would have pleased her, or what she would have said on this or that occasion.

All her little belongings filled a cupboard in the two-bedded room. Madame Aubin looked at them as seldom as possible. One summer day she made up her mind to do so, and some moths flew out of the cupboard.

Virginie's dresses were all in a row underneath a shelf on which there were three dolls, some hoops, some little pots and pans, and the basin she had used. They took out her petticoats as well, and her stockings and handkerchiefs, and spread them out on the two beds before folding them up again. The sunlight shone on these poor things, bringing out their stains and the creases made by the little girl's movements. The sky was warm and blue, a blackbird warbled, and life seemed bathed in a deep sweet peace. They came across a little plush hat with thick, chestnut-colored fur, but the moths had eaten it. Félicité begged for it. They gazed at each other and their eyes filled with tears. At last the mistress opened her arms, the servant threw herself into them, and they clasped each other in a hearty embrace, staunching their grief with a kiss that made them equal.

It was the first time in their lives, for Madame Aubin was not expansive by nature.

Félicité was as grateful as though she had received a great favor, and from that day she cherished her mistress with an animal's devotion and religious worship.

The kindness of her heart opened out.

When she heard the drums of a regiment marching in the street, she would stand at the door with a pitcher of cider and offer it to the soldiers to drink. She took care of cholera patients. She protected the Polish refugees, and one of these proposed to marry her. They quarreled, nevertheless; for as she returned from the Angelus one morning, she found he had got into her kitchen and made with vinegar a salad for himself, which he was eating quietly.

After the Poles came Père Colmiche, an ancient man who was reputed to have committed atrocities in '93. He lived beside the river in a ruined pig-sty. The little boys used to stare at him through the cracks in his wall, and to throw pebbles at him, which fell on the mattress upon which he lay constantly shaken with catarrh. His hair was very long, his eyes were inflamed, and he had a tumor on his arm that was bigger than his head. Félicité found him some linen and tried to clean up his miserable den. She longed to establish him in the bakehouse without letting him annoy Madame. When the tumor burst, she used to dress it every day. Sometimes she would bring him cake and put him out in the sunlight on a truss of straw. The poor old man, slobbering and trembling, would thank her in a faint voice, fearful of losing her, and would stretch out his hand as he saw her going away. He died; and she had a Mass said for the repose of his soul.

That very day a great happiness befell her. Just at dinner time Madame de Larsonnière's Negro appeared, carrying the parrot in its cage, with perch, chain, and padlock. There was a note from the Baroness informing Madame Aubin that her husband had been promoted to a

Prefecture, and they were going away that evening. She begged her to accept the bird as a memento and a token of her esteem.

For a long time the parrot had absorbed Félicité's attention, because he came from America. The name reminded her of Victor, so much so that she had asked the Negro about it. Once she had gone so far as to say: "How happy Madame would be to have him!"

The Negro had repeated this remark to his mistress. Since she could not take the bird away with her, this was how she got rid of him.

IV

His name was Loulou. His body was green, the tips of his wings were rosy pink, his brow was blue, and his throat was golden.

But he had a tiresome habit of biting his perch, tearing out his feathers, flinging his dirt about, and spattering the water from his bath. He annoyed Madame Aubin, and she presented him to Félicité.

She undertook to train him. Soon he could repeat: "Good boy! Your servant, sir! How dy'ye do, Marie?" He was placed beside the door, and several people were surprised to find that he did not answer to the name of Jacquot, for all parrots are called Jacquot. He was compared to a turkey and a log, and this always stabbed Félicité to the heart. And Loulou was strangely obstinate. If you looked at him, he wouldn't speak!

All the same, he was fond of society. On Sunday, when the Rochefeuille girls, Monsieur de Houppeville, and some new acquaintances—Onfroy the chemist, Monsieur Varin, and Captain Mathieu —were playing cards, he used to beat the windows with his wings and fling himself about so furiously that you couldn't hear yourself talk.

It would seem as if Bourais' face struck him as extremely funny. The moment he saw it he began to laugh, and he laughed with all his might. His shrieks rang through the courtyard, and the echo repeated them. The neighbors would come to their windows and laugh too, while Monsieur Bourais, to escape the parrot's eye, would slip along under the wall, hiding his face in his hat, reach the river, and enter by the garden gate. There was no tenderness in the scowls that he darted at that bird.

Loulou had been buffeted by the butcher's boy for daring to stick his head into his basket. Ever since, he had been trying to nip him through his shirt. Fabu threatened to wring his neck, although he was by no means cruel in spite of his tattooed arm and great whiskers. On the contrary, he secretly liked the parrot and in his merry humor even wanted to teach him to swear. Félicité, alarmed by such doings, put the bird in the kitchen. His little chain was removed and he wandered round the house.

When he wanted to come downstairs, he used to lean on each step with his beak, raise his right foot, and then his left. Félicité was afraid such gymnastics made him giddy. He fell ill and could neither talk nor eat any longer. He had a growth under his tongue as birds often have. She cured him by tearing the skin off with her fingernails. One day Monsieur Paul thoughtlessly blew some cigar smoke into his face, and another day when Madame Lormeau was teasing him with the tip of her umbrella, he snapped at the ferrule. At last he got lost.

Félicité had set him down on the grass to get some fresh air and went away for a moment. When she came back, there was no parrot to be seen. First she hunted for him in the shrubbery, on the river bank, and over the roofs, paying no attention to her mistress's cries of "Take care! You've lost your wits!" Then she explored all the gardens in Pont-L'Évêque and stopped everyone who passed by.

"You haven't happened to have seen my parrot by any chance, have you?" She described the parrot to those who did not know him. All at once, she seemed to see something green fluttering behind the mills at the foot of the hill. But there was nothing on the hilltop. A pedlar assured her that he had just come across the parrot in Mère Simon's shop at Saint-Melaine. She hurried there. They had no idea what she meant. At last she came home exhausted, with her slippers in tatters and despair in her soul. As she was sitting beside Madame on the garden seat, telling her the whole story of her adventures, something light dropped on to her shoulder. It was Loulou! What on earth had he been doing? Taking a walk in the neighborhood, perhaps!

She had some trouble in getting over this, or rather she never did get over it. After a chill she had quinsy, and soon afterwards an earache. Three years later she was deaf, and she spoke very loudly, even in church. Although Félicité's sins might have been shouted in every corner of the diocese without dishonoring her or scandalizing anybody, the priest thought it advisable to hear her confession in the sacristy.

Imaginary noises in her head completed her misfortune. Her mistress would often say to her: "Good heavens! how stupid you are!"

And she would reply: "Yes, madame," and look round for something.

Her little circle of ideas grew narrower and narrower. The peal of church bells and the lowing of cattle no longer existed for her. Human beings moved in ghostly silence. Only one sound reached her ears now—the parrot's voice.

Loulou, as if to amuse her, copied the clatter of the turnspit, the shrill cry of a man hawking fish, and the noise of the joiner's saw in the opposite house. Whenever the doorbell rang, he used to mimic Madame Aubin's "Félicité! the door! the door!"

They used to carry on conversations. He would repeat endlessly the three phrases in his repertory, and she would answer in words that were just as disconnected but expressed what lay in her heart. In her isolation, Loulou was almost a son and a lover to her. He would climb up her fingers, nibble at her lips, and cling to her shawl. When she bent her forehead and shook her head gently, as nurses do, the great wings of her bonnet and the wings of the bird fluttered together.

When the clouds gathered and the thunder rumbled, Loulou would shriek, possibly remembering the downpours in his native forests. The streaming rain would drive him absolutely mad. He would flap about wildly, dash up to the ceiling, upset everything, and go out through the window to splash about in the garden. But he would soon come back to perch on one of the andirons, and would hop about drying his feathers, showing his tail and his beak in turn.

One morning in the terrible winter of 1837, she had put him in front of the fire because of the cold. She found him dead in the middle of his cage, head down, with his claws in the bars. No doubt he had died of congestion. But Félicité decided that he had been poisoned with parsley, and though she had no proof of it, she was inclined to suspect Fabu.

She wept so bitterly that her mistress said to her: "Well, then, have the bird stuffed!"

She asked the chemist's advice, for he had always been kind to the parrot. He wrote to Havre, and a man called Fellacher undertook the job. But as parcels sometimes got lost in the mail coach, she decided to take the parrot as far as Honfleur herself.

Along the roadside were leafless apple trees stretching endlessly. The ditches were covered with ice. Dogs barked on the farms, and Félicité, with her hands under her cloak, and her little black wooden shoes and her basket, walked quickly in the middle of the road.

She crossed the forest, passed Le Haut-Chêne, and came to St. Gatien.

The mail coach rushed at full gallop like a hurricane behind her in a cloud of dust with gathering momentum down the steep hill. Seeing this woman, who did not get out of the way, the driver stood up in front and the postilion shouted, while the four horses which he could not control increased their speed, and the two leaders grazed her just as he threw them to one side with a jerk of the reins. He was wild with fury and, raising his arm as he raced by, he gave her such a lash from her waist to her neck with his long whip that she fell on her back.

The first thing she did, when she recovered consciousness, was to open her basket. Fortunately, Loulou was none the worse. She felt her right cheek bleeding, and when she put her hand on it, it was red. The blood was flowing.

She sat down on a pile of stones and bandaged her face with her handkerchief. Then she ate a crust which she had put in her basket as a precaution, and consoled herself for her wound by gazing at the bird.

When she reached the hilltop of Ecquemauville, she saw the lights of Honfleur twinkling in the night like a host of stars. Far off, the sea stretched dimly. Then she was seized with faintness and paused. Her miserable childhood, the wreck of her first love, her nephew's departure, Virginie's death, all flooding in on her at once like the waves of a making tide, rose in her throat and choked her.

Later she made a point of speaking to the captain of the boat and besought him to take care of the package, but she did not tell him what it contained.

Fellacher kept the parrot a long time. He kept promising to send it back the following week. After six months he announced that a case was on its way, and then she heard no more of it. It seemed as if Loulou would never come back. "They have stolen him," was her thought.

At last he arrived, and he looked magnificent. There he stood, erect, on a branch screwed into a mahogany base, with one claw in the air and his head cocked on one side, biting at a nut, which the ornithologist, with a sense of drama, had gilded.

Félicité shut him up in her room. Very few people were admitted to this place, which held so many religious objects and varied odds and ends that it looked like a chapel turned into a bazaar.

A huge wardrobe interfered with the door as you came in. Opposite the window which overlooked the garden, a little round window offered a glimpse of the courtyard. There was a table beside the folding bed with a jug, two combs, and a cube of blue soap on a chipped plate. The walls were covered with rosaries, medals, several gracious Virgins, and a holy water stoup made out of a coconut. On the chest of drawers, which was covered with a cloth like an altar, were the shell box that Victor had given her, a watering-pot, a toy balloon, copybooks, the illustrated Geography, and a pair of girl's boots. And, tied by its ribbons to the nail of the looking glass, hung the little felt hat. Félicité carried her ritual so far as to keep one of Monsieur's frock coats. All the old rubbish which Madame Aubin had cast aside she carried off to her room. And so there were artificial flowers along the edge of the chest of drawers and a portrait of the Comte d'Artois in the tiny window recess.

Loulou was set on a bracket over the chimneypiece which jutted out into the room. Every morning when she woke, she saw him there in the dawn and remembered old times and the least details of insignificant acts in a painless and peaceful quietude.

She had intercourse with no one, and lived like one who walks in her sleep. Only the Corpus Christi processions were able to rouse her. Then she would go about begging mats and candlesticks from the neighbors to ornament the altar that was put up in the street.

In church she was always gazing at the Holy Ghost in the window, and noticed that he looked rather like the parrot. The likeness was more remarkable, she thought, on a crude chromo representing the baptism of Our Lord. With his purple wings and emerald body, the dove was the image of Loulou.

She bought the picture and hung it up in place of the Comte d'Artois, so that she could see them both together at a single glance. They were united in her thoughts, and the parrot was consecrated by his connection with the Holy Ghost, which grew more and more vivid and intelligible to her. The Father could not have chosen to express Himself through a dove, for these birds cannot speak. He must have chosen one of Loulou's ancestors. Though Félicité used to look at the picture while she was saying her prayers, now and then her glance turned toward the parrot.

She was anxious to join the Ladies of the Blessed Virgin, but Madame Aubin dissuaded her.

Then a great event loomed up before their eyes—Paul's marriage.

He had been successively a solicitor's clerk, in business, in the Customs, in the Internal Revenue, and had even made an effort to get into the Bureau of Forestry, when, at the age of thirty-six, he was inspired to discover his real vocation—the Registrar's Office. There he had shown such marked talent that an inspector had offered him his daughter's hand and promised him his patronage. Paul, now grown serious, brought the girl to see his mother.

She criticized the ways of Pont-L'Évêque sharply enough, gave herself high and mighty airs, and hurt Félicité's feelings. Madame Aubin was glad when she went away.

A week later news came of Monsieur Bourais' death at an inn in Lower Brittany. The rumor of his suicide was confirmed, and doubts arose about his honesty. Madame Aubin scrutinized his accounts and soon learned the whole story of his misdeeds—embezzled arrears, secret sales of lumber, forged receipts, and so on. Besides all that, he had an illegitimate child and "relations with a person at Dozulé."

These disgraceful facts greatly upset her. In March, 1853, she was seized with a pain in the chest. Her throat seemed to be coated with film, and leeches did not help the difficulty she found in breathing. She died on the ninth evening of her illness.

She was just seventy-two.

She passed as being younger, thanks to the bands of brown hair that framed her pale, pockmarked face. She left few friends to regret her passing, for she had a haughtiness of manner that kept folk off.

But Félicité mourned for her as servants seldom mourn for their mistresses. It upset her notions and seemed to reverse the whole order of things, that Madame should die before her. It was inconceivable and monstrous.

Ten days later the heirs hastily arrived from Besançon. The daughter-in-law ransacked the drawers, chose some pieces of furniture, and sold the remainder. Then they went back to their Registrar's business.

Madame's armchair, her little round table, her foot-warmer, her eight chairs, were all gone. Yellow patches in the middle of the panels showed where the engravings had hung. They had carried off the two little beds and mattresses, and all the relics of Virginie had disappeared from the cupboard. Félicité wandered from floor to floor in a sorrowful daze.

Next day there was a notice on the door, and the chemist shouted in her ear that the house was for sale.

She tottered, and had to sit down. What distressed her most of all was giving up her room, which was so suitable for poor Loulou. She wrapped him in a gaze of anguish as she implored the Holy Ghost, and formed the idolatrous habit of kneeling in front of the parrot whenever she said her prayers. Occasionally the sun shone through the little window of her attic and caught his glass eye, and a great luminous ray would shoot out from it and put her in an ecstasy.

Her mistress left her three hundred and eighty francs a year. The garden kept her in vegetables, and as for clothes, she had enough to last her until the end of her days. She saved candles by going to bed at twilight.

She seldom went out, as she did not like to pass the dealer's shop in which some of the old furniture was exposed for sale. Since her fit of giddiness she dragged one leg and, as her strength was fading, Mère Simon, whose grocery business had come to grief, came every morning to split wood and pump water for her.

Her sight grew feeble. She no longer opened the shutters. Years went by, and the house was neither let nor sold.

Félicité never asked for repairs because she was afraid of eviction. The boards on the roof rotted. Her bolster was damp all one winter. After Easter she spat blood. Then Mère Simon called in a doctor. Félicité wanted to know what was the matter with her. But she was too deaf to hear. The only word which reached her ears was "pneumonia." It was a familiar word to her, and she answered softly: "Ah! like Madame!" thinking it only natural that she should follow her mistress.

The time for the Corpus Christi shrines drew nigh. The first shrine was always at the bottom of the hill, the second in front of the Post Office, and the third halfway up the street. There was some rivalry about the last shrine, and finally the women of the parish chose Madame Aubin's courtyard.

The difficult breathing and fever increased. Félicité was vexed that she could do nothing for the shrine. If only she could put something on it! Then she thought of the parrot. The neighbors protested that it would not be decent, but the curé gave her permission, which delighted her so much that she begged him to accept Loulou, her only treasure, when she died.

From Tuesday till Saturday, the eve of the feast-day, she coughed more often. By evening her face shriveled up, her lips stuck to her gums, and she had attacks of vomiting. At dawn next morning, feeling very low, she sent for the priest.

Three kind women were beside her during the Extreme Unction. Then she said that she must speak to Fabu. He came in his Sunday best, quite ill at ease in the funereal atmosphere.

"Forgive me," she said, making an effort to stretch out her arms, "I thought it was you who had killed him."

What did she mean by such nonsense? She had suspected him of murder—a man like him. He was furious and started to make a row.

"Don't you see," said the women, "that she has lost her senses?"

From time to time Félicité talked with shadows around her bed. The women went away, and Mère Simon had her breakfast. A little later she took Loulou and laid him close to Félicité, saying:

"Come, now, say good-bye to him!"

Loulou was not a corpse, but the worms had devoured him. One of his wings was broken, and the stuffing was coming out of his stomach. But Félicité was blind now. She kissed him on the forehead and held him close against her cheek. Mère Simon took him back from her and placed him on the shrine.

V

The fragrance of summer rose from the meadows, flies were buzzing, the sun made the river shine and heated the slates on the roof. Mère Simon came back into the room and fell asleep softly. She was roused by the sound of church bells. The people were coming out from Vespers. Félicité's delirium subsided. She thought of the procession, and saw it as if she were taking part in it herself.

All the school children, the choir, and the firemen walked on the pavement, while in the middle of the road the verger led the way with his halberd, and the beadle with a large cross. Then came the schoolmaster watching the little boys, and the Sister Superior anxious about the little girls. Three of the most adorable little girls, with curls like angels, were scattering rose petals in the air, the deacon conducted the band with outstretched arms, and two thurifers turned back at every step toward the Blessed Sacrament, which was carried by Monsieur the Curé, wearing his beautiful chasuble, under a canopy of rich red velvet held up by the four churchwardens. A crowd of people surged behind between the white draperies covering the walls of the houses, and they reached the bottom of the hill.

A cold sweat moistened Félicité's temples. Mère Simon sponged them with a piece of linen, saying to herself that one day she would have to go the same road.

The roar of the crowd increased, was very loud for a moment, and then died away.

A fusillade shook the window. It was the postilions saluting the monstrance. Félicité turned her eyes round and said as loud as she could: "Does he look well?" The parrot was on her mind.

Her agony began.

The death rattle became faster and faster and made her sides heave. Bubbles of foam came at the corners of her mouth, and her whole body trembled.

Soon the booming of the ophicleides, the high voices of the children, and the deep voices of the men could be distinguished. Now and then all was silent, and the tread of feet, deadened by the flowers on which they trampled, sounded like a flock drifting across grass.

The clergy appeared in the courtyard. Mère Simon climbed up on a chair to reach the attic window, and so looked down on the shrine. Green garlands hung over it, and it was adorned with a flounce of English lace. In the middle of it was a small frame with relics in it. There were two orange trees at the corners, and all along stood silver candlesticks and china vases full of sunflowers, lilies, peonies, fox-gloves and tufts of hortensia. This blazing mass of color from the altar to the carpet spread over the pavement. Some rare objects caught the eye. There was a silver-gilt sugar bowl with a crown of violets, pendants of Alençon stone sparkled on moss, and two Chinese screens unfolded their landscapes. Loulou was smothered in roses, and showed nothing but his blue forehead, like a bar of lapis lazuli.

The churchwardens, the choir, and the children took their places round the three sides of the courtyard. The priest went slowly up the steps, and placed his great, radiant golden sun upon the lace of the shrine. They all knelt down. There was a great silence. The censers swung slowly to and fro on the full length of their chains.

An azure vapor rose and entered Félicité's room. It came to her nostrils. She inhaled it sensuously, mystically. She closed her eyes. Her lips smiled. Her heartbeats dwindled one by one, more fleeting and soft each moment, as a fountain sinks, an echo vanishes. When she sighed her last breath, she thought she saw an opening in Heaven, and a gigantic parrot fluttering over her head.

James Joyce, who some have said was the greatest writer of our time, used to walk the streets of Dublin trying to capture the feelings of the moment—the "epiphanies" he called it—those moments almost transfixed in time and transmuted by emotion that we never forget. In "Araby" the story of first love is indeed an epiphany.

ARABY

JAMES JOYCE

North Richmond Street, being blind, was a quiet street except at the hour when the Christian Brothers' School set the boys free. An uninhabited house of two storeys stood at the blind end, detached from its neighbors in a square ground. The other houses of the street, conscious of decent lives within them, gazed at one another with brown imperturbable faces.

The former tenant of our house, a priest, had died in the back drawing-room. Air, musty from having been long enclosed, hung in all the rooms, and the waste room behind the kitchen was littered with old useless papers. Among these I found a few paper-covered books, the pages of which were curled and damp: *The Abbot*, by Walter Scott, *The Devout Communicant* and *The Memoirs of Vidocq*. I liked the last best because its leaves were yellow. The wild garden behind the house contained a central apple-tree and a few straggling bushes under one of which I found the late tenant's rusty bicycle-pump. He had been a very charitable priest; in his will he had left all his money to institutions and the furniture of his house to his sister.

When the short days of winter came dusk fell before

we had well eaten our dinners. When we met in the street the houses had grown somber. The space of sky above us was the color of ever-changing violet and towards it the lamps of the street lifted their feeble lanterns. The cold air stung us and we played till our bodies glowed. Our shouts echoed in the silent street. The career of our play brought us through the dark muddy lanes behind the houses where we ran the gantlet of the rough tribes from the cottages, to the back doors of the dark dripping gardens where odors arose from the ashpits, to the dark odorous stables where a coachman smoothed and combed the horse or shook music from the buckled harness. When we returned to the street light from the kitchen windows had filled the areas. If my uncle was seen turning the corner we hid in the shadow until we had seen him safely housed. Or if Mangan's sister came out on the doorstep to call her brother in to his tea we watched her from our shadow peer up and down the street. We waited to see whether she would remain or go in and, if she remained, we left our shadow and walked up to Mangan's steps resignedly. She was waiting for us, her figure defined by the light from the half-opened door. Her brother always teased her before he obeyed and I stood by the railings looking at her. Her dress swung as she moved her body and the soft rope of her hair tossed from side to side.

Every morning I lay on the floor in the front parlor watching her door. The blind was pulled down to within an inch of the sash so that I could not be seen. When she came out on the doorstep my heart leaped. I ran to the hall, seized my books and followed her. I kept her brown figure always in my eye and, when we came near the point at which our ways diverged, I quickened my pace and passed her. This happened morning after morning. I had never spoken to her, except for a few casual words, and yet her name was like a summons to all my foolish blood.

Her image accompanied me even in places the most hostile to romance. On Saturday evenings when my aunt went marketing I had to go to carry some of the parcels. We walked through the flaring streets, jostled by drunken men and bargaining women, amid the curses of laborers, the shrill litanies of shop-boys who stood on guard by the barrels of pigs' cheeks, the nasal chanting of street-singers, who sang a *come-all-you* about O'Donovan Rossa, or a ballad about the troubles in our native land. These noises converged in a single sensation of life for me: I imagined that I bore my chalice safely through a throng of foes. Her name sprang to my lips at moments in strange

prayers and praises which I myself did not understand. My eyes were often full of tears (I could not tell why) and at times a flood from my heart seemed to pour itself out into my bosom. I thought little of the future. I did not know whether I would ever speak to her or not or, if I spoke to her, how I could tell her of my confused adoration. But my body was like a harp and her words and gestures were like fingers running upon the wires.

One evening I went into the back drawing-room in which the priest had died. It was a dark rainy evening and there was no sound in the house. Through one of the broken panes I heard the rain impinge upon the earth, the fine incessant needles of water playing in the sodden beds. Some distant lamp or lighted window gleamed below me. I was thankful that I could see so little. All my senses seemed to desire to veil themselves and, feeling that I was about to slip from them, I pressed the palms of my hands together until they trembled, murmuring: O love! O love! many times.

At last she spoke to me. When she addressed the first words to me I was so confused that I did not know what to answer. She asked me was I going to *Araby*. I forget whether I answered yes or no. It would be a splendid bazaar, she said; she would love to go.

—And why can't you? I asked.

While she spoke she turned a silver bracelet round and round her wrist. She could not go, she said, because there would be a retreat that week in her convent. Her brother and two other boys were fighting for their caps and I was alone at the railings. She held one of the spikes, bowing her head towards me. The light from the lamp opposite our door caught the white curve of her neck, lit up her hair that rested there and, falling, lit up the hand upon the railing. It fell over one side of her dress and caught the white border of a petticoat, just visible as she stood at ease.

—It's well for you, she said.

—If I go, I said, I will bring you something.

What innumerable follies laid waste my waking and sleeping thoughts after that evening! I wished to annihilate the tedious intervening days. I chafed against the work of school. At night in my bedroom and by day in the classroom her image came between me and the page I strove to read. The syllables of the word *Araby* were called to me through the silence in which my soul luxuriated and cast an Eastern enchantment over me. I asked for leave to go to the bazaar on Saturday night. My aunt was surprised and hoped it was not some Freemason affair. I answered few questions in class. I watched my master's face pass from amiability to sternness; he hoped I was not beginning to idle. I could not call my wandering thoughts together. I had hardly any patience with the serious work of life which, now that it stood between me and my desire, seemed to me child's play, ugly monotonous child's play.

On Saturday morning I reminded my uncle that I wished to go to the bazaar in the evening. He was fussing at the hallstand, looking for the hat-brush, and answered me curtly:

—Yes, boy, I know.

As he was in the hall I could not go into the front parlor and lie at the window. I left the house in bad humor and walked slowly towards the school. The air was pitilessly raw and already my heart misgave me.

When I came home to dinner my uncle had not yet been home. Still it was early. I sat staring at the clock for some time and, when its ticking began to irritate me, I left the room. I mounted the staircase and gained the upper part of the house. The high cold empty gloomy rooms liberated me and I went from room to room singing. From the front window I saw my companions playing below in the street. Their cries reached me weakened and indistinct and, leaning my forehead against the cool glass, I looked over at the dark house where she lived. I may have stood there for an hour, seeing nothing but the brown-clad figure cast by my imagination, touched discreetly by the lamplight at the curved neck, at the hand upon the railings and at the border below the dress.

When I came downstairs again I found Mrs. Mercer sitting at the fire. She was an old garrulous woman, a pawnbroker's widow, who collected used stamps for some pious purpose. I had to endure the gossip of the tea-table. The meal was prolonged beyond an hour and still my uncle did not come. Mrs. Mercer stood up to go: she was sorry she couldn't wait any longer, but it was after eight o'clock and she did not like to be out late, as the night air was bad for her. When she had gone I began to walk up and down the room, clenching my fists. My aunt said:

—I'm afraid you may put off your bazaar for this night of Our Lord.

At nine o'clock I heard my uncle's latchkey in the halldoor. I heard him talking to himself and heard the hallstand rocking when it had received the weight of his overcoat. I could interpret these signs. When he was midway through his dinner I asked him to give me the money to go to the bazaar. He had forgotten.

—The people are in bed and after their first sleep now, he said.

I did not smile. My aunt said to him energetically:

—Can't you give him the money and let him go? You've kept him late enough as it is.

My uncle said he was very sorry he had forgotten. He said he believed in the old saying: *All work and no play makes Jack a dull boy.* He asked me where I was going and, when I had told him a second time he asked me did I know *The Arab's Farewell to His Steed.* When I left the kitchen he was about to recite the opening lines of the piece to my aunt.

I held a florin tightly in my hand as I strode down Buckingham Street towards the station. The sight of the streets thronged with buyers and glaring with gas recalled to me the purpose of my journey. I took my seat in a third-class carriage of a deserted train. After an intolerable delay the train moved out of the station slowly. It crept onward among ruinous houses and over the twinkling river. At Westland Row Station a crowd of people pressed to the carriage doors;

but the porters moved them back, saying that it was a special train for the bazaar. I remained alone in the bare carriage. In a few minutes the train drew up beside an improvised wooden platform. I passed out on to the road and saw by the lighted dial of a clock that it was ten minutes to ten. In front of me was a large building which displayed the magical name.

I could not find any sixpenny entrance and, fearing that the bazaar would be closed, I passed in quickly through a turnstile, handing a shilling to a weary-looking man. I found myself in a big hall girdled at half its height by a gallery. Nearly all the stalls were closed and the greater part of the hall was in darkness. I recognized a silence like that which pervades a church after a service. I walked into the center of the bazaar timidly. A few people were gathered about the stalls which were still open. Before a curtain, over which the words *Café Chantant* were written in colored lamps, two men were counting money on a salver. I listened to the fall of the coins.

Remembering with difficulty why I had come I went over to one of the stalls and examined porcelain vases and flowered tea-sets. At the door of the stall a young lady was talking and laughing with two young gentlemen. I remarked their English accents and listened vaguely to their conversation.

—O, I never said such a thing!

—O, but you did!

—O, but I didn't!

—Didn't she say that?

—Yes. I heard her.

—O, there's a . . . fib!

Observing me the young lady came over and asked me did I wish to buy anything. The tone of her voice was not encouraging; she seemed to have spoken to me out of a sense of duty. I looked humbly at the great jars that stood like eastern guards at either side of the dark entrance to the stall and murmured:

—No, thank you.

The young lady changed the position of one of the vases and went back to the two young men. They began to talk of the same subject. Once or twice the young lady glanced at me over her shoulder.

I lingered before her stall, though I knew my stay was useless to make my interest in her wares seem the more real. Then I turned away slowly and walked down the middle of the bazaar. I allowed the two pennies to fall against the sixpence in my pocket. I heard a voice call from one end of the gallery that the light was out. The upper part of the hall was now completely dark.

Gazing up into the darkness I saw myself as a creature driven and derided by vanity; and my eyes burned with anguish and anger.

*James Joyce used words with the beauty of a magician.
He made each one count. Each one was a glossy new
coin—so much so that if he could not find the word he
wanted, he often coined a new one. But the opposite of
the new is the cliché, and one of the greatest makers
of clichés is our delightful American humorist Frank
Sullivan. He has been collecting clichés describing almost every area of human feeling, but none more success-
fully than the hackneyed words of love.*

THE CLICHÉ EXPERT
TESTIFIES ON LOVE

FRANK SULLIVAN

Q: Mr. Arbuthnot, as an expert in the use of the cliché, are
you prepared to testify here today regarding its application in topics of sex, love, matrimony, and so on?

A: I am.

Q: Very good. Now, Mr. Arbuthnot, what's love?

A: Love is blind.

Q: Good. What does love do?

A: Love makes the world go round.

Q: Whom does a young man fall in love with?

A: With the Only Girl in the World.

Q: Whom does a young woman fall in love with?

A: With the Only Boy in the World.

Q: When do they fall in love?

A: At first sight.

Q: How?

A: Madly.

Q: They are then said to be?

A: Victims of Cupid's darts.

Q: And he?

A: Whispers sweet nothings in her ear.

Q: Who loves a lover?

A: All the world loves a lover.

Q: Describe the Only Girl in the World.

A: Her eyes are like stars. Her teeth are like pearls. Her lips are ruby. Her cheek is damask, and her form divine.

Q: Haven't you forgotten something?

A: Eyes, teeth, lips, cheek, form—no, sir, I don't think so.

Q: Her hair?

A: Oh, certainly. How stupid of me. She has hair like spun gold.

Q: Very good, Mr. Arbuthnot. Now will you describe the Only Man?

A: He is a blond Viking, a he-man, and a square shooter who plays the game. There is something fine about him that rings true, and he has kept himself pure and clean so that when he meets the girl of his choice, the future mother of his children, he can look her in the eye.

Q: How?

A: Without flinching.

Q: Are all the Only Men blond Vikings?

A: Oh, no. Some of them are dark, handsome chaps who have sown their wild oats. This sort of Only Man has a way with a maid, and there is a devil in his eye. But he is not a cad; he would not play fast and loose with an Only Girl's affections. He has a heart of gold. He is a diamond in the rough. He tells the Only Girl frankly about his Past. She understands—and forgives.

Q: And marries him?

A: And marries him.

Q: Why?

A: To reform him.

Q: Does she reform him?

A: Seldom.

Q: Seldom what?

A: Seldom, if ever.

Q: Now, Mr. Arbuthnot, when the Only Man falls in love, madly, with the Only Girl, what does he do?

A: He walks on air.

Q: Yes, I know, but what does he do? I mean, what is it he pops?

A: Oh, excuse me. The question, of course.

Q: Then what do they plight?

A: Their troth.

Q: What happens after that?

A: They get married.

Q: What is marriage?

A: Marriage is a lottery.

Q: Where are marriages made?

A: Marriages are made in heaven.

Q: What does the bride do at the wedding?

A: She blushes.

Q: What does the groom do?

A: Forgets the ring.

Q: After the marriage, what?

A: The honeymoon.

Q: Then what?

A: She has a little secret.

Q: What is it?

A: She is knitting a tiny garment.

Q: What happens after that?

A: Oh, they settle down and raise a family and live happily ever afterward, unless—

Q: Unless what?

A: Unless he is a fool for a pretty face.

Q: And if he is?

A: Then they come to the parting of the ways.

Q: Mr. Arbuthnot, thank you very much.

A: But I'm not through yet, Mr. Untermyer.

Q: No?

A: Oh, no. There is another side to sex.

Q: There is? What side?

A: The seamy side. There are, you know, men who are wolves in sheep's clothing and there are, alas, lovely women who stoop to folly.

Q: My goodness! Describe these men you speak of, please.

A: They are snakes in the grass who do not place woman upon a pedestal. They are cads who kiss and tell, who trifle with a girl's affections and betray her innocent trust. They are cynics who think that a woman is only a woman, but a good cigar is a smoke. Their mottoes are "Love 'em and leave 'em" and "Catch 'em young, treat 'em rough, tell 'em nothing." These cads speak of "the light that lies in woman's eyes, and lies—and lies—and lies." In olden days they wore black, curling mustachios, which they twirled, and they invited innocent Gibson girls to midnight suppers, with champagne, at their bachelor apartments, and said, "Little girl, why do you fear me?" Nowadays they have black, patent-leather hair, and roadsters, and they drive up to the curb and say, "Girlie, can I give you a lift?" They are fiends in human form, who would rob a woman of her most priceless possession.

Q: What is that?

A: Her honor.

Q: How do they rob her?

A: By making improper advances.

Q: What does a woman do when a snake in the grass tries to rob her of her honor?

A: She defends her honor.

Q: How?

A: By repulsing his advances and scorning his embraces.

Q: How does she do that?

A: By saying, "Sir, I believe you forget yourself," or "Please take your arm away," or "I'll kindly thank you to remember I'm a lady," or "Let's not spoil it all."

Q: Suppose she doesn't say any of those things?

A: In that case, she takes the first false step.

Q: Where does the first false step take her?

A: Down the primrose path.

Q: What's the primrose path?

A: It's the easiest way.

Q: Where does it lead?

A: To a life of shame.

Q: What is a life of shame?

A: A life of shame is a fate worse than death.

Q: Now, after lovely woman has stooped to folly, what does she do to the gay Lothario who has robbed her of her most priceless possession?

A: She devotes the best years of her life to him.

Q: Then what does he do?

A: He casts her off.

Q: How?

A: Like an old shoe.

Q: Then what does she do?

A: She goes to their love nest, then everything goes black before her, her mind becomes a blank, she pulls a revolver, and gives the fiend in human form something to remember her by.

Q: That is called?

A: Avenging her honor.

Q: What is it no jury will do in such a case?

A: No jury will convict.

Q: Mr. Arbuthnot, your explanation of the correct application of the cliché in these matters has been most instructive, and I know that all of us cliché-users here will know exactly how to respond hereafter when, during a conversation, sex—when sex—when—ah—

A: I think what you want to say is "When sex rears its ugly head," isn't it?

Q: Thank you, Mr. Arbuthnot. Thank you very much.

A: Thank *you*, Mr. Untermyer.

Each person reacts differently to love. Although everyone wants to be loved, there are some people who are incapable of loving another human being realistically. Instead, they pour most of their love into creating a "work of love." In this little-known story, "The Oval Portrait," Edgar Allan Poe relates the tragic tale of a painter so immersed in painting his loved one that he is unaware she is dying before his eyes.

THE OVAL PORTRAIT

EDGAR ALLAN POE

The château into which my valet had ventured to make forcible entrance, rather than permit me, in my desperately wounded condition, to pass a night in the open air, was one of those piles of commingled gloom and grandeur which have so long frowned among the Apennines, not less in fact than in the fancy of Mrs Radcliffe. To all appearance it had been temporarily and very lately abandoned. We established ourselves in one of the smallest and least sumptuously furnished apartments. It lay in a remote turret of the building. Its decorations were rich, yet tattered and antique. Its walls were hung with tapestry and bedecked with manifold and multiform armorial trophies, together with an unusually great number of very spirited modern paintings in frames of rich golden arabesque. In these paintings, which depended from the walls not only in their main surfaces, but in very many nooks which the bizarre architecture of the château rendered necessary—in these paintings my incipient delirium, perhaps, had caused me to take deep interest; so that I bade Pedro to close the heavy shutters of the room

—since it was already night—to light the tongues of a tall candelabrum which stood by the head of my bed, and to throw open far and wide the fringed curtains of black velvet which enveloped the bed itself. I wished all this done that I might resign myself, if not to sleep, at least alternately to the contemplation of these pictures, and the perusal of a small volume which had been found upon the pillow, and which purported to criticize and describe them.

Long, long I read—and devoutly, devoutly I gazed. Rapidly and gloriously the hours flew by and the deep midnight came. The position of the candelabrum displeased me, and outreaching my hand with difficulty, rather than disturb my slumbering valet, I placed it so as to throw its rays more fully upon the book.

But the action produced an effect altogether unanticipated. The rays of the numerous candles (for there were many) now fell within a niche of the room which had hitherto been thrown into deep shade by one of the bedposts. I thus saw in vivid light a picture all unnoticed before. It was the portrait of a young girl just ripening into womanhood. I glanced at the painting hurriedly, and then closed my eyes. Why I did this was not at first apparent even to my own perception. But while my lids remained thus shut, I ran over in mind my reason for so shutting them. It was an impulsive movement to gain time for thought—to make sure that my vision had not deceived me —to calm and subdue my fancy for a more sober and more certain gaze. In a very few moments I again looked fixedly at the painting.

That I now saw aright I could not and would not doubt; for the first flashing of the candles upon that canvas had seemed to dissipate the dreamy stupor which was stealing over my senses, and to startle me at once into waking life.

The portrait, I have already said, was that of a young girl. It was a mere head and shoulders, done in what is technically termed a *vignette* manner; much in the style of the favorite heads of Sully. The arms, the bosom, and even the ends of the radiant hair melted imperceptibly into the vague yet deep shadow which formed the background of the whole. The frame was oval, richly gilded and filigreed in *Moresque*. As a thing of art nothing could be more admirable than the painting itself. But it could have been neither the execution of the work, nor the immortal beauty of the countenance, which had so suddenly and so vehemently moved me. Least of all, could it have been that my fancy, shaken from its half slumber, had mistaken the head for that of a living person. I saw at once that the peculiarities of the design, of the *vignetting*, and of the frame, must have instantly dispelled such idea—must have prevented even its momentary entertainment. Thinking earnestly upon these points, I remained, for an hour perhaps, half sitting, half reclining, with my vision riveted upon the portrait. At length, satisfied with the true secret of its effect, I fell back within the bed. I had found the spell of the picture in an absolute *lifelikeliness* of expression, which, at first startling, finally confounded, subdued, and appalled me. With deep and reverent awe I replaced the candelabrum in its former position. The cause of my deep agitation being thus shut from view, I sought eagerly the volume which discussed the paintings and their histories. Turning to the number which designated the oval portrait, I there read the vague and quaint words which follow:

"She was a maiden of rarest beauty, and not more lovely than full of glee. And evil was the hour when she saw, and loved, and wedded the painter. He, passionate, studious, austere, and having already a bride in his Art: she a maiden of rarest beauty, and not more lovely than full of glee; all light and smiles, and frolicsome as the young fawn; loving and cherishing all things; hating only the Art which was her rival; dreading only the pallet and brushes and other untoward instruments which deprived her of the countenance of her lover. It was thus a terrible thing for this lady to hear the painter speak of his desire to portray even his young bride. But she was humble and obedient, and sat meekly for many weeks in the dark high turret-chamber where the light dripped upon the pale canvas only from overhead. But he, the painter, took glory in his work, which went on from hour to hour, and from day to day. And he was a passionate, and wild, and moody man, who became lost in reveries; so that he *would* not see that the light which fell so ghastly in that lone turret withered the health and the spirits of his bride, who pined visibly to all but him. Yet she smiled on and still on, uncomplainingly, because she saw that the painter (who had high renown) took a fervid and burning pleasure in his task, and wrought day and night to depict her who so loved him, yet who grew daily more dispirited and weak. And in sooth some who beheld the portrait spoke of its resemblance in low words, as of a mighty marvel, and a proof not less of the power of the painter than of his deep love for her whom he depicted so surpassingly well. But at length, as the labor drew nearer to its conclusion, there were admitted none into the turret; for the painter had grown wild with the ardor of his work, and turned his eyes from the canvas rarely, even to regard the countenance of his wife. And he *would* not see that the tints which he spread on the canvas were drawn from the cheeks of her who sat beside him. And when many weeks had passed, and but little remained to do, save one brush upon the mouth and one tint upon the eye, the spirit of the lady again flickered up as the flame within the socket of the lamp. And then the brush was given, and then the tint was placed; and, for one moment, the painter stood entranced before the work which he had wrought; but in the next, while he yet gazed, he grew tremulous and very pallid, and aghast, and crying with a loud voice, 'This is indeed *Life itself!*' turned suddenly to regard his beloved:—*She was dead!*"

"I have wanted to know what there is to know," Sean O'Faolain has written, "to possess life and be its master. The moment I found out that nobody knows, I had exposed myself to myself, I would never do it again. The shame of it was too much to bear. Like everybody else, I would pretend for the rest of my life. I would compound; I would invent—poetry, religion, common sense, kindness, good cheer, the sigh, the laugh, the shrug— everything that saves us from having to admit that beauty and goodness exist here only for as long as we create and nourish them by the force of our dreams; that there is nothing outside ourselves apart from our imaginings."

These intense words of Sean O'Faolain's describe a boy's experience in a disappointment in love. Throughout our lives few of our dreams will be fulfilled, but perhaps with love more than with anything else, we are often likely to dream more than we act, to imagine more than we experience, to want more than is ever given. Some even follow love's young dream so assiduously that they lose track of the beauty of today's reality.

LOVE'S YOUNG DREAM

SEAN O'FAOLAIN

I don't remember my first visits to that part of Ireland, although my father often told me that since I was four years old I used to be sent there every year, sometimes twice a year. He was a ship's captain, my mother had died when I was three, and whenever he was at sea and no nearer relative could have me I would be sent off for safekeeping to the County Kildare.

The first visit I remember at all clearly was when I was ten, to my Uncle Gerry's farm near the town of Newbridge. I remember it because it was during this visit that Noreen Coogan pushed me into the Liffey. (Noreen was the only child of my aunt's servant, Nancy Coogan; that year she must have been about twelve or thirteen.) I can still see myself standing dripping on the bank, crying miserably, and my uncle assuring me that Noreen—"the bold, bad slut!"— would be kept far away from me for the rest of the holidays; at which I began to wail more loudly than before, and he, guessing the state of my heart, began to laugh so loudly at me that I fairly bawled.

I have no clear image of what Noreen looked like at the time, or, indeed, at any later time. All I have clearly in my memory is a vision of a cloud of corn-fair hair, and large eyes, and for some reason or other, I always want to say that she had a complexion like sweet peas. Perhaps I saw her at some time with a big bunch of cream-and-pink sweet peas in her arms or standing in the garden with a lot of sweet peas in it and felt that the delicate blend of colors and scents was a perfect setting for her. But all my memories of those early visits are like that—both actual and dim, like the haze of heat that used to soften the soft surfaces of the far meadows across the river or the swarms of gnats rising and sinking hazily over the reeds below the bridge. I am sure I saw my uncle's stableman, Marky Fenelon, quite clearly, a little man with a face all composed of marbles, from his blackberry eyes to his crumpled chin or his tightly wound ears, but when I heard that he was a Palatine, I never asked what it meant and did not care.

I was very clearly aware of Nancy Coogan, big, bustling, bosomy, bare-armed, with a laugh like a thunderclap, but when I gathered somehow that she and Marky were courting and would marry someday, all that this "someday" meant to me was never. Is all childhood made up of facts of nature that are accepted beyond questioning? Perhaps mine was prolonged. When I was thirteen I was so vague as to what marrying meant that I much amused Nancy by asking her why some ladies are called Miss and some Mrs. She laughed and said the misses are the ones that miss, which I thought very clever indeed.

One reason why Noreen and my clearer memories of Newbridge go together is that she focused my holidays for me. She was their one clear center from which everything went outward and to which everything returned. For after I was ten she became as certain and

fixed a part of those visits as my first sight of the elongated Main Street of Newbridge, with the walls of the cavalry barracks all along one side of it and the sutlers' shops all along the other, or the peaceful sound of the gun wagons jingling along the dusty roads—they suddenly sounded less peaceful the year the Great War broke out—or the happy moment of arrival at the farm when I would run to meet Marky Fenelon in the wide, cobbled yard and at once hand him his ritual present of a pound of sailor's twist, bought for him by my father, or—one of the happiest moments of all—when I would run into the flagged kitchen to Nancy with her ritual present, which was always a lacy blouse bought in some port like Gibraltar, or Naples, or Genoa. At the sight of me, she would let out a welcoming roar of laughter, squash me up against her great, soft, bulging bosom, give me a smacking kiss and lift me, laughing and shrieking, high in the air until my head nearly touched the ceiling.

It was the year in which I asked my famous question about the difference between misses and missises that I also felt the first faintest, least stir of questioning interest in Nancy's and Marky's marathon courtship. It was really no more than an idle question and I had only a small interest in the answer. That day she was making soda bread on the kitchen table and I was sitting up on the end of the table watching her knead and pound the dough.

"Nancy!" I said pertly. "What's up with you at all that you're not marrying Marky? When are you going to marry him? Marry him tomorrow, Nancy! Go on! Will you marry him tomorrow?"

She let out one of her wild laughs and began to scrape the dough from her fingers and fling the scrapings down on the kneading board, saying gaily with each flap of her hands, "This year! Next year! Sometime! Never!"

"Is it the way, Nancy, that you're not in love with Marky?"

This time her laughter was a quarry blast. "God love you, you poor child, that has nothing at all to do with it! It's just that he doesn't like having Noreen living with us. Now, go off and play with the cat," she added crossly, and began to carve a deep cross into the flattened loaf. But at once I wanted to stab her cake myself and began begging her for the knife. Anyway, this talk about Noreen and Marky merely meant what I had always known—that they would all be always there waiting for me at the start of every holiday.

One reason why I know I was thirteen that year was that the next time I went to stay with Uncle Gerry I was fifteen, and this I know because I very soon found out that those two extra years made a great difference to all of us. What made the difference was that in my fourteenth year I spent a long summer spell with my three Feehan cousins, some seven or eight miles away from the Newbridge farm over on the plain of the Curragh. There I had another uncle, Ken Feehan, who had some sort of job in connection with the racecourse.

The Curragh is famous for two things: its racecourse on one side of the plain and on the other the extended military settlement which seems to outline the farthest edge of green with the long faint stroke of a red pencil. This settlement is still known as The Camp, long after its original tent canvas has been transformed into barrack squares in red brick, wooden huts, tin chapels and tin shops. Sheltering belts of stunted firs have now been planted along its entire length to protect it from the bitter winds blowing down from the mountains whose slow drum-roll closes the view to the southeast. From the door of my Uncle Ken's house, a long, whitewashed cottage near the grandstand, we looked southeast at the far-off red pencil line across a rolling expanse of short grass, empty except for a few cropping sheep, scattered tufts of furze and an occasional car slowly beetling along the road that crosses the Curragh from Newbridge to the south.

It was an empty place for three girls to live in. It is also to the point that the plain is of great age. The couple of roads that cross it are the old woolpack roads into Danish Dublin. The distant finger of the round tower of Kildare, to the west, was gray with age in the twelfth century. There was a racecourse here some two thousand years ago. Weapons of the Stone Age have been dug up in various parts of the plain.

I like to think of this silent antiquity whenever I think of Philly, the eldest of my three cousins, standing at night at the door of the cottage—it is the way I always remember her now—staring across the plain at the only thing there that really interested her, the remote lights of the military camp. Whether The Camp had always excited her or not I do not know, but when I first met her, after the outbreak of the war, everything about it did—the news of departing or arriving regiments, the crackle of gunfire from the pits, the distant flash of a heliograph on bright days, the faint sound of regimental bands borne to us on the southeasterly wind. Standing there at the cottage door she would talk endlessly of all the handsome and brave poor boys fighting and falling at that very moment on the plains of Flanders. She inferred the whole war from the flash of a mirror, the short rattle of rifle fire, the faint beating of drums, a wavering bugle call. She was eighteen.

I have no doubts at all about Philly's looks. She was not pretty, but she was not plain. I grant that her nose was a bit peaky, her teeth slightly prominent, her figure almost skinny, but she had two lively brown eyes, like an Italian girl, and her dark, shining hair was combed slick back from her prominent profile with the effect of a figurehead on a ship's prow. Her lower lip was always moistened by her upper teeth, her hands were nervous, her laughter on a hair-trigger, her moods unpredictable and turning as rapidly as a trout in a stream, and she was a magnificent liar. This, I see, is as much an implication of her nature as a description of her appearance, but it is how she struck everybody who met her—an unflattering impression dispelled completely in one second.

That I have no wish to do more than mention her two sisters, Moll and Una, may suggest further the force of her personality. She overshadowed them completely, although both of them were capable and pleasing girls. She bullied Moll all the time and she forced all the housework on her simply by refusing to do her own share of it. Poor Moll, a soft, rotund, pouting girl, was no match for her and never did anything in self-defense except complain feebly, weep a little, then laugh despairingly and go on cheerfully with her double chores. Philly did not need to bully Una, a gentle, fair-flaxen girl of about my own age—she was too young and delicate for bullying, cycled into Newbridge every day to school at the local convent, and studied endlessly when at home. I think she had realized very early that the cottage was a place to get out of as quickly as possible.

I liked the three of them, but I far preferred Philly. She was more fun, and I liked the streak of boyish devilment in her that always made her ready for any escapade. I suppose she suffered me as being better company than none, and I also suppose that the main thing in my favor was that, although a child to her eyes, I was at least male. This is not merely an unkind remark. Her reputation had preceded my meeting with her. Back in Newbridge the general attitude to her was that she was a foolish virgin. At the mention of her name, my Uncle Gerry had just phewed out a long, contemptuously good-humored breath.

My aunt laughed at her. Once she made the witty and shrewd remark, "That girl has far too many beaus to her string."

Nancy sniffed mockingly, "That featherhead!" But she may have jealously compared her to her own adored Noreen.

Marky said, "Aha! A bold lassie!"

Noreen was, by turns, respectfully and scornfully silent, but, young as I was, I smelled envy.

As for her own sisters, they admired her and feared her and did not love her. They assured me privately that her list of boys was as long as my arm. ("Boys" was a popular word at that time—the "boys" at the front; our "boys" in Flanders; and so on.) Their list included a rich trainer from the County Meath; a subaltern from The Camp; a jockey; a farmer from behind Kildare; a publican's son in Newbridge; a young lawyer from Dublin; even a stableboy from the stables of one of the wealthy trainers, who, then as now, lived in half-timbered houses all around the edge of the plain behind white rails and clipped privet hedges.

I gathered that all of these beaus were met on race days in the Enclosure, on the Members' stand, in the Restaurant—to all of which places, because of her father, she had complete access. There was more than a suggestion that she met her admirers on varying terms, playing whatever role pleased her fancy and suited their class. In those days when everybody of her own class swarmed on the open plain outside the rails and only the comparatively few paid to go inside them, the daughter of an employee of the Turf Club would have had to present herself very well indeed to be accepted by a lieutenant, a lawyer or a trainer.

I was torn this way and that by her. In loyalty to Newbridge I knew I should think her a figure of fun, and I could see that she was a little bully and a shrew, but she would sweep me off my feet whenever she started to talk about that Camp whose lights flickered at night across the empty plain. She turned it into a magic doorway to the world. In Newbridge, everything, I have said, had been actual but hazy. When she talked to me about the real world I heard Life begin to paw its stable floor.

"Listen, lad! When you grow up, take the King's shilling! Be a soldier! See the world!" And then, with her wide, wild, white-toothed laugh, "Or, if it has to be, see the next world!"

I shall never have a dim or hazy notion of Philly Feehan as long as I remember the baking day when the four of us stood at the door of the cottage, the racecourse behind us as empty as a ballroom on the morning after a dance, the plain before us as empty as a bed at noon, and watched a small, slow cloud of dust move at marching pace from The Camp toward the railway station at Kildare, and heard the clear rattle of the parting snare drums.

She shocked us all by suddenly crying out with passion, her brown eyes fixed on the little creeping dust cloud, her face pale under her shiny, black coif, "I wish to God I was a hussar!"

She taught me how to smoke. I drank my first beer with her in a hotel bar across the plain in Kilcullen. She gave me my first lesson in dancing. Looking back at her now, I see why her type of girl was the ideal of the soldiers of the 1914 war. They had been made to think of themselves as "boys." Their ideal woman was the young virgin, still with her hair down, the flapper, a blend of devilment and innocence—their most highly desired antithesis to rain-filled trenches, mud above their puttees and shells whining over their heads all day long.

So, you can guess why my next visit to Newbridge was different to any that went before. I was now turned fifteen. Noreen was eighteen. The others were beyond the years. They behaved to me as always, but I was not the same with them. I had become wary. It began the minute I arrived. When my Uncle Gerry drove the old tub trap into the cobbled yard through the big tarred gates, opened by Marky immediately he heard the familiar clop of the pony coming along the road, I handed the ritual pound of twist over the side to Marky, alighted, asked the usual questions, said, "I suppose ye're not married yet?" and then, as if on an other thought, "Oh, and how's our little Noreen these days?"

She must have done something to annoy him specially that day, because he said grimly and shortly, "Oh, very well, I believe! A bit rakish, now and again! But very well. In the best of health."

I was alert at once.

"In what way rakish, Marky?" I laughed innocently.

"Ah!" He shook his head upward. If he had been a horse I would have heard the rattle of the bit and seen the yellow teeth. "I suppose it might be through having no father to keep her in order."

I nodded in sage agreement.

"How long is it now, Marky, since he died?"

He was untackling the pony, detaching the traces from the hames, his face against the pony's neck, but though I could not see him, I knew from his voice that he was not going to pursue the subject.

"Well!" he growled into the pony's neck. "It was all a long time ago. Nancy's inside, expecting you."

He could hardly have said it plainer. I went indoors to her and produced the usual Italian blouse. She hugged me and kissed me, but I was too grown-up now to be lifted to the ceiling, and I hugged her back hard and thought she had fine eyes and was a handsome woman yet.

Finally I said it, "And how's Noreen these days?"

She turned back to the table and gently lifted the white silk blouse and said in a thick, oozy voice, " 'Tis lovely. 'Twill suit Noreen down to the ground."

"But," I protested, "it's for you! My father sent it for you!"

"Tshah! What do I want with finery? I'm gone beyond fineries. But"—smiling fondly and lifting up the blouse again by the points of the shoulders to look it all over—"Noreen will look a masher in that."

No age is at once so insensitive and so sensitive as adolescence. It is one reason why young people are so exasperating to adults. I looked at her with curiosity, oblivious of her maternal devotion, and elegantly leaning against the table I ventured, "Nancy! If you were married, the three of ye would be as happy as three kittens in a basket. And Marky would be a father to Noreen."

She dropped the blouse in a silken heap, gave me a sharp look and flounced to the fireplace.

"Noreen," she said to the range, banging in the damper, "doesn't want him as long as he has me! Anyway, since he won't have both of us, he can have neither of us. Have you seen your aunt yet? She'll be expecting you."

The flick of her skirt frightened me. I did not know what I had touched, but it felt red hot. All I knew was that this prolonged courtship of theirs was going, if not gone, on the rocks.

That first day I did not run down the road in search of Noreen, as I would have done two years before. I walked down to where Coshea's Boreen comes out on River Road and I came on her there, beyond the laundry, leaning over the wall, showing the hollow backs of her knees, chewing a bit of straw, looking across the river at the meadows and the Dublin road beyond them.

I stole up behind her, slipped my arm about her waist and said gaily, "Hello!" She just glanced at me and said, "Do you mind removing your arm?"

"Oho!" Very loftily. "Touch me not, eh?"

I was so mad I could have spat in her eye, but I pretended nothing —I would not give her that much satisfaction. Instead, I started chatting away about what I had been doing since I saw her two summers ago. She kept chewing the straw and looking idly across the river. I do not remember what precisely I said that made her begin to pay heed to me, except that it was my idea of a gentle probe about Marky and her mother, but it made her give me a slow, mocking smile that said, as plainly and scornfully as if she had spoken the actual words of an American phrase that was beginning to be current at the time: "Well, and what do you know?"—meaning that I had surprised her, and that I knew nothing, not only about Marky and her mammy but about everything in general, and that I could just as well stop pumping her and go away and find it all out for myself the way she had done. I expected her to say at any moment, "Hump off, kid!" She conveyed it silently. Women do not talk to small boys.

If I had had any pride I would have walked away from her. But at fifteen years and a couple of months you are so frantic to know all about everything in general that you have no pride, only lots of cunning.

I said, very sadly, "I suppose, Noreen, you think I'm only a kid?"

"How old are you?" she asked, with just a faint touch of sympathy in her voice.

"Going on to sixteen. But everybody," I said bitterly, "talks to me as if I was still ten. Have a fag?"

I flashed out my new mock-silver cigarette case. I observed with satisfaction the way she glanced down the road toward the bridge and the end of Main Street, and then turned and leaned her back on the wall and glanced idly up Cat Lane before saying, in a bored voice, "I suppose, really, I might as well."

I noted that she smoked the way all girls smoke who are not smokers, continually corking and uncorking her mouth.

I kept up the role of downtrodden youth. " 'Tis well for you, Noreen. I wish I was eighteen. You can do what you like. My da would leather me if he caught me smoking. The way he talks about stamina and muscles, you'd think he wants me to be another Jack Dempsey. Would Nancy be cross with you?"

"I'd like to see her!" she boasted.

"I know a girl in Dublin who smokes thirty a day."

This was too much for her. "You know nothing about girls!"

"Oho! We grow up fast in Dublin!"

I blew smoke down my nose and turned around and leaned over the river wall and spat in the river. She also turned and blew smoke down her nose and spat in the river. For a moment or two she looked across at the golden meadows. Then, "I'm engaged to be married."

I was shocked upright. "You can't be! Not at eighteen! You're too young!"

"I won't get married for a year or two, of course. But I'll get married when I'm twenty. You don't think I'm going to hang around here tied to my ma's apronstrings all my bloomin' life?"

"Where's your engagement ring?"

"It's a secret yet," she said, with another, slow, hot look.

I looked at her for a while, torn between disbelief and a disappointment that had something in it of despair. Then I let my cigarette fall into the river. It was like a fellow throwing down his gun.

She said, "Come on and we'll walk down by the weirs."

I walked by her side until we came to a hawthorn in full spate, listening to her telling me all about her boy. He was a sergeant on the Curragh. He cycled over from The Camp whenever he was off duty and she went out to meet him halfway. He was not going to re- main a sergeant for long; he was "going for an officer" and when he got his commission, they would live in London. I asked her if Nancy knew about all this. It was the only thing I said that upset her.

"If you say one word to her," she threatened, "I'll cut the thripes out of you."

After a bit, I risked saying, "If he saw us together now would he be jealous?"

She was pleased to laugh condescendingly. "I'd love to see him jealous. He's simply mad about me."

And she drowned me with talk of the life she was having now as his "belle," and the life she would have after she was married, until it was I who became mad with jealousy. Do you doubt it? Even if I was only fifteen and three months? Dear heaven! Does no- body in the world know how old it is to be fifteen and three months? Whenever now I see a group of boys returning, say after holi- days, to school, of any age from twelve on, I look most carefully into their faces in search of eyes that correspond to my unalterable concept of fifteen and three months.

I look at myself through those eyes. I see my own frustration in them. For how can anybody who has to come close to them not feel their helplessness? Each of them is imprisoned in childhood and no one can tell him how to escape. Each of them must, blind-eyed, gnaw his way out secretly and unaided. That they may be the eyes of boys who are mathematically fourteen, seventeen, even—I have met them—nineteen, does not matter.

All that matters is the fear of being on a brink and not knowing what is beyond it. At certain moments all through our lives we touch a point where ignorance is teetering on the brink of some es- sential revelation which we fear as much as we need. These brinks, these barriers, these No Road signs recur and recur. They produce our most exhausting and hateful dreams. They tell us every time that we have to be born all over again, grow, change, free ourselves yet once again. Each teetering moment is as terrible as the imaginary point of time in Eastern philosophy when a dying man, who knows that within a few seconds he will be reincarnated, clings to life in terror of his next shape or dies in the desire to know it. The particular ten- derness attaching to the age which I call "fifteen and three months" is that it is the first of many such steps and trials and must affect the nature of all that follow.

Since that July I have been in love half a dozen times, but I have never felt anything since like the tearing torment of those few weeks of summer. How I used to fawn on this creature whose beauty, I now know, was an illusion! How I used to flatter this girl whom, I was so soon to realize, I should never have trusted, merely to be allowed to sit beside her and secretly feel the edge of her skirt!

"And does he take you to many dances in The Camp, Noreen? But where do you get the dance dresses? I'd love to see you dressed for a dance! You must look smashing! But where do you get this little card that you write the dances on? Did you say that it is a pink pencil that's attached to it? By a pink thread? You didn't really mean, did you, Noreen, that they have six wineglasses?"

Her least word could crush me like a moth. But from that summer on, she had a power over all of us that was like a tyrant's. One night when Nancy flounced in with the supper and banged down the teapot, and whisked out again with a flick of her rear, my uncle said crossly, "What's up with that one now?"—implying that things had been "up with" her before now.

My aunt shot a glance at me and said, "Our ladyship is gone to the pictures without taking Nancy. And Marky is gone off to a whist drive."

I wonder they didn't notice me. Cinema, indeed! I saw the road to the Curragh, dark, secret, scented. Thinking of that sergeant, I must have had eyes like two revolvers. Yet I never realized the extent of Nancy's miseries and suspicions until, one day, she frightened me by saying, "What are you always mooning about for by yourself? You have no life in you at all this year. Was it you I saw wandering out the road by yourself the other night?"

I knew then that she also had been wandering along the roads at dark.

For three whole despairing weeks I did not see Noreen at all. Then, quite suddenly, one Sunday morning I collapsed at Mass. My uncle's doctor diagnosed my illness as acute anemia, but I am satisfied now that it was a traumatic illness. On August the ninth I was sent home. My father got three months' leave to be near me and I remained at home under his care for the rest of the summer and most of the autumn.

Then, toward the end of October, I began to get a bit brighter in myself when he said that I should go to the Feehans and he would join me there for Christmas with his brother, Kenneth, whom he had not seen for some years. I argued to myself that Newbridge would be only a few miles away and that I could more tactfully spy out the land from the slopes of the Curragh. As it happened, things turned out very differently to the way I expected.

I had not reckoned with the weather. To understand this you should see the place as I did that November. In the winter the Curragh seems older and wider. The foggy air extends its size by concealing its boundaries. The grass is amber as if from the great age of the plain. For one week that November a sprinkle of snow fell almost every day, so that all the bottoms were white and the crowns of their slopes were melted green. At dusk the whole plain seemed to surge against the glimmering cliffs of the distant camp, and then only the lights of a traveling car would restore to the earth its natural solidity. In the cottage, life became as restricted as aboard a ship. Only easygoing Moll was content, her tubby figure always moving busily through the pale glow of the house.

On most days there was little to do but watch the horses at the morning workouts—whenever a horse halted, steam enveloped its jockey—or, if the air cleared, walk across to The Camp. It was always Philly who proposed this expedition—no other walk appealed to her—even if we did nothing when we got there except buy some trifle at the stores, such as the latest copy of *The Strand* or the *Red Magazine*, or, if she had the money, she might treat herself to a small bottle of scent. Her favorite, I remember, was some allegedly Oriental perfume called Phul-Nana. We might go into the red-painted tin chapel to say a prayer for the boys. Its candles were as calm as light gone to sleep, its tin roof creaking faintly in the wind.

I had always thought The Camp a bleak and empty place. During the winter it was as blank and cold as a plate of sheet iron, and as silent as an abandoned factory building. One wondered where all the soldiers were. It was so silent that it was startling to hear a lorry zooming up the hill toward the tower with its Union Jack hanging soggily from the flagstaff. After the lorry had passed into The Camp there was a ghostliness about the long tracks that it had left behind it on the slight snow. Noreen had talked about "all the fun" that took place here in the winter. When I asked Philly where all the fun was, she said crossly that it all took place at night. I could only imagine or overimagine its supposed liveliness at those hours when she and I would stand in the porch of the cottage gazing fixedly at its flickering line until the cold defeated her curiosity and desire.

After about three weeks I suddenly began to feel one night that something had happened between us, standing there every night under the porch, watching those distant fireflies, sometimes talking, sometimes hardly speaking at all. At first I had the feeling of some form of complicity or collusion. I even wondered whether it might not be that the years between us had dwindled since I last stayed in the cottage. She had been eighteen then. I had been fourteen, divided from her by childhood. Now that she was twenty and I on the brink of sixteen there was barely a rivulet between us. I noted, too, that she had recently begun to converse more seriously with me. Perhaps it was merely because she was bored? Or perhaps it was because I no longer felt obliged by loyalty to Newbridge to think of her as a comic figure, and so felt a greater sympathy with her? She continued to impress me.

The season induced her to do something else that she had never done during the summer: to practice on the old upright piano with its pale-green, fluted satin shining behind its mahogany fretwork. Its strings sounded very tinkly during that snowy week. During the thaw they jangled.

One night I found her reading, pencil in hand, and asked, "What's the book?" It was Moran's French Grammar. She was trying unaided to learn the language. I noted the books she was reading—histories, travel books, famous biographies. She borrowed most of these from a widow, much older than herself, living in Kildare, a colonel's widow whom she had met by chance at one of the meetings on the Curragh.

After I had heard about the colonel's widow I guessed the truth. With the diabolical shrewdness of my age I saw that she was playing, for me, the part of a woman of a certain age with nothing left for her to do but to encourage a young man who still had the world before him. She once even dared to say, "Ah! If I only had my life to live over again!" But, in the end this pretending to be so much older than she was worked in a manner directly opposite to her intentions. Lost in her sense of the dramatic difference between our ages, she let down all her defenses, as if she were a very, very old lady thinking, "Nothing that I can say can possibly matter from one as old as me."

The result was inevitable. When a passionate sigh or a deliberate profanity led her to expose her hand I quietly read the hand and, excited by what I saw, encouraged her without guile. In proportion as she responded to the rising sap of my wonder, she lapsed into sincerity, I achieved equality. It was for this unguarded moment that I was lying in wait, as my earlier experience with Noreen had taught me that I must if I wished to be treated as an equal.

I think she first realized how far she had lowered her defenses the night when, as we sat alone over the parlor fire—Moll was singing in the kitchen, Uncle Ken in bed with his rheumatics and Una studying in her bedroom—I looked at her after she had told some wildly romantic story of army life in India, and said, in a tone of voice with which I hoped her older admirers had made her familiar, "Philly, you have lovely hair too. I'm sorry you put it up since I was here before. I'd love to see you letting it all ripple down your back."

I knew by the start she gave and the abrupt way she said "My hair is all right," that she had recognized the tone. When I kept looking at her with a curved smile and lowering eyes, I was gratified to see the frightening look in her eyes. It meant that I was able to interest her not as a boy, but as a man, so that I was merely amused to see her trying to flounder back quickly to the role of the grown woman talking graciously to the young boy.

I was content with this new situation for about a week—that is to say, I played the role of the sixteen-year-old pupil with a twenty-year-old teacher who knows that he is attracted by her, but who feels that it is her duty to keep him in his place as it is her pleasure to hold his admiration. Then, suddenly, I got tired of it. One night, in a temper at some correction she had made, I shut the book with a bang, glared at her and said that I preferred to work alone.

"But"—she smiled sweetly—"I only want to help you!"

"I don't want you to help me!" I cried haughtily.

"Believe me, my child," she said sarcastically, "you need a great deal of help."

"Not from you!" I retorted.

"Master Know All!"

"And I'm not a child!"

"You are a schoolboy."

I screamed at her, "I'm not! I'm not! I'm not!"

She flew into a rage herself, "Be quiet! Remember that if you can't behave yourself you can't stay here!"

I swept the books from the table and raced out of the parlor, and the cottage, into the garden, and so through the wicket gate straight on to the darkness and emptiness of the plain.

The night was frosty. Not only The Camp but the whole plain was an iron dish. But I was not aware of the cold as I walked straight ahead, as hot with anger as a man might be with alcohol—that anger of resentment which makes young people cry at the very injustice of being born. It began to die in me only as the exhaustion induced by constant stumbling in the dark, the splendor of the sky, the magnitude of the plain and the cold night air worked on me to cool my rage and fan my passion.

I lay down under the shelter of a furze clump between the camp lights and the cottage lights. Once I thought I heard the coughing of a sheep. Then I realized that I was hearing only the wind rattling through some withered thistles near my feet. The wind, the darkness, the stars, the lights, the size of the plain dwindled me and isolated me. My isolation turned all these human and sky-borne lights into my guides and companions. When my head rolled to the north to the lone cottage, to the south to the wind-washed campfires, and looked straight up to the stars of the Charioteer, I remember shouting out in my excitement, without knowing what I meant, "The lights! The lights!" as if I wanted some pyrotechnic convulsion in nature to occur, some flashing voice to speak. Only the wind whispered. Only the dried thistles coughed. I knew that I must be the one who should say the releasing word.

It was long after midnight when I re-entered the garden. The cottage was quiet. She would have heard the sweetbrier squeaking over the porch, the soft snoring of her daddy, and after a little while, her bedroom door being opened. She must have thought it was Moll, because she said nothing. I heard her gasp when my hand fell on her bare arm, and I whispered, "It's me, Philly."

She sat up, whispering, "What's wrong?" and I heard her fumbling with the matches.

"Don't light a light!" I begged.

"What is wrong?" she whispered again and the rest of our talk was carried on like that, whispering in the dark.

"Philly, I don't want to fight with you."

"That's all right; we both lost our tempers."

"I'm very fond of you, Philly."

"So am I, of you. Good night, now."

"But I'm not a schoolboy."

"Yes, yes. Go to your room now. Daddy will be raging if he hears you."

"Philly! You are a grown woman. And I am not a boy."

"I only said it to tease you."

"Philly!"

I could feel my heart pounding.

"Yes?"

"Kiss me!"

"If you don't go back to bed at once, I will call Molly."

"If you don't kiss me I'll run out of the house and never come back again. Never! Never again!"

(She said that my voice rose. "You were sort of gasping. You were threatening me. I was sure Daddy would hear.") Now she whispered, "If I give you one kiss will you go right back to bed?"

I still feel that first kiss, her parted lips, the gateways of the world opening, the stars over the plain shivering, the wind blowing, and her terror as she said, "Now go!"

"Another!"

She struck a match, lit her candle and saw me in my pants, shirt and bare feet. She started to upbraid me, but I saw that she saw that she was no longer dealing with a boy. I sat on the side of her bed, filled with wonder and delight at her bare shoulders and her dark, shining hair down about them, and the knowledge that she was not looking at me as a boy nor speaking to me as a boy. She gripped my hand and she assured me that in future I would have to keep to myself or leave the house, that she knew now that she had been stupid and foolish to have treated me as a boy, because any woman should have known better, but that she understood now and she hoped I understood, so would I please realize that I was a man and behave like a man? And as she whispered, like this, so seriously, I stroked her bare forearm, and felt the trembling of it and the weakness entering into it, and so must she because she stretched out her clenched knuckles to the wall.

"I am going to call Molly!"

"Just one last kiss?" I begged, staring at the whiteness of her neck and bosom.

Still holding her knuckles to the wall, "On your word of honor, you will go then?"

"On my word of honor."

When we parted, two hours later, she upbraided me with a gentleness that affected me far more than anything else that had happened since our quarrel in the parlor.

I lay awake until I heard the cock crowing. I felt no triumph. My delight was chastened by its own wonder. If she thought that I was in love with her she was deluded. I was too supremely astonished by my adventure to be fully aware of her, and when we met in the morning and I looked at her as if she were a mirror, I did not recognize myself. Totally unaware that what appealed to her in me was my utter innocence, taking her to be a woman who had seen strange places, known strange people, heard strange things that I had never seen, known or heard, fearing that she was aware only of my utter inexperience, I behaved unnaturally and self-consciously, hurting her cruelly by what I considered were the proper airs of any man of the world on such occasions. I spoke coolly to her, smiled cynically, once I even winked at her. Whatever I did, I knew that I must conceal my ignorance from her; for during those two hours, lying close together, we had been as harmless as doves, as innocent as lambs simply because I—as I thought then, but as I see now, both of us—had not known what else to do.

Besides, I now needed above everything else a retirement into silence, secrecy, self-contemplation, spiritual digestion, a summoning of shocked resources. I put on my cap after breakfast, borrowed one of my uncle's walking sticks, put a cigarette into the side of my mouth, waved a "Tol-loll" to the three girls and spent the whole day wandering, blind and lost, about the back roads that lead into the great central bogland of Ireland, an earth-lake of purple heather where you might tramp all day and see nothing stir except a snipe rising with a whir or, far away, a sloping pillar of blue peat smoke from a turf cutter's fire. Its emptiness suited my sense of lostness. I had no wish to arrive anywhere. I wanted to remain undestined. All I wanted was that my other lost self should come back to me.

In much the same spirit I so obviously avoided every chance of being alone with her that she must surely have begun to ask herself, "Does he loathe the sight of me?" just as I kept saying to myself, "Does she despise me now? Did it really happen at all? Did she upbraid me, and push me away and draw me toward her again and again?"

At last my awe began to defog. Passing her in the little corridor one afternoon, I gripped her hand and said, "Tonight?" She nodded, then to my astonishment burst into tears and slipped from me into her room.

That night the barriers rose between us at once. I was frightened by her silence into silence. I was repelled, even disgusted, by the stuffiness of the room, the smelly candle, the tousled bed, our humiliating

248 *§ Love's Young Dream

stealth. We gripped each other at every creak, lying rigid to listen. I could have cried for rage when I was alone again. Our public behavior become correspondingly gracious. It was of what I would now call a Byzantine formality, a mandarin formality. My manner would not have shamed a grand seigneur; hers a princess. There also began between us a series of long, maundering talks about love and marriage which could come to no conclusion, which indeed could hardly have made sense, since each of us was trying to instruct the other without admitting that neither of us had anything to reveal.

The fact is only too obvious, we both had within us the same monstrous weapon of destruction. She had imagined too many romantic stories; I had imagined too luxuriantly; both of us had imagined outside ourselves. Fountains and flags and flowers were elsewhere, always elsewhere—under the Himalayas, on the plains of France, an eye-cast across the plain. So, when I asked her about those wonderful winter dances in The Camp and she admitted that she had not yet been to one, the thought had no sequence unfavorable to her because, after all, she had met a real lieutenant at the races. Still, her nature's lighthouse was not roving as it used to rove for me at my pier's end. What had attracted me in her had been the flare that said, "This way to the open sea!" I could not avoid seeing that we had both suddenly become dependent: on this cottage—to which we had so often turned our backs to look at the lights across the plain—on my uncle, on my father, on the few shillings that they yielded us for pocket money, on the stuffy little timber-lined room, with the chamber pot under the bed, and the varnish blistered from the summer heat and one corner of the ceiling damp.

The day she clutched me and said miserably, "Do you love me at all?" I realized that she had become dependent on me. My father came next day. I immediately asked him if I might go to the farm at Newbridge for Christmas. I went there that very evening.

It was like going out of a dim room into full sunshine. I saw everything clearly. They had all been right about Philly; she was a silly featherhead, full of vaporings and nonsense. I no sooner mentioned The Camp to Noreen than she at once made me see it for what it was. Even during the two months while I had been at the cottage looking across at The Camp she had cycled there to three dances which she described to me fully and simply. There was nothing now about pink cards, and pink pencils and six wineglasses; only

Love's Young Dream ᴇ§ 249

when I cried, "But you told me!" she only laughed and said she had been making fun of me. That sort of thing might happen in the officers' mess on a special occasion, such as a big dinner dance—she was not certain because she had never been to such an event—but I surely did not think that it was the form at the sergeants' mess? She said that if I wanted badly to take her to a dance there, her man would arrange it. And it was clear that she meant this, and that she was now in the habit of going wherever she liked, and in every other way behaving like a grown young woman.

Within an hour I was under her spell again. She seemed to me more beautiful than ever. She was the actuality of all I had imagined Philly to be. But it was not only her beauty that held me now—the mane of sunlight about her head, her full lips the color of a pale tea rose, her body that was just beginning to take on her mother's plump strength. Her real attraction for me now was her matter-of-factness, her willfulness which produced more and more sighs from my aunt, and frowns from my uncle, and growls from Marky, and—a thing I could never have expected—a sudden flood of tears from Nancy on the only occasion that she talked about her.

"But why?" I asked my uncle. "Why?"

The pitying look he gave me said more than his words. "Nancy gave up a great deal for that girl. I warned her! But nobody can save a mother from herself!"

I discussed it with Marky. "People have to grow up!" I protested to him. "Noreen must be near twenty."

"I foresaw it," he growled. "And I was dead right."

None of them understood her. And yet I could sympathize with them. There were times when I almost hated her myself, so greatly did I need her, and so well did she know it, and so ruthlessly did she exact the price of my need. When she started again to dodge me for days, it was solely, I knew well, for the pleasure of making me realize how essential she was to me.

I realized it only too well. Within two weeks the pattern of the previous summer began to repeat itself—one day made radiant by her company, followed by three without her, so miserably blank by comparison that I could imagine that she had plotted the contrast; appointments made only to be broken or kept briefly and summarily interrupted. It would not have been so humiliating if she had made it clear to me that I was only a foil or a fill-in for her sergeant, but there were days when she treated me as much more than that, and then, without warning, she would slap me down with those damned three years between us.

The end came after I had spent six whole, empty days cycling around the country desperately searching for her. On the afternoon of that fateful seventh day, just as the first suggestion of twilight was entering the chilly air, I turned down one of those aimless side lanes that lead under the railway toward the level bog. I had come there across the Curragh. After the plain, open as a tennis lawn, this hollowed lane, deep under trees slung like hammocks from ditch to ditch, gave me a queer feeling of enclosure, secrecy and remoteness. I had been there once before during the summer, also in search of her, and I had then got exactly the same feeling that I was going underground. That summer's day the lane had been a pool of tropical heat, a clot of mingled smells from the overgrown ditches teeming with various weeds and flowers.

This winter's evening these flowers and weeds were a damp catacomb of moldy bones. It became dark where the lane descended under a stone railway bridge before emerging to end at a wooden gate, leading out to the bog, now so vague in the half-light that all I saw of it clearly was the occasional eye of a pool catching the last gleams from the watery sky.

She stood with her back to me, leaning over the old gate, gazing out over the bog. She started when she heard my step. My heart was battering, but I managed to say, with a pretense of gaiety, "Hello, Noreen! Waiting for your beau?"

"And what if I am, nosy?"

"Oho! Nothing at all! Is he letting you down tonight?"

For a second she seemed to bend and slacken, and I relished the sight. She recovered herself with a wicked grin.

"You can be my beau tonight. You're not so awful-looking. You'd pass in a crowd, I suppose."

I had leaned idly against the gate. I was wearing my school cap. She took it off, threw it on the ground and brushed back my hair with her palm. A brighter gleam flitting through the clouds. A bog pool glinted greenly behind her shoulder. The smells of the dank vegetation grew thicker. My breath came faster.

"You know, kid, if you did your hair properly—Have you no sweetie of your own?"

"Yes!" I said. "Up in Dublin."

"What's she like?"

I could only think of Philly, red-eyed from weeping. I could not talk about that goose to a girl who was going to marry a sergeant who would soon take his commission as an officer and carry her off to England, a married woman. I shook my head dumbly and gazed into her eyes.

"Well," she said impatiently, "what does she say to you when you walk her out? What do you say to her?" She suddenly dragged my arm behind her waist. "Here! Suppose I was her, what would I be saying to you now?" I shivered at her touch. "Go on!" she mocked.

"I don't think you'd say anything. You'd just look at me."

She looked at me sidewards and upwards from under droopy lids. "This way?"

"No!" I said furiously. "More like——I dunno how! More like a sheep?"

She detached my arm irritably. Then she laughed at me pitilessly and put my arm back again around her waist.

"You're a very timid courter. Say something to me. As if I was your girl."

I whispered, seeing her cloud of flaxen hair against a pale star, "You're like an angel, Noreen."

She sighed a happy sigh that was almost a groan. She looked past me up the dark tunnel with heavy eyelids.

" 'Tis like the pictures," she said sleepily. "Go on."

"I could pray to you, Noreen."

"Go on," she murmured throatily, leaning against me.

"When I see the sun through the window in the priory, I think of you, Noreen."

Her eyes were closed. She muttered, as if barely awake, "Why does nobody talk to me like that?"

"Doesn't your sergeant?"

She opened her eyes wide, and stared at me enormously. "What window?"

"The window of Mary Magadalene with the long golden hair."

She pushed me away and roared, laughing at me—perhaps, I now think, at the pair of us—and was there, I have sometimes wondered, a bitterness in her laughing?

"Honest to God, you're a scream!" She quietened and looked seriously at me. "You poor little fool!" she said. "I don't know what I'm going to do with you."

And she really did seem to be considering the problem, so that I felt a great warmth of happiness that she should be thinking kindly about me even if she was a grown woman and even if she still thought I was only a boy. Then she stiffened suddenly and shoved me away. She had lifted her head like a bird that hears a warning screech from its mate.

"Hop it!" she rapped at me. "Clear out!" and began to clamber over the gate into the field beyond.

It did not occur to me to disobey. In a daze of shame I went slowly back up the lane to where I had thrown my bicycle against the ditch. Only when I was on the road did I remember my cap, and laying the bicycle aside, I went back for it, thinking she had run off into the field beyond the gate.

As I came to the bridge I saw them on the other side of the gate framed by the stone arch, in each other's arms, their mouths locked. Knowledge turned me into a statue. He was not a sergeant. He was not even a private soldier. He was a little buttoned-up lump of a fellow with a coarse cap on his head, peaked upward so that what there was left of salvaged daylight on his little, wizened horse's face made me realize that he could only be a stableman like Marky Fenelon. As I stood there, petrified, his fist clutched her yellow mop and slowly dragged her head backward. Her mouth fell open like a cat's red gullet, yawning widely.

I slunk into the ditch. Then I crept away up the lane, jumped on my bicycle and rode off like a madman. I was aware of a star through black branches. Behind me, far away across the plain, a bugle began to unfold its gay, elaborate call. As it came and died away, I imaged the illusory lights of The Camp flickering in the wind that had silenced the wavering notes, and I thought of that flickering line not as lights, but as lies. Yet I did not feel anger or disgust. I did not feel deceived, or betrayed, or derided. I felt only a hollow in me full of defeat, now and forever after. It was a secret moment. Nobody knew it. Nobody would ever know it. But as I rode through the Main Street of Newbridge, along one side of which the shops were now lighted, with the girls already parading the pavement, and the soldiers coming out of the barracks across the street in twos and threes for a night's pleasure, I kept my head lowered over the handle bars, as if I were afraid that somebody would guess my shame in my knowledge of my defeat, see my fear at my discovery of my own helpless loneliness.

I had wanted to know what there is to know; to possess life and be its master. The moment I found out that nobody knows, I had exposed myself to myself. I would never do it again. The shame of it was too much to bear. Like everybody else, I would pretend for the rest of my life. I would compound; I would invent—poetry, religion, common sense, kindness, good cheer, the sigh, the laugh, the shrug, everything that saves us from having to admit that beauty and goodness exist here only for as long as we create and nourish them by the force of our dreams; that there is nothing outside ourselves apart from our imaginings.

I rode home. I was in nice time for supper. My uncle said, "That's a fine complexion you have. Been cycling?"

"It was a grand day for it!" I smiled. "And a grand night of stars."

He winked at me and began mockingly to hum the Barcarole from The Tales of Hoffman.

The next morning as I passed the gate lodge, Noreen came out and with one of her slow, smiling looks, as of a fellow conspirator, she handed me my cap, wet, crumpled and muddy. When I unfolded it I found the silver track of a snail across the lining. I let it fall into the Liffey, where it slowly floated away.

I did not go down there again for a couple of years. By then I was doing Medicine at the university. When my Uncle Gerry met me at the station, he laughed loudly, "By gor, John, I hardly recognized you. They're after making a grand straight fellow out of you. You'd better stop growing up now and start growing out for a change."

As I watched him lumbering into the old tub trap, I said, "You're after getting a bit on the logy side yourself, Uncle Gerry."

"Anno Domini!" he said, flicking up the pony, which had also got so fat that he had rubbed the paint off the insides of the shafts.

As we trotted along the road I asked after my aunt, and Marky, and Nancy, and the farm, but what I wanted to get on to as quickly as I decently could was whether he had any tips for the July races. It was not until I was unpacking and came on my father's usual presents for Marky and Nancy that I remembered that Noreen had got married a few months back; for there were two Italian blouses this time, one white for Nancy, and one pale blue marked "For Noreen," which I took to be a wedding token. I found Nancy in the kitchen, and I could see no great change in her, apart from a few gray streaks of hair, and that she was getting "right logy" too. She shouted with delight when she saw me, "Aha! You're not a child any more! God be with the days when I used to throw you up to the ceiling. But I'm going to kiss you all the same."

And we kissed with double-hearty smacks and laughs. Then I handed over the two blouses with a mock bow, "With my papa's compliments, madame!"

"They're gorgeous!" she said, laying the two of them side by side. The arm of the blue fell on the arm of the white. Gently she lifted the blue sleeve and let it sink on its own blouse. "I'll post it to her. You heard she went off from me in the heel of the hunt? Aye! She fell in with a soldier here in the barracks and followed him to London. It wouldn't surprise me to hear one of these days that his regiment was posted overseas, to India, or Africa, or Egypt. Then she'll be gone from me entirely." She smiled, but it was a sad smile.

"I'm sorry, Nancy. You'll miss her."

Her smile went. She said vehemently, "I will not! There was a time I'd have laid down my life for that girl. I don't care no more about her now than the child unborn." She smiled sadly again. "Ye used to be great pals at one time."

"Yes," I agreed shortly, and I was glad to turn round and see Marky darkening the doorway.

We greeted each other warmly. I handed him the sailor's twist. As we were flattering each other I wondered if I was expected to make the old joke about his getting married to Nancy, but that year I was in love with a girl at the university and he looked so gray and wizened that the joke seemed rather stale and even a little unseemly. I got him to talk about the July races, because my uncle had said that he was interested in a horse called Flyaway, and he started to tell me all about it.

Suddenly, as we talked, there was a noise behind us, like a clatter of pigeons rising. It was Nancy rending the blue blouse from top to bottom, tearing at it savagely again and again, her teeth bared, her eyes out on pins. Marky, undeflected, merely glanced at her and went on talking in his slow, steady voice about Flyaway. We heard the bang of the range lid. Staring at him, I got the smell of burning silk. Marky, seeing that I was too dazed to listen, took me by the arm and guided me out into the hot sun of the cobbled yard. I looked back at the kitchen door.

"Never heed her," he said. "She's upset. She feels very lonely in herself this long time."

"Marky! Did Noreen get into trouble or something?"

"No! She just hoisted her sails, and off with her. It was just as well! Seeing her going off there every night with common fellows around the town, and poor Nancy in that kitchen, sitting looking at the fire in the range——"

"Wasn't it a pity yourself and Nancy didn't make a match of it?"

He looked at me from under his gray eyebrows and said quietly, "And give it to say to everyone that I had another man's child under my roof?"

"What matter!" I cried.

He shook his little bullet head slowly, and slowly pronounced judgment, "It does matter. I heard it said too often that no man nor beast ever loved their young with the fierce love of a woman for her by-child." He tapped me lightly on the arm with the twist tobacco. "If I was you, I'd put ten shillings on Flyaway," and he limped away about his affairs.

The natural way back into the house was through the kitchen. Nancy was standing by the range with the poker in her fist and her head to the door. I knew she had heard the lifted latch, but she held her rounded back rigidly against me. I waited.

She turned, looked at me and said coldly, "Well? Do you want something?"

As I looked at her, a bugle began to unfold its far-carrying notes from the distant barracks. Then its elaborate call wavered on the changing wind and died away. Did I hear the sparrows chirruping in the walled orchard? Did the ivy at the window rustle? I saw the evening star, and the west was already a cold green. It was the hour when the soldiers would soon be coming out to meet their girls. I made a feeble gesture with my hands and walked off to another part of the house. I wanted badly to read about Flyaway.

All that happened over forty years ago. I have three children of my own now. One is fourteen, one is nearly sixteen and the eldest is a few months over eighteen. The middle one is my son. When I happened to look at him the other night across the fire I saw a familiar look in his eyes and all this came back to me. After all, I have now come to the age when memories are meaningful—the age when a man knows that he has lived. The farm has descended to a second cousin, but my family goes down there now and again for a holiday. They tell me that the cottage on the Curragh is completely disappeared, knocked down to make room for a car park. When I talk to them about bugle calls, they laugh at me and say, "Daddy! Buglers and drummer boys and gun wagons and semaphores and all that sort of thing belong to the time of the Boer War."

They say you cannot see the lights of The Camp any more because of the spruce and firs that have been planted there as a shelter belt. But I could always go to the Curragh for the races.

Neither trained horses nor wild horses would drag me down there now. The only thing that would tempt me there would be to feel and smell the dark night over the plain. I daren't do it. I would still see the flickering lights. I would hear the wavering sound of a far-off bugle. And I would know that these things that I could neither see nor hear are the only reality. This I know to be the truth about life, as surely as I know that I am too old to embrace it now.

And then there is the most mature love of all—marital love that has endured for many years composed of reality, tragedy, affection, and then, finally, loss. Colette, who wrote some of the most haunting autobiographical pieces that have ever been put down on paper, has captured a picture of marital love and the intense pain of loss in this charming and enduring cameo of her mother's reaction to the death of her husband.

LAUGHTER

COLETTE

She was easily moved to laughter, a youthful, rather shrill laughter that brought tears to her eyes, and which she would afterwards deplore as inconsistent with the dignity of a mother burdened with the care of four children and financial worries. She would master her paroxysms of mirth, scolding herself severely, "Come, now, come! . . ." and then fall to laughing again till her pince-nez trembled on her nose.

We would jealously compete in our efforts to evoke her laughter, especially as we grew old enough to observe in her face, as the years succeeded each other, the ever-increasing shadow of anxiety for the morrow, a kind of distress which sobered her whenever she thought of the fate of her penniless children, of her precarious health, of old age that was slowing the steps—a single leg and two crutches—of her beloved companion. When she was silent, my mother resembled all mothers who are scared at the thought of poverty and death. But speech brought back to her features an invincible youthfulness. Though she might grow thin with sorrow, she never spoke sadly. She would escape, as it were in one bound, from a painful reverie, and pointing her knitting needle at her husband would exclaim:

"What? Just you try to die first, and you'll see!"

"I shall do my best, dear heart," he would answer.

She would glare at him as savagely as if he had carelessly trodden on a pelargonium cutting or broken the little gold-enameled Chinese teapot.

"Isn't that just like you! You've got all the selfishness of the Funels and the Colettes combined! Oh, why did I ever marry you?"

"Because, my beloved, I threatened to blow out your brains if you didn't."

"True enough. Even in those days, you see, you thought only of yourself! And now here you are talking of nothing less than of dying before me. All I say is, only let me see you try!"

He did try, and succeeded at the first attempt. He died in his seventy-fourth year, holding the hands of his beloved, and fixing on her weeping eyes a gaze that gradually lost its color, turned milky blue and faded like a sky veiled in mist. He was given the handsomest of village funerals, a coffin of yellow wood covered only by an old tunic riddled with wounds—the tunic he had worn as a captain in the 1st Zouaves—and my mother accompanied him steadily to the grave's edge, very small and resolute beneath her widow's veil, and murmuring under her breath words of love that only he must hear.

We brought her back to the house, and there she promptly lost her temper with her new mourning, the cumbersome crape that caught on the keys of doors and presses, the cashmere dress that stifled her. She sat resting in the drawing-room, near the big green chair in which my father would never sit again and which the dog had already joyfully invaded. She was dry-eyed, flushed and feverish and kept on repeating:

"Oh, how hot it is! Heavens! The heat of this black stuff! Don't you think I might change now, into my blue sateen?"

"Well . . ."

"Why not? Because of my mourning? But I simply loathe black! For one thing, it's melancholy. Why should I present a sad and unpleasant sight to everyone I meet? What connection is there between this cashmere and crape and my feelings? Don't let me ever see you in mourning for me! You know well enough that I only like you to wear pink, and some shades of blue."

She got up hastily, took several steps towards an empty room and stopped abruptly:

"Ah! . . . Of course. . . ."

She came back and sat down again, admitting with a simple and humble gesture that she had, for the first time that day, forgotten that *he* was dead.

"Shall I get you something to drink, mother? Wouldn't you like to go to bed?"

"Of course not. Why should I? I'm not ill!"

She sat there and began to learn patience, staring at the floor, where a dusty track from the door of the sitting-room to the door of the empty bedroom had been marked by rough, heavy shoes.

A kitten came in, circumspect and trustful, a common and irresistible little kitten four or five months old. He was acting a dignified part for his own edification, pacing grandly, his tail erect as a candle, in imitation of lordly males. But a sudden and unexpected somersault landed him head over heels at our feet, where he took fright at his own temerity, rolled himself into a ball, stood up on his hind legs, danced sideways, arched his back, and then spun round like a top.

"Look at him, oh, do look at him, Minet-Chéri! Goodness! Isn't he funny!"

And she laughed, sitting there in her mourning, laughed her shrill, young girl's laugh, clapping her hands with delight at the kitten. Then, of a sudden, searing memory stemmed that brilliant cascade and dried the tears of laughter in my mother's eyes. Yet she offered no excuse for having laughed, either on that day, or on the days that followed; for though she had lost the man she passionately loved, in her kindness for us she remained among us just as she always had been, accepting her sorrow as she would have accepted the advent of a long and dreary season, but welcoming from every source the fleeting benediction of joy. So she lived on, swept by shadow and sunshine, bowed by bodily torments, resigned, unpredictable and generous, rich in children, flowers and animals like a fruitful domain.

"I am living today in yesterday"

A GATHERING OF GREAT
LOVE LETTERS

Letters are perhaps the most direct expression of love, because the spoken words of love seem to disappear the way spring days disappear, the way rain evaporates after it glistens on a blade of grass. Captured in letters, however, such words may be returned to repeatedly. The great letter writers, those who have been able to express such feelings, are the counselors and comforters of others in love.

Here is a handful of love letters, some old, some new, but all tremendously enduring, by people who have felt deeply and meaningfully and have been able to express what they feel. Although each of these letters was directed to one individual, their intensity of emotion and the clarity of expression have made them speak to every young lover.

The poet John Keats, a superb letter writer, wrote a series of haunting love letters to Fanny Brawne. A young man, he already knew he was dying, and that his love would be unfulfilled, when he wrote "My Sweet Girl."

"MY SWEET GIRL . . ."

LETTERS FROM JOHN KEATS TO FANNY BRAWNE

To FANNY BRAWNE. *Monday 11 Oct. 1819.*

College Street.

My sweet Girl,

I am living to day in yesterday: I was in a complete fa[s]cination all day. I feel myself at your mercy. Write me ever so few lines and tell you [*for* me] you will never for ever be less kind to me than yesterday—. You dazzled me. There is nothing in the world so bright and delicate. When Brown came out with that seemingly true story again[s]t me last night, I felt it would be death to me if you had ever believed it—though against any one else I could muster up my obstinacy. Before I knew Brown could disprove it I was for the moment miserable. When shall we pass a day alone? I have had a thousand kisses, for which with my whole soul I thank love—but if you should deny me the thousand and first—'twould put me to the proof how great a misery I could live through. If you should ever carry your threat yesterday into execution—believe me 'tis not my pride, my vanity or any petty passion would torment me—really 'twould hurt my heart—I could not bear it. I have seen Mrs Dilke this morning; she says she will come with me any fine day.

Ever yours

Ah hertè mine!

John Keats

To FANNY BRAWNE. *Wednesday 13 Oct. 1819.*

25 College Street.

My dearest Girl,

This moment I have set myself to copy some verses out fair. I cannot proceed with any degree of content. I must write you a line or two and see if that will assist in dismissing you from my Mind for ever so short a time. Upon my Soul I can think of nothing else. The time is passed when I had power to advise and warn you against the unpromising morning of my Life. My love has made me selfish. I cannot exist without you. I am forgetful of every thing but seeing you again—my Life seems to stop there—I see no further. You have absorb'd me. I have a sensation at the present moment as though I was dissolving—I should be exquisitely miserable without the hope of soon seeing you. I should be affraid to separate myself far from you. My sweet Fanny, will your heart never change? My love, will it? I have no limit now to my love—You[r] note came in just here—I cannot be happier away from you. 'Tis richer than an Argosy of Pearles. Do not threat me even in jest. I have been astonished that Men could die Martyrs for religion—I have shudder'd at it. I shudder no more—I could be martyr'd for my Religion—Love is my religion—I could die for that. I could die for you. My Creed is Love and you are its only tenet. You have ravish'd me away by a Power I cannot resist; and yet I could resist till I saw you; and even since I have seen you I have endeavoured often 'to reason against the reasons of my Love'. I can do that no more—the pain would be too great. My love is selfish. I cannot breathe without you.

Yours for ever

John

To FANNY BRAWNE. *Tuesday 19 Oct. 1819.*

Great Smith Street
Tuesday Morn

My sweet Fanny,

On awakening from my three days dream ("I cry to dream again") I find one and another astonish'd at my idleness and thoughtlessness. I was miserable last night—the morning is always restorative. I must be busy, or try to be so. I have several things to speak to you of tomorrow morning. Mrs Dilke I should think will tell you that I purpose living at Hampstead. I must impose chains upon myself. I shall be able to do nothing. I sho[u]ld like to cast the die for Love or death. I have no Patience with any thing else—if you ever intend to be cruel to me as you say in jest now but perhaps may sometimes be in earnest be so now—and I will—my mind is in a tremble, I cannot tell what I am writing.

Ever my love yours

John Keats

To Fanny Brawne. [*Friday 4 Feb. 1820?*]
Dearest Fanny, I shall send this the moment you return. They say I must remain confined to this room for some time. The consciousness that you love me will make a pleasant prison of the house next to yours. You must come and see me frequently: this evening, without fail—when you must not mind about my speaking in a low tone for I am ordered to do so though I *can* speak out.

Yours ever

sweetest love.—

turn over

J. Keats

Perhaps your Mother is not at home and so you must wait till she comes. You must see me to-night and let me hear your promise to come to-morrow.

Brown told me you were all out. I have been looking for the stage the whole afternoon. Had I known this I could not have remain'd so silent all day.

To Fanny Brawne. [*Thursday 10 Feb. 1820?*]
My dearest Girl,
If illness makes such an agreeable variety in the manner of your eyes I should wish you sometimes to be ill. I wish I had read your note before you went last night that I might have assured you how far I was from suspecting any coldness. You had a just right to be a little silent to one who speaks so plainly to you. You must believe—you shall, you will—that I can do nothing, say nothing, think nothing of you but what has its spring in the Love which has so long been my pleasure and torment. On the night I was taken ill—when so violent a rush of blood came to my Lungs that I felt nearly suffocated— I

assure you I felt it possible I might not survive, and at that moment though[t] of nothing but you. When I said to Brown 'this is unfortunate' I thought of you. 'Tis true that since the first two or three days other subjects have entered my head. I shall be looking forward to Health and the Spring and a regular routine of our old Walks.

Your affectionate

J.K.

To FANNY BRAWNE. [*Feb. 1820?*]

My sweet love, I shall wait patiently till to-morrow before I see you, and in the mean time, if there is any need of such a thing, assure you by your Beauty, that whenever I have at any time written on a certain unpleasant subject, it has been with your welfare impress'd upon my mind. How hurt I should have been had you ever acceded to what is, notwithstanding, very reasonable! How much the more do I love you from the general result! In my present state of Health I feel too much separated from you and could almost speak to you in the words of Lorenzo's Ghost to Isabella

> *Your Beauty grows upon me and I feel*
> *A greater love through all my essence steal.*

My greatest torment since I have known you has been the fear of you being a little inclined to the Cressid; but that suspicion I dismiss utterly and remain happy in the surety of your Love, which I assure you is as much a wonder to me as a delight. Send me the words 'Good night' to put under my pillow.

Dearest Fanny,

Your affectionate

J.K.

To FANNY BRAWNE. [*Feb.1820?*]

My dearest Girl,

According to all appearances I am to be separated from you as much as possible. How I shall be able to bear it, or whether it will not be worse than your presence now and then, I cannot tell. I must be patient, and in the mean time you must think of it as little as possible. Let me not longer detain you from going to Town—there may be no end to this imprisoning of you. Perhaps you had better not come before tomorrow evening: send me however without fail a good night.

You know our situation—what hope is there if I should be recovered ever so soon—my very health with [*for* will] not suffer me to make any great exertion. I am recommended not even to read poetry, much less write it. I wish I had even a little hope. I cannot say forget me—but I would mention that there are impossibilities in the world. No more of this. I am not strong enough to be weaned—take no notice of it in your good night.

Happen what may I shall ever be my dearest Love

Your affectionate

J—K—

To FANNY BRAWNE. [*Feb.* 1820?]

My dearest Girl, how could it ever have been my wish to forget you? how could I have said such a thing? The utmost stretch my mind has been capable of was to endeavour to forget you for your own sake seeking what a change [*for* chance] there was of my remaining in a precarious state of health. I would have borne it as I would bear death if fate was in that humour: but I should as soon think of choosing to die as to part from you. Believe too my Love that our friends think and speak for the best, and if their best is not our best it is not their fault. When I am better I will speak with you at large on these subjects, if there is any occasion—I think there is none. I am rather nervous today perhaps from being a little recovered and suffering my mind to take little excursions beyond the doors and windows. I take it for a good sign, but as it must not be encouraged you had better delay seeing me till tomorrow. Do not take the trouble of writing much: merely send me my good night.

Remember me to your Mother and Margaret.

Your affectionate

J.K

This short love letter is one of the most famous in English literature. It was written by Mary Wollstonecraft Godwin immediately before she eloped with Percy Bysshe Shelley.

"MY OWN LOVE"

LETTER FROM
MARY WOLLSTONECRAFT GODWIN TO
PERCY BYSSHE SHELLEY

My own love:

I do not know by what compulsion I am to answer you, but your porter says I must, so I do. By a miracle I saved your five pounds & I will bring it. I hope, indeed, oh my loved Shelley, we shall indeed be happy. I meet you at three and bring heaps of Skinner street news. Heaven bless my love and take care of him!

His Own Mary

Two well-known lovers were Elizabeth Barrett and Robert Browning. *Their work brought them together—she the invalid, he the famous poet—and here, in the very first exchange of letters between them, is that mutual dignity and joy that was to become enduring happiness.*

"I LOVE YOUR VERSES
WITH ALL MY HEART . . ."

LETTER FROM ROBERT BROWNING TO
ELIZABETH BARRETT
AND HER REPLY

New Cross, Hatcham, Surrey,
January 10th, 1845

I love your verses with all my heart, dear Miss Barrett—and this is no off-hand complimentary letter that I shall write—whatever else, no prompt matter-of-course recognition of your genius, and there a graceful and natural end of the thing. Since the day last week when I first read your poems, I quite laugh to remember how I have been turning and turning again in my mind what I should be able to tell you of their effect upon me, for in the first flush of delight I thought I would this once get out of my habit of purely passive enjoyment, when I do really enjoy, and thoroughly justify my admiration—perhaps even, as a loyal fellow-craftsman should, try and find fault and do you some little good to be proud of hereafter!—but nothing comes of it all—so into me has it gone, and part of me has it become, this great living poetry of yours, not a flower of which but took root and grew—Oh, how different that is from lying to be dried and pressed flat, and prized highly, and put in a book with a proper account at top and bottom, and shut up and put away . . . and the book called a 'Flora,' besides! After all, I need not give up the thought of doing that, too, in time; because even now, talking with whoever is worthy, I can give a reason for my faith in one and another excellence, the fresh strange music, the affluent language, the exquisite pathos and true new brave thought; but in thus addressing myself to you—your own self, and for the first time, my feeling rises altogether. I do, as I say, love these books with all my heart—and I love you too. Do you know I was once not very far from seeing—really seeing you? Mr. Kenyon said to me one morning, 'Would you like to see Miss Barrett?' then he went to announce me—then he returned . . . you were too unwell, and now it is years ago, and I feel as at some untoward passage in my travels, as if I had been close, so close, to some world's-wonder in chapel or crypt, only a screen to push and I might have entered, but there was some slight, so it now seems, slight and just sufficient bar to admission, and the half-opened door shut, and I went home my thousands of miles, and the sight was never to be!

Well, these Poems were to be, and this true thankful joy and pride with which I feel myself.

Yours ever faithfully,
Robert Browning

HER REPLY

50 Wimpole Street,
Jan. 11th, 1845

I THANK you, dear Mr. Browning, from the bottom of my heart. You meant to give me pleasure by your letter—and even if the object had not been answered, I ought still to thank you. But it is thoroughly answered. Such a letter from such a hand! Sympathy is dear—very dear to me: but the sympathy of a poet, and of such a poet, is the quintessence of sympathy to me! Will you take back my gratitude for it?—agreeing, too, that of all the commerce done in the world, from Tyre to Carthage, the exchange of sympathy for gratitude is the most princely thing!

For the rest you draw me on with your kindness. It is difficult to get rid of people when you once have given them too much pleasure going to say—after a little natural hesitation—is, that if ever you —*that* is a fact, and we will not stop for the moral of it. What I was emerge without inconvenient effort from your 'passive state,' and will *tell* me of such faults as rise to the surface and strike you as important in my poems (for of course, I do not think of troubling you with criticism in detail), you will confer a lasting obligation on me, and one which I shall value so much, that I covet it at a distance. I do not pretend to any extraordinary meekness under criticism and it is possible enough that I might not be altogether obedient to yours. But with my high respect for your power in your Art and for your experience as an artist, it would be quite impossible for me to hear a general observation of yours on what appear to you my master-faults, without being the better for it hereafter in some way. I ask for only a sentence or two of general observation—and I do not ask even for *that*, so as to tease you—but in the humble, low voice, which is so excellent a thing in women—particularly when they go a-begging! The most frequent general criticism I receive, is, I think, upon the style— 'if I *would* but change my style'! But *that* is an objection (isn't it?) to the writer bodily? Buffon says, and every sincere writer must feel, 'Le style c'est l'homme'; a fact, however, scarcely calculated to lessen the objection with certain critics.

Is it indeed true that I was so near to the pleasure and honour of making your acquaintance? and can it be true that you look back upon the lost opportunity with any regret? *But*—you know—if you had entered the 'crypt,' you might have caught cold, or been tired to death, and *wished* yourself 'a thousand miles off'; which would have been worse than travelling them. It is not my interest, however, to put such thoughts in your head about its being 'all for the best'; and I would rather hope (as I do) that what I lost by one chance I may recover by some future one. Winters shut me up as they do dormouse's eyes; in the spring, *we shall see:* and I am so much better that I seem turning round to the outward world again. And in the meantime I have learnt to know your voice, not merely from the poetry but from the kindness in it. Mr. Kenyon often speaks of you— dear Mr. Kenyon!—who most unspeakably, or only speakably with tears in my eyes—has been my friend and helper, and my book's friend and helper! critic and sympathizer, true friend of all hours! You know him well enough, I think, to understand that I must be grateful to him.

I am writing too much—and notwithstanding that I am writing too much, I will write of one thing more. I will say that I am your debtor, not only for this cordial letter and for all the pleasure which came with it, but in other ways, and those the highest: and I will say that while I live to follow the divine art of poetry, in proportion to my love for it and my devotion to it, I must be a devout admirer and student of your works. This is in my heart to say to you—and I say it.

And for the rest, I am proud to remain,

Your obliged and faithful

Elizabeth B. Barrett

The separations of love have occasioned exquisite love letters. No two lovers were more star-crossed nor doomed to separation than Heloise and Abelard, who loved not wisely but too well. (She was his student, he her tutor.) As was the custom of the Middle Ages, the time in which they lived, they retired respectively to a convent and to monastic solitude, after the discovery of their love became a matter of public scandal. These are some of the words Abelard wrote when he knew he would never see Heloise again.

The couple were finally buried together in the Pére-Lachaise cemetery in Paris, where you can still read these words on their tombstone:

> *Here, under the same stone, repose, of this monastary the founder Peter Abelard, and the first abbess, Heloise, heretofore in study, genius, love, inauspicious marriage, and repentance now, as we hope, in eternal happiness united. Peter died April 21, 1142. Heloise May 17, 1164.*

"TO LOVE HELOISE TRULY IS TO LEAVE HER . . ."

LETTER FROM ABELARD TO HELOISE

I intend to mix my grief with yours, and pour out my heart before you: in short, to lay open before your eyes all my trouble, and the secret of my soul, which my vanity has hitherto made me conceal from the rest of the world, and which you now force from me, in spite of my resolutions to the contrary.

It is true, that in a sense of the afflictions which have befallen us, and observing that no change of our condition could be expected; that those prosperous days which had seduced us were now past, and there remained nothing but to erase from our minds, by painful endeavors, all marks and remembrances of them. I had wished to find in philosophy and religion a remedy for my disgrace; I searched out an asylum to secure me from love. I was come to the sad experiment of making vows to harden my heart.

But what have I gained by this? If my passion has been put under a restraint my thoughts yet run free. I promise myself that I will forget you, and yet cannot think of it without loving you. My love is not at all lessened by those reflections I make in order to free myself. The silence I am surrounded by makes me more sensible to its impressions, and while I am unemployed with any other things, this makes itself the business of my whole vocation. Till after a multitude of useless endeavors I begin to persuade myself that it is sufficient wisdom to conceal from all but you how confused and weak I am.

I remove to a distance from your person with an intention of avoiding you as an enemy; and yet I incessantly seek for you in my mind; I recall your image in my memory, and in different disquietudes I betray and contradict myself. I hate you! I love you! Shame presses me on all sides.

I am at this moment afraid I should seem more indifferent than you fare, and yet I am ashamed to discover my trouble. How weak are we in ourselves if we do not support ourselves on the Cross of Christ. Shall we have so little courage, and shall that uncertainty of serving two masters which afflicts your heart affect mine too? You see the confusion I am in, how I blame myself and how I suffer.

Religion commands me to pursue virtue since I have nothing to hope for from love. But love still preserves its dominion over my fancies and entertains itself with past pleasures. Memory supplies the place of a mistress. Piety and duty are not always the fruits of retirement; even in deserts, when the dew of heaven falls not on us, we love what we ought no longer to love.

The passions, stirred up by solitude, fill these regions of death and silence; it is very seldom that what ought to be is truly followed here and that God only is loved and served. Had I known this before I had instructed you better. You call me your master; it is true you were entrusted to my care. I saw you, I was earnest to teach you vain sciences; it cost you your innocence and me my liberty.

You tell me that it is for me you live under that veil which covers you; why do you profane your vocation with such words? Why provoke a jealous God with blasphemy? I hoped after our separation you would have delivered me from the tumult of my senses. We commonly die to the affections of those we see no more, and they to ours; absence is the tomb of love. But to me absence is an unquiet remembrance of what I once loved which continually torments me. I flattered myself that when I should see you no more you would rest in my memory without troubling my mind; that Brittany and the sea would suggest other thoughts; that my fasts and studies would by degrees delete you from my heart. But in spite of severe fasts and redoubled studies, in spite of the distance of three hundred miles which separates us, your image, as you describe yourself in your veil, appears to me and confounds all my resolutions—the beginning of my guilt; your eyes, your discourse, pierced my heart; and in spite of that ambition and glory which tried to make a defense, love was soon the master.

God, in order to punish me, forsook me. You are no longer of the world; you have renounced it: I am a religious devoted to solitude; shall we not take advantage of our condition? Would you destroy my piety in its infant state? Would you have me forsake the abbey into which I am but newly entered? Must I renounce my vows? I have made them in the presence of God; whither shall I fly from His wrath should I violate them? Suffer me to seek ease in my duty . . .

Regard me no more, I entreat you, as a founder or any great personage; your praises ill agree with my many weaknesses. I am a miserable sinner, prostrate before my Judge, and with my face pressed to the earth I mix my tears with the earth. Can you see me in this posture and solicit me to love you? Come, if you think fit, and in your holy habit entrust yourself between my God and me, and be a wall of separation. Come and force from me those sighs and thoughts and vows I owe to Him alone. Assist the evil spirits and be the instrument of their malice. What cannot you induce a heart to do whose weakness you so perfectly know?

Nay, withdraw yourself and contribute to my salvation. Suffer me to avoid destruction, I entreat you by our former tender affection and by our now common misfortune. It will always be the highest love to show none; I here release you from all your oaths and engagements. Be God's wholly, to whom you are appropriated; I will never oppose so pious a design. How happy shall I be if I thus lose you! Then shall I indeed be a religious and you a perfect example of an abbess.

Make yourself amends by so glorious a choice; make your virtue a spectacle worthy of men and angels. Be humble among your children, assiduous in your choir, exact in your discipline, diligent in your reading; make even your recreations useful.

But to forget Heloise, to see her no more, is what Heaven demands of Abelard; and to expect nothing from Abelard, to forget him even as an idea, is what Heaven enjoins on Heloise. To forget, in the case of love, is the most necessary penance, and the most difficult. It is easy to recount our faults; how many, through indiscretion, have made themselves a second pleasure of this instead of confessing them with humility. The only way to return to God is by neglecting the creature we have adored, and adoring the God whom we have neglected. This may appear harsh, but it must be done if we would be saved . . .

This is the thought you ought to have of a fugitive who desires to deprive you of the hope of ever seeing him again . . . When love has once been sincere how difficult it is to determine to love no more! 'Tis a thousand times more easy to renounce the world than love. I hate this deceitful, faithless world; I think no more of it; but my wandering heart still eternally seeks you, and is filled with anguish at having lost you, in spite of all the powers of my reason. In the meantime, though I should be so cowardly as to retract what you have read, do not suffer me to offer myself to your thoughts save in this last fashion.

Remember my last worldly endeavors were to seduce your heart; you perished by my means and I with you: the same waves swallowed us up. We waited for death with indifference, and the same death had carried us headlong to the same punishments. But Providence warded off the blow, and our shipwreck has thrown us into a haven.

There are some whom God saves by suffering. Let my salvation be the fruit of your prayers; let me owe it to your tears and your exemplary holiness. Though my heart, Lord, be filled with the love of Thy creature, Thy hand can, when it please, empty me of all love save for Thee.

To love Heloise truly is to leave her to that quiet which retirement and virtue afford. I have resolved it: this letter shall be my last fault. Adieu.

If I die here I will give orders that my body be carried to the house of the Paraclete. You shall see me in that condition, not to demand tears from you, for it will be too late; weep rather for me now and extinguish the fire which burns me.

You shall see me in order that your piety may be strengthened by horror of this carcass, and my death be eloquent to tell you what you brave when you love a man. I hope you will be willing, when you have finished this mortal life, to be buried near me. Your cold ashes need then fear nothing, and my tomb shall be the more rich and renowned.

Nathaniel Hawthorne was one of the great American letter writers. But less well known is that he wrote some immortal love letters to Sophia Peabody, who was to become his wife.

"MY LOVE"

LETTER FROM NATHANIEL HAWTHORNE TO SOPHIA PEABODY

I do trust, my dearest, that you have been employing this bright day for both of us; for I have spent it in my dungeon, and the only light that broke upon me was when I opened your letter. I am sometimes driven to wish that you and I could mount upon a cloud (as we used to fancy in those heavenly walks of ours), and be borne quite out of sight and hearing of all the world; for now all the people in the world seem to come between us. How happy were Adam and Eve! There was no third person to come between them, and all the infinity around them only served to press their hearts closer together. We love one another as well as they; but there is no silent and lovely garden of Eden for us. Will you sail away with me to discover some summer island? Do you not think that God has reserved one for us, ever since the beginning of the world? Foolish that I am to raise a question of it, since we have found such an Eden—such an island sacred to us two—whenever we have been together! Then, we are the Adam and Eve of a virgin earth. Now, good-by; for voices are babbling around me, and I should not wonder if you were to hear the echo of them while you read this letter.

Great love letters written after marriage are more rare than letters of courtship. This beautiful letter by William Penn, the Quaker founder of Pennsylvania, was written as he left England for America, leaving his wife and children behind him.

"NEITHER SEA, NOR LAND, NOR DEATH CAN EXTINGUISH . . ."

LETTER FROM WILLIAM PENN TO HIS FAMILY

Worminghurst,
4th of the 6th
month, 1682

My dear Wife and Children,

My love, which neither sea, nor land, nor death can extinguish towards you, most endearedly visits you with eternal embraces, and will abide with you for ever. My dear wife, remember thou wast the love of my youth and the joy of my life, the most beloved, as well as most worthy of all my earthly comforts. God knows and thou knowest it, it was a match of Providence's own making. Now I am to leave thee, and that without knowing whether I shall ever see thee more in this life.

Take my counsel to thy bosom:

Firstly. Let the fear of the Lord dwell in you richly.

Secondly. Be diligent in meetings and worship and business, and let meetings be kept once a day in the family, and, my dearest, divide thy time and be regular. In the morning, view the business of the house. Grieve not thyself with careless servants, they will disorder thee, rather pay them and let them go. It is best to avoid many words, which I know wound the soul.

Thirdly. Cast up thy income and see what it daily amounts to, and I beseech thee live low and sparingly until my debts are paid. I write not as doubtful of thee, but to quicken thee.

Fourthly. My dearest, let me recommend to thy care the dear children abundantly beloved of me. Breed them up in the love of virtue. I had rather they were homely than finely bred. Religion in the heart leads into true civility, teaching men and women to be mild and courteous.

Fifthly. Breed them up in a love one of another. Tell them it is the charge I left behind me. Tell them it was my counsel, they should be tender and affectionate one to another. For their learning be liberal, spare no cost. Rather keep an ingenuous person in the house to teach them, than send them to schools, too many evil impressions being commonly received there. And now, dear children, be obedient to your dear mother, whose virtue and good name is an honour to you, for she hath been exceeded by none in integrity, industry, and virtue, and good understanding, qualities not usual among women of her worldly condition and quality. Be temperate in all things, watch against anger, and avoid flatterers, who arc thieves in disguise. Be plain in your apparel, let your virtue be your ornament. Be not busy-bodies, meddle not with other folk's manners, and for you who are likely to be concerned in the Government of Pennsylvania, especially my first born, be lowly, diligent and tender. Keep upon the square, for God sees you. Use no tricks, but let your heart be upright before the Lord. So may my God, who hath blessed me with abundant mercies, guide you by His counsel, bless you, and bring you to His eternal glory. So farewell to my thrice beloved wife and children.

Yours as God pleaseth, which no waters can quench, no time forget, nor distance wear away, but remains for ever,

William Penn

About the Contributors

PETER ABELARD,
the French philosopher, was born near Nantes, in Brittany, in 1079. He studied theology and philosophy in Paris and became master of a philosophical school that inaugurated what has been called "the Renaissance of the Twelfth Century." His philosophy, known as conceptualism, was condemned by the Church as heretical in 1121. He secretly married Heloise, whose uncle, Fulbert, had him mutilated. Abelard then led a wandering life from monastery to monastery and died on his way to Rome to present his defense in 1142. His body was given to Heloise, then prioress of a convent, and after her death their bodies were buried together. Their tomb at the Pere Lachaise cemetery in Paris is still visited by lovers. His chief philosophical work, *Yes and No*, gives both positive and negative answers to a number of questions. More famous is his correspondence with Heloise.

THOMAS LOVELL BEDDOES,
poet and physiologist, was the son of an eminent physician. Beddoes was born at Clifton, England, in 1803 and was educated at Charterhouse and Oxford. He died in 1849. His drama, *Death's Jest-Book or the Fool's Tragedy,* was published in 1850, a year after his death, and his poems were published the year after that.

ANITA ROWE BLOCK
began writing to speed the hours while her husband was in the Air Force during the Second World War. She has continued writing since, but instead of speeding time, she must now find time, as she serves on a hospital board, does gardening, collects antiques, and cares for her family. Her collection of stories entitled *Love Is a Four Letter Word,* from which "One Day in April" was taken, attracted wide acclaim when it was published.

ANNE BRADSTREET
was born in England in 1612 and died in Massachusetts in 1672. Most of her adult life was spent in the wilderness of the new world. She and her husband raised eight children. She is the first important poet America produced.

ELIZABETH BARRETT BROWNING
was born on March 6, 1806. Her first epic poem was privately printed when she was fourteen. She fell from a pony shortly afterward and acquired an injury which plagued her for the rest of her life. Her marriage to Robert Browning, however, seemed to cure her invalidism. She died in 1862.

ROBERT BROWNING,
an English poet, was born in 1812 and died in 1889. He decided at the age of seventeen to be a poet, and his first poem, "Pauline," shows the influence of Shelley. However, little notice was taken of it, and it was partly this early failure that turned him to the form of dramatic monologue that he made peculiarly his own. In 1846 he married Elizabeth Barrett, often considered to be the greatest English poetess.

ROBERT BURNS,
the Scottish poet, put a fresh, new face upon the traditional ballads of his native country. In his own words, he was "little indebted to scholastic education and was bred at a plough tail." Rustic or not, his fine poetry has stirred the hearts of the world since its first publication. He was born in 1759 and died in 1796.

GEORGE GORDON, LORD BYRON
was born in London in 1788 and died in Greece in 1824. He was a poet who captured the popular imagination of his day. For example, when Tennyson was a boy of fourteen, Byron died. Tennyson always remembered that he carved the words, "Byron is dead," on a rock, and declared, "The whole world seemed darkened to me."

JOHN CLARE,
the English poet known as "the Northamptonshire Peasant Poet," was particularly sensitive to the natural world around him. He was born in 1793 and died in 1864.

COLETTE,
the pen name of Sidonie Gabrielle Claudine, a French writer, was born in 1875. She wrote forty-four books, the first, *Claudine at School*, published in 1900, and the last, *Five Seasons*, published posthumously. Her works include a series of stories centering about a partly autobiographical character, Claudine. Her mother, Sidonie, known as Sido, repeatedly appeared under that name in Colette's stories about her, translated in English as *My Mother's House*, from which the beautiful selection "Laughter" was taken. *Gigi*, published when Colette was seventy, was her only novelette with a happy ending. As a book, as a film and as a play, in France and in the United States and in other countries in translations, it proved the biggest financial success of her career. However, it was Chéri, published in 1920, that first brought her international recognition. When she died in 1954, the city of Paris ordered a plaque to be placed on the garden wall of her home, reading, "Here lived, here died Colette, whose work is a window wide-open on life."

MAUREEN DALY
was born in Ireland but grew up in Wisconsin. She now lives in New York with her husband, William McGivern, who writes mystery stories. They have two children. Miss Daly has had a consuming interest in young adults for many years. She

has written many books and articles that have especial appeal for young people.

CHARLES DICKENS,
one of the world's greatest novelists, was born in England in 1812. The son of a navy clerk, he grew up in London. During one of his father's imprisonments for debt, the twelve-year-old Charles was apprenticed in a blacking warehouse and learned firsthand the horror of child labor. At seventeen he became a court shorthand reporter and subsequently was a parliamentary reporter for the London *Chronicle*. His sketches of London types (signed "Boz") began appearing in periodicals in 1833, and *Collected Sketches of Boz* (1836) enjoyed a great success. *The Posthumous Papers of the Pickwick Club* (1836–37) made Dickens and his characters Sam Weller and Mr. Pickwick famous. For his eager and ever more numerous readers Dickens worked vigorously, publishing first in monthly installments and then as books *Oliver Twist* (1838), *Nicholas Nickleby* (1839), *The Old Curiosity Shop* (1841). He often worked on more than one novel at a time. After a visit to America in 1842, he wrote *American Notes* (1842) and *Martin Chuzzlewit* (1843), both sharply criticizing America's shortcomings. His many other novels, of which *David Copperfield* was his own favorite, were written while he was lecturing, managing his amateur theatrical company and editing successively two magazines, *Household Words* and *All the Year Round*. Dickens died in 1870, but he remains one of the most widely read authors of all time.

EMILY ELIZABETH DICKINSON,
considered by many to be America's greatest woman poet, was born in 1830 at Amherst, Massachusetts, and spent nearly all her life there. Educated at Amherst Academy and Mount Holyoke Female Seminary, she was noted for her wit and love of fun and as a young woman took a normal part in village social activities. At twenty-three she accompanied her lawyer father, then a congressman, to Washington and Philadelphia, and it was then that she began the mysterious love affair that is supposed to have broken her life. She returned to Amherst and retired gradually into seclusion. About 1862, she began writing the poems that have made her one of the classic poets of America. The best of her short lyrics rank with the finest of modern poetry and her work has been a great molding force in twentieth-century poetry. Practically none of her works appeared in her lifetime. She died in 1886.

HILDEGARDE DOLSON
was born in Pennsylvania, where her life as a teen-ager was filled with the excitement engendered by her brothers and sister. She has experienced all kinds of feelings from the day, as a thirteen-year-old sophisticate, she had to share the bathtub with a live bass caught by her brothers, to the day she made humor history by publishing *We Shook the Family Tree*.

RALPH WALDO EMERSON,
essayist, poet and philosopher, was born in Boston in 1803. He studied for the ministry but in 1832 resigned because his religious views had changed and he felt that "the day of formal religion was past."

At this time, he made his first visit to Europe. In England he met Coleridge and Wordsworth and commenced a lifelong friendship with Carlyle. He stands out in American literature as the greatest of the "transcendentalist" group, which included Thoreau and Hawthorne. He died in 1882.

JACK FINNEY,
the American writer, was born in 1912. Mr. Finney is best known for his short stories and science fiction.

GUSTAVE FLAUBERT,
the French novelist, was born at Rouen in 1821. The son of a surgeon, he studied law unsuccessfully and early settled down to the life of a writer. In 1857 was published, after five years of work, *Madame Bovary*, which, in spite of his romantic inclinations, is a masterpiece of realism, written in a supremely fastidious style. The book resulted in his being prosecuted on moral grounds, but he won the case. The volume *Three Tales*, which contained the great short story "A Simple Heart," was published in 1877. Flaubert is the model of the scrupulous writer intent on the exact word and complete objectivity. He died in 1880.

ANNE FRANK
was born in 1929 in Frankfurt-on-Main. In 1933, her family emigrated to Holland because of Hitler's anti-Jewish laws. For two years, Anne and her family lived in the "secret annex" behind her father's shop in Amsterdam. On August 4, 1944, the annex was raided, and the occupants were sent to concentration camps. Anne died in the infamous concentration camp of Bergen-Belsen, but the writing she left behind will live forever.

NATHANIEL HAWTHORNE,
the American novelist and short story writer, was born in Salem, Massachusetts, in 1804. His father died when he was four years old, and from his widowed mother, almost a recluse, the boy learned solitary ways that were to prepare him to become a writer. From his youngest years he was fascinated by stories of Salem's history before the seafaring days, and it was this era that he recorded in his later writing. Hawthorne graduated from Bowdoin in 1825, and for the next twelve years devoted himself to writing stories, which were published in *Token* and *New England Magazine*. His magazine stories first made him known, and they were collected as *Twice-Told Tales* (1837; second series 1842). With his later stories, they remain among the best American short stories. In 1842 he married Sophia Peabody, through whom he came to know such writers as Ralph Waldo Emerson, Henry David Thoreau, Louisa May Alcott, and Margaret Fuller. His book *Mosses from an Old Manse* (1842) was written at the home in Concord where he took his bride. In Salem, when he was surveyor of the port (1846–49), he began his masterpiece, *The Scarlet Letter* (1850). For this and later stories of the Puritan mind, he has been called the founder of the American psychological novel. Living at "Tanglewood," near Lenox, Massachusetts, Hawthorne wrote the novel he liked best of his works, *The House of the Seven Gables* (1851). His *Wonder-Book* (1852) and *Tanglewood Tales*

(1853) remain children's favorites. He was appointed United States Consul at Liverpool (1853–58) by his college friend, President Franklin Pierce. He continued to write and live abroad for several years after the termination of his consular appointment. He returned to Concord and his literary life in 1860. Hawthorne died at Plymouth, New Hampshire, in 1864, having made a timeless contribution to American literature.

O. HENRY
was the pen name of William Sydney Porter, who was born in Greensboro, North Carolina, in 1862 and died in New York City in 1910. He worked as a drugstore clerk and cowboy and finally became a writer. He first laid eyes on New York in 1902 and was in love with the city for the rest of his life. When he died he left over six hundred complete stories behind him, and the bulk of them are about New York City. His stories are mellow, humorous, ironic, ingenious, and shot through with that quality known as "human interest."

JAMES JOYCE,
the Irish novelist and a major figure of modern world literature, was born in Dublin in 1882. He was educated at Jesuit schools and was graduated from a well-known Jesuit center of higher education, University College in Dublin. Both his native city and his Jesuit training are reflected in his work, although he cut himself off from both his home and his church and spent almost all of the rest of his life in self-imposed exile on the Continent. He died in Zurich in 1941.

JOHN KEATS
was born in London in 1795 and died in Rome in 1821. He trained as a medical student, but soon his interest was diverted to poetry. One of the best-loved poets of all time, he was a careful craftsman and a warm human being.

KATHERINE MANSFIELD,
British short story writer, whose real name was Kathleen Beauchamp, was born at Wellington, New Zealand in 1888. Her first story was published when she was nine, and later, when at Queens College, London, she edited the college magazine, but her plans then were for a musical career. She married an English literary critic, John Middleton Murry, in 1918. Ill-health due to lung trouble made her move about seeking a congenial climate, and she spent most of her adult life in England, France and Germany. Her first volume of short stories, *In a German Pension*, was published in 1911. In 1920, *Bliss and Other Stories* made her famous. Other collections were *The Garden Party, The Dove's Nest, Something Childish*, and *The Aloe*. In her mastery of the short story, depending on atmosphere rather than on incident, she has been compared to Chekhov. Her work has strongly influenced recent writers of the short story. Her *Poems* were published in 1923, and her autobiographical *Journal* (1927), *Letters* (1928), and *Scrapbook* (1940) were all edited by her husband. She died at Fontainebleau, France, in 1923.

CHRISTOPHER MARLOWE,
English dramatist and poet, was born in 1564 and died in 1593.

Marlowe is considered the innovator of the modern form of blank verse. In imagination, richness of expression, originality, and general poetic and dramatic power, he surpasses all the Elizabethans except Shakespeare.

THOMAS MOORE
was born in Dublin in 1779 and died in England in 1852. After his education at Trinity College, Dublin, he studied law in London and was sent to a government post in Bermuda. He was a biographer and a satirist, but it is his Irish songs that give him a lasting place in literature.

SEON O'FAOLAIN,
novelist, short-story writer, and biographer, was born in Dublin in 1900, and was educated at the National University of Ireland and at Harvard. He took the Republican side in the civil conflict of 1922 and was Director of Publicity for the Irish Republican Army. He then became a teacher, and in 1932 his first book appeared, a collection of short stories entitled *Midsummer Night's Madness.*

MARGARET OLIFANT,
novelist and biographer, was born at Walbyford, Scotland, in 1828. In 1857 she married her cousin, Francis Wilson Olifant, an artist. Her literary output began when she was little more than a girl and continued almost up to the end of her life. Her first novel, *Mrs. Margaret Maitland,* appeared in 1849, and its humor, pathos, and insight into character gave the author an immediate position in literature. She died in 1897.

WILLIAM PENN,
the English essayist and lawgiver, was born in London in 1644, and died near Reading, Pennsylvania in 1718. He was the son of Admiral Sir William Penn, the conqueror of Jamaica and one of the few prominent Englishmen to make personal profit out of both the Civil Wars and the Restoration. As a young man Penn became a Quaker and suffered a number of imprisonments for his views. He became one of the chief Quaker propagandists and wrote scores of religious books and tracts. Of these only *No Cross, No Crown* is still much read. His best-known work is a collection of aphorisms, *Fruits of Solitude,* written while he was waiting out the aftermath of the Revolution of 1688. From Charles II he received proprietorship of Pennsylvania in settlement of debts owed to his father by the crown. He advertised the new province throughout Europe as a refuge for the oppressed of whatever belief. His greatest contribution was his "Frame of Government" for Pennsylvania, in which he gathered all the most enlightened ideas of his time into a flexible and lasting constitution.

EDGAR ALLAN POE,
American writer, was born in Boston in 1809 and died in 1849. His tragic life gave his poetry a haunting melancholy and his stories great imaginative depth. It was his poem "The Raven," published in 1845, that brought him fame. He initiated the detective short story with "The Murders in the Rue Morgue" and "The Gold Bug."

About the Contributors 285

WILLIAM SAROYAN,
playwright, novelist and short story writer, was born at Fresno, California, of Armenian parents. After leaving school, he worked variously as telegraph boy, office boy and farm laborer, then settled in San Francisco. He first gained notice with a volume of short stories, *The Daring Young Man on the Flying Trapeze* (1934). His earliest play, *My Heart's in the Highlands* (1939), was followed in the same year by *The Time of Your Life*, which was awarded the Pulitzer Prize. Others are *Love's Old Sweet Song, The Beautiful People, Get Away Old Man*, and *Jim Dandy*. Novels and books of short stories are *The Human Comedy, Dear Baby, Adventures of Wesley Jackson, Tracy's Tiger*, and *The Laughing Matter*. *The Bicycle Rider in Beverly Hills* is an autobiography.

WILLIAM SHAKESPEARE
was born in Stratford-on-Avon in 1564 and died in 1616. We know very little about his life before 1582, when he married Anne Hathaway. They had three children; Susanna, Hamnet, and Judith. The most brilliant dramatist English literature has ever known, Shakespeare was also an actor and a poet.

MARY W. SHELLEY,
a novelist, was born in London in 1797, the only daughter of William Godwin and Mary Wollstonecraft. In 1816, she married Percy Bysshe Shelley and went to the Continent. While abroad, she saw much of Byron, and it was at his villa on the Lake of Geneva that she conceived the idea of her famous novel *Frankenstein*. She wrote other novels, contributed biographies of for-

eign artists and authors to *Lardner's Cabinet Encyclopaedia*, and edited her husband's poems after his death. She died in 1851.

PERCY BYSSHE SHELLEY
was born in England in 1792 and died by drowning in 1822. From boyhood, he disliked authority and convention. Despite the fact that his best work was produced within the space of five years, Shelley ranks with the greatest English poets.

FRANK SULLIVAN,
born in Saratoga Springs, New York, in 1892, is an example of America's favorite success story. He's the local boy who made good —at practically everything. He graduated from the Saratoga High School, got his degree at Cornell University, and was a second lieutenant in the First World War. A journalist since youth, he has perfected a kind of commentary which has been described as "a little like a brief informal essay and a lot like a brisk extravaganza. A calculating humorist, he remains incalculable.

MARK ALBERT VAN DOREN,
poet and critic, was born at Hope, Illinois, in 1894, and educated at the University of Illinois and Columbia, where he became Professor of English. From 1924 to 1928, he was literary editor of the *Nation*, and in 1940 he was awarded the Pulitzer Prize for his *Collected Poems*. Separate volumes of his verse are *Spring Thunder, 7 P.M., Now the Sky, Jonathon Gentry, A Winter Diary, The Last Look, The Mayfair Deer, The Seven Sleepers, The Country Year, New*

Poems, and *Spring Birth.* Among his critical works are studies of Thoreau, Dryden, Shakespeare and Hawthorne.

JESSAMYN WEST,
the creator of *Cress Delahanty,* spent her early childhood in Indiana but has lived in California since the age of six. She attended a small Quaker college in southern California and began graduate study at the University of California for a Ph.D. degree. Tuberculosis put an end to her study, and she spent ten years in convalescence. During these years she began to write. In the *Friendly Persuasion* she has portrayed the simple and satisfying world of her great-grandparents on the Indiana frontier. *The Witch Diggers* is a novel of small-town life in Indiana at the turn of the century. In *Cress Delahanty* she describes small-town life in California during her own youth.

SEON MANLEY
GOGO LEWIS

Seon Manley and Gogo Lewis, who are sisters, have long practiced the gentle art of collaboration in many books ranging over a wide variety of topics. Immediately after college they owned and operated their own printing press, and they have been active in all phases of the publishing world for two decades.

Mrs. Manley is the wife of Robert Manley, a Management Consultant, and the mother of a daughter, Shivaun. She lives in Greenwich, Connecticut.

Mrs. Lewis, whose husband is an audio-visual specialist, is the mother of two daughters, Carol and Sara. She lives in Bellport, Long Island.

Jointly and individually, Seon Manley and Gogo Lewis have over twenty books currently in print.